THE WHOLE TEN YARDS

FRANK GIFFORD
and Harry Waters

THE
WHOLE
TEN
YARDS

RANDOM HOUSE
NEW YORK

Library of Congress Cataloging-in-Publication Data

Gifford, Frank
The whole ten yards / Frank Gifford and Harry Waters
        p.   cm.
ISBN 0-679-41543-2
1. Gifford, Frank. 2. Football players—United States—Biography.
3. Sportscasters—United States—Biography.
I. Waters, Harry. II. Title. III. Title: Whole 10 yards.
GV939.G5A3 1993
796.332'092—dc20
[B]   93-17806

Manufactured in the United States of America

98765432

FIRST EDITION

Book design by Carole Lowenstein

94-112

ACKNOWLEDGMENTS

The Whole Ten Yards came about in a rather strange way. A couple of years before the legendary author Fred Exley passed away, we were yakking on the phone, as we had on many occasions over the years. We had pretty much covered the wild success of Fred's beloved Giants on the way to their thrilling Super Bowl win over Buffalo, when for one of the first times in over twenty-five years our conversation took on a serious note. I knew that Fred was seriously ill. He knew I knew, and we both had, for a long time, avoided bringing it up. This time, however, I just blurted it out. "How is it, Fred?" I asked. "As bad as I've heard?" There was a long, uncomfortable silence. Then a raspy clearing of one of the most abused throats of all time. "Real bad, I guess," he said slowly. Another long awkward pause and then Fred let me off the hook. First came the chuckle, then the low rumbling laugh that was so familiar. "I think everything will be okay," he said. "There's this hot shit up in Canada who's got some sort of radical way to treat the thing, and I don't know"—another long pause—and then the finality of his observation, "I'll be okay, Frank."

Even though we spoke often after that, we never again talked openly about the inevitable end we both knew was near. In one of our conversations, I suggested that I do a book and that Fred should be the writer. I was only kidding, but Fred really got off on that. He had suffered greatly from the negative reception that the last book of his trilogy, *Last Notes from Home,* had gotten, and I think he would have loved to have gone back to work. We both knew that wasn't going to happen, and I cooled things off by joking, "You can write my story and I can help write yours." Again the silence and then again the laugh—"Hey, man, we did that already, didn't we?" The reference, of course, was to *A Fan's Notes,* his brilliant first novel, much of which drew parallels between his life and mine.

Some time later, as my longtime friend Art Cooper of *GQ* magazine and I were comparing notes on what we had heard about Fred, I laughingly related the story. Art was a huge fan of Fred's and on several occasions had reached out to help him by offering him work at *GQ.* "Good idea," mused Art. "You should do a book." Several lunches later and after some very wise advice and direction from Art, *The Whole Ten Yards* began to take shape. My first thought was to do the whole thing myself. My second thought, after discussions with Art, was that I needed a real pro. That's when Harry Waters came into my life, again at the suggestion of Art.

Harry and I had first met in Sarajevo, Yugoslavia, when he was there for *Newsweek* magazine covering our ABC coverage of the 1984 Winter Olympics. That was a brief encounter. What was coming up was to be a marathon of laughter, stories I thought were dumb and he loved, stories he thought were dumb and I loved, and a unique bonding much like what I suppose happens between a shrink and a patient.

In short, the following pages accomplish several things for me. First and foremost, my editor, David Rosenthal, let me write about growing up. That was important for me. I hope that my two sons, Jeff and Kyle, and my daughter, Vicki, from my first marriage, will learn a little more about the old man and that it wasn't all bright lights, Yankee Stadium, and the tube. As for Cody, my grandchildren's uncle, and little Cassidy, their aunt, I hope they'll all enjoy reading about their dad and "Poppy Grandpa" and the "good ol' days."

As for the great pals I played with, and not-so-great guys I played against, I hope I haven't hurt any feelings. Honestly, guys, we were not even close to the athletes that play our game today. Not in size, speed, or skill. I do hope, however, that some of today's players get a chance to read *The Whole Ten Yards*. We were the guys who paved the way for your multiyear, multimillion-dollar deals. Most of us don't begrudge you guys one cent. Like you, we know what a knee feels like when it "blows," and we know what it's like to play out a game wondering where the hell you are and what day it is. You owe us only one thing—take good care of the game we left for you.

Finally, some thanks go to a few people who have been so supportive in making *Yards* happen. Pat Connell, my secretary and assistant, has been invaluable. She has remembered what I've forgotten, she's located the irretrievably lost photographs and other items, and has obediently laughed and sighed at all the right moments. And then there's Harry's Ruth. Man, would he be lost without her. As for my Kathie, when I first told her I was going to write a book, she said, "What a great idea." So great, she thought, she promptly wrote her own, which became a runaway bestseller. Now that *The Whole Ten Yards* has finally hit the bookstores, so too has Kathie's paperback. Well, it is the Year of the Woman, and I love this one a whole bunch.

CONTENTS

THE WHOLE TEN YARDS

*I*t was a terrible day. It was a terrific week.

On December 28, 1958, the New York Giants and the Balti-more Colts squared off in what became known as "the greatest football game ever played." For a Giant named Gifford, that NFL title match would turn out anything but great. Yet to me there was a lot more going on that day than championship football.

In the Yankee Stadium stands sat a very special visitor: my father, Weldon Gifford. Dad was an oil worker who had come down from the Point Barrow, Alaska, oil field to spend a week in New York with his athlete son. An oil worker's life meant hopping from town to town and job to job. Consequently, I had never gotten to know my dad well; he'd been gone for much of my youth. Now, at the age of fifty-eight, he was about to witness me play professionally for the first time. So that week was really important to us.

Dad did everything with me. He went to the Giants' practices, sat in on my press interviews, and watched me do my radio show. In the evenings, we hung out at Toots Shor's saloon. I introduced him to all the regulars—Jackie Gleason, Rocky Graziano, Mickey Mantle,

Whitey Ford, my buddy Charlie Conerly, and, of course, Toots himself, who kind of took Dad under his wing. That wasn't terribly healthy for my father, because Toots drank Hennessy brandy with both fists and expected his friends to match him blast for blast. Pretty soon my dad was calling him "Toooots." One night, as we were riding home from Shor's on the D train, he gave me a big, glassy-eyed grin and proclaimed, "That Toooots is one hell of a guy." I groaned and replied, "Right, and it looks like he buried you again tonight."

But I was enormously proud of my father because he wasn't impressed by any of these celebrities. They just weren't his world. Hell, his heroes were guys who capped burning oil wells. Even so, he really got into the scene. He'd perch at Toots's bar wearing his ten-year-old suit—it still looked good because he wore it only on Sundays—and chat up movie stars, writers, and famous athletes as if they were lifelong buddies (and as if he had a clue who they were). Watching him, I realized how much I'd missed by not knowing my dad. I realized we could have had a lot of laughs because he was such a wonderfully fun guy. And you could see he loved being "Frank Gifford's father," which made me especially happy. I got more pleasure being the football hero through his eyes than actually living the part. It was the closest we had ever been.

The Giants went into that historic championship an exhausted, ripped-up team. To clinch our conference title, we had had to beat the Cleveland Browns twice over the two previous weeks. Both those games were played on frozen fields, and we had the wounds to prove it. The bursa sac in my elbow was swollen the size of a tennis ball, both knees were hurting, and a hip bruise had hemorrhaged blood into my leg. Most of us could barely walk through practice. Man, we were a wreck.

Not only did the Colts enter the game with two weeks' rest, but they were simply a better football team. That day they fielded no fewer than four future Hall of Famers: Johnny Unitas, Lenny Moore, Ray Berry, and Gino Marchetti. Despite all that, we took them into a sudden-death overtime—the first time one had ever decided an NFL championship.

We probably would have won the game if I hadn't fumbled twice in the second period. The Colts recovered both times, and each led to Colt touchdowns. At the intermission, we trailed 14–3, so you can see what those two fumbles meant. Early in the second half, however, one of our defense's patented goal-line stands charged us up enough to come back. We took a 17–14 lead, the go-ahead TD coming on a sideline pass from Charlie Conerly to me. But I was still thinking about those costly fumbles.

Then came the most crucial, and controversial, play of our season. With only a few minutes remaining, we faced a third-and-four on our own 39. Up in the stands, optimistic fans were already filing out, and, in the press box, the writers were voting Conerly a Corvette as the game's Most Valuable Player. For the first down that could lock up the championship, I took a handoff from Charlie on a 47 power over right tackle. Gino Marchetti, the best defensive end in football, fought through our right tackle and grabbed me. Then all hell broke loose as three hundred pounds of Big Daddy Lipscomb, the Colts' massive tackle, piled on both of us. Marchetti's leg snapped like a twig.

As Gino screamed in agony, the ref picked up the ball and held it, rather than marking the spot. Then he started pulling players off Marchetti. Finally, he put the ball down a couple of inches short of a first down.

I was stunned. I knew I had that first. When you've played nearly twenty years of football, you know when you've either made it or you haven't. But the ref apparently became so distracted by Marchetti's screams that he didn't focus on where the ball should be marked. All of the Giants and most of the stadium felt I'd made it. A lot of the sportswriters who reported on the game agreed.

Now we confronted a fourth and inches at our 43. Charlie Conerly wanted to go for it. Vince Lombardi, our offensive coach, wanted to go for it. Most of all, I wanted to go for it—and with the exact same play. Hell, I'd just gotten four yards with it, and the guy who stopped me was carried out of the game. But because we had the best defense in football, as well as the second-best kicker, head coach Jim Lee Howell called for a punt. Logically, it wasn't a bad call. It just turned out to be the wrong call.

Following Don Chandler's perfect punt, it took Johnny Unitas less than a minute to coolly pass the Colts from their own 14 to our 13. Five perfect throws—bang, bang, bang, bang, bang—including three to the great Ray Berry, who caught more passes that day than any receiver ever had in a title game. From the bench, Charlie and I watched their drive with a mixture of agony and exhaustion.

"Can you believe what's happening?" I asked him.

Charlie just grunted. Then he wearily said, "Shit, man, I don't think I can go anymore."

I looked at the old goat I loved so much and said, "I don't think I can either."

After a Colt field goal sent the game into sudden death, Unitas did it again. This time it took him thirteen plays to move them eighty yards to the winning touchdown. We were tired, they were a better team, and they earned their victory. But I was still so upset about that third-down call that I did something I had never, ever done. After the game ended, I followed the ref off the field and said, "Boy, you really got us, didn't you?"

My dad, who'd watched the game from Toots Shor's private box, reunited with me in our locker room. I was devastated by the realization that my fumbles had probably cost us the championship. Plus, I was really beaten up, with a huge gash in my leg. I couldn't even cut my tape off. Then Vince Lombardi did something very un-Lombardi-like. He came up to my father and me, threw an arm around my shoulder, squeezed the back of my neck, and said, "Don't take it so hard, Frank, because we wouldn't have gotten here without you." I will always remember those words and forever be grateful to him for that gesture. Meanwhile, my poor dad felt so sorry for me that he almost started crying. That was the last thing I wanted. So I looked up at him and told him what his being there meant to me. Then we both kind of ran out of words.

Sure, it would have been a lot better had I played the Johnny Unitas role that day. Yet it didn't really matter. For the first time, my father had seen me do what I did. I don't know whether it truly was the greatest game ever played. All I know is that it was one of the best weeks of my life.

CHAPTER 1

THIS PARTY'S STILL NOT OVER

*A*t this point in my life, I'm perceived as several different persons. Women see me as Kathie Lee's husband. Young kids see me as Cody's (and now Cassidy's) father. Old football fans see me as a former New York Giant and even older ones as an All-American from USC. But as far as I'm concerned, I'm a broadcaster. That's the hat I've worn for the last thirty years and the hat I'm still wearing. As a matter of fact, a guy in ABC's research department recently told me that I've appeared more hours on prime-time television than anyone in the medium's history. For some reason, I felt tired the rest of the day.

Most of those appearances, of course, have been on a series that's earned its own niche in TV history. Don Meredith called it *Mother Love's Traveling Freak Show*. Howard Cosell, rarely at a loss for too many words, called it a "happening." Others have likened it to a zoo, a tribal ritual, and an electronic church. As for me, I feel sorry for anyone who has never been involved in something like *Monday Night Football*.

In the beginning, the sheer craziness of it overwhelmed the game.

When we came to town, we were received like royalty. There were motorcades and mayoral receptions and chamber-of-commerce luncheons and postgame champagne parties. I've got the keys to so many cities I feel as if I've been running for president for the last twenty years. Our traveling style was right up there with rock stars'. Don dubbed it "silk shorts, limousines, and Learjets," and some of those limousines were so long they had to have hinges on them. You'd alight in front of the stadium, and handmaidens would escort you to the booth. The place would be jumping, signs and banners everywhere, and the first thought you had was, _It must have been like this in the Roman Colosseum._

At times we could have used less excitement. First of all, football fans going to 9:00 P.M. games in the Eastern Time Zone tend to make lubrication stops after work. Four hours later, they're often more a mob than a crowd. We needed guards to keep them from knocking down the door to our booth and police escorts to get out of the stadium. Sometimes they shook our limos so violently they almost turned over. I always tried to avoid getting into the one with Howard. A few of those people wanted Howard dead. Seriously dead. Like on that weird Monday night in Buffalo in 1973.

It started on the plane when I noticed two somber-looking guys getting aboard with Howard. "Giffer," he informed me, "these gentlemen are FBI agents here to protect me. There's been a threat on my life."

Naturally, Don and I laughed like hell. "Don't worry, old pal," we assured him. "We'll look after you." Then, on the way to the hotel, Howard filled us in a bit more. The crazy who had threatened him—via a postcard postmarked Buffalo—had promised to blow up the ABC booth at halftime. Since Don and I would also occupy that booth, we no longer saw quite so much humor in Howard's predicament. As a matter of fact, we were suddenly seriously concerned about his well-being.

That was the longest two quarters I ever broadcast. And when halftime finally arrived, an odd thing happened. First Don stood up, stretched his legs, and announced, "I'm a-goin' to the head." Then Howard arose, patted me on the shoulder, and said, "Giffer, I've got to do a couple of radio spots. I'll be right back." For the next twenty minutes, I felt like Gary Cooper in _High Noon._

Though we didn't explode, Buffalo wasn't finished with us. Toward the end of the game, a well-oiled fan climbed up on a cable that ran across the stadium at the back of the end zone. The cable held up a screen that prevented extra points from going into the crowd.

As he inched along his death-defying route, I'm trying to do the play-by-play. Meanwhile, Howard is off on another of his fan-bashing acts: "Giffer, it is beyond my perspicacity why spectators of this once-splendiferous sport behave the way they do. How can the NFL allow this execrable rowdiness to continue?" Don, on the other hand, had concluded that the Houdini act was better than the game. Echoing the crowd, he started chanting, "Go, sucker, *GO!*"

Mercifully, the police eventually talked the guy down and, I presume, took him away in a net.

Leaving the game ourselves, we felt so drained that we decided we needed nutrition. All of a sudden, everyone wanted a cheeseburger. Since our hotel didn't have room service, we instructed our limo driver to find us a McDonald's. He did—in the toughest part of town. When we pulled into the parking lot, a half-dozen of the meanest-looking dudes I've ever seen were lounging against some cars.

Howard took one peek out the window and quickly said, "Giffer, perhaps we better move on."

"Hell, no," I replied. "I'm hungry." So Don and I got out and headed for the entrance, Don in his cowboy hat and walking like Marshal Dillon.

"It's Dandy Don, it's Dandy Don!" one of the loungers started screaming. "Where's Howard, Dandy? Where's that son of a bitch?"

Don strolled back to the car and told Howard, who by then was scrunched into a corner: "Hahrd, they want you. It's your constituency. You know, the poor, the downtrodden. You're always talking about them. Shit, Hahrd, *here they are!*"

Howard finally did get out, and of course they loved him. They even sprang for his cheeseburger. Nevertheless, none of us were sorry to end that particular visit to Buffalo.

In terms of broadcasting techniques, the early years of *MNF* resembled the early days of television. We made it up as we went along.

No one improvised more ingeniously than our director, the diminutive, talented, but hugely volatile Chet Forte. In my mind, Chet was the best live director in the business. He was pure genius at grasping the moment. For instance, he would change the entire opening of a show at the very last minute, a skill I'm sure he learned from the guru of TV sports, ABC's Roone Arledge.

Once in Chicago, Chet noticed a beautiful sunset unfolding over Lake Michigan. He slapped up a tape of Sinatra singing, "In Chicago, Chicago . . ." then cut to a sunset shot as he counted down the seconds.

"This is great, Giff . . . eight, seven, six . . . Wow, what a shot . . . four, three, two . . ."

"My God, Chet," I yelled. "What am I supposed to say?"

"Just talk about fucking Chicago in the fucking sunset!"

So that's how we came on the air. And just as Chet sensed, it gave the show a unique spontaneity.

Of course, the true guru of *Monday Night Football* was Arledge, the president of ABC Sports when that division led the TV league in innovation. Right from the very beginning, Roone recognized that the prime-time audience wasn't like the audience on weekend afternoons. They expected something different from their TV sets. So from the moment Pete Rozelle suggested *MNF,* Roone saw it not so much as a football game as an entertainment show. And he put that show together like a Hollywood casting director, looking for types who would fit clearly defined roles. Howard was the elitist New York know-it-all, the bombastic lawyer middle America loved to hate. Don was the good ol' country boy who put Howard in his place. Actually, all Don usually said was, "Aw, get off it, Hahrd." But the next morning, every redneck in America was telling his buddies, "Did you hear what ol' Don said last night? He just cut the shit out of that sumbitch."

As for me, I was cast as the nice guy, the guy who got the numbers out and the names down and the game played. Some writer called me "the bland leading the blind," which we all loved. But it didn't make any difference if the media liked us or not. The formula has overwhelmed the media. It's kept feeding on itself until we've become, next to *The Ed Sullivan Show,* the longest-running prime-time series in television history. And in 1994 we pass Sullivan!

Even though my original partners are long gone from the "Freak Show," whenever I go out into the heartland to make a speech these days, people still want to hear about Don and Howard. "How's Don and Howard?" is always the first question I get, as if we all live together. The second is, "What are Don and Howard really like?" If I had to give a short answer, it would be this: One became as close to me as a brother, and the other will always remain an enigma.

HOWARD

I recently heard a joke that was making the rounds at ABC: "Howard Cosell has written four books—one for each face."

While I couldn't help laughing, I knew it was a cheap shot. The Howard I knew had at least forty sides. By God, he carried around a whole busload of people inside his head. What the rest of the world saw, however, was basically two personalities. Howard was like the little girl with the little curl in the old nursery rhyme. When he was good, he was very, very good, and when he was bad, he was horrid.

By and large, Howard and I had a great time together (even though you couldn't tell that from the way he bad-mouthed me in the ABC hallways and carved me up in his books). In any case, my intention here is not to criticize him but to try to explain him. As I said, that's a tall order: Howard Cosell is the most complex person ever to walk into my life. Still, you can't sit next to someone for fifteen years, nearly four hours every Monday night, without acquiring at least some insights into what makes him tick.

My first encounter with Howard came in 1956. At the time, he was a rookie radio host, a thirty-eight-year-old sports addict who had left the profession of law for something more stimulating. One day he came up to me at Yankee Stadium, his back bent under the weight of his suitcase-sized tape recorder, and said, "Frank, I want you to be a guest on my radio show."

"Fine, Howard," I replied. "But on one condition. I don't want to talk about the Philadelphia Eagles." Earlier that week, *Life* magazine had come out with a cover story about dirty play in pro football, and the team it accused of playing the dirtiest was the Eagles. Since the Giants had to meet the Eagles the next week, the last thing I wanted was to say something that might wind up on their bulletin board, pissing them off as well as my teammates. I explained that to Howard.

"I absolutely understand, Frank." He nodded. "I won't bring up the Eagles. I would never put you on the spot like that. You know me better than that."

Actually, I didn't know him at all. But I went on his show and, after he introduced me, his very first words were, "Giffer, there's a highly disturbing story out of Philadelphia. The Eagles have been labeled the dirtiest team in football. I would like your . . ."

Once I got over my shock, I wiggled out of it with a few we-all-play-hard clichés. And I didn't complain to Howard. In fact, Howard and I have never once exchanged an angry word in the thirty-plus years we've known each other.

But I also never went on his show again.

The Howard Cosell whom I teamed up with in 1971, the year I joined *Monday Night Football,* was as short on curls as he was on hair—but, God, was he good. He had a memory like a data bank. Plug him in, and he could probably recite the 1950 spring-training rosters of the entire American League, then tell you each player's astrological sign and taste in haberdashery.

Even though Howard never seemed to sleep, he had amazing energy. Following a Monday-night game, he'd tape his next morning's network radio show right there in the booth. Then off he'd go, regaling reporters or hangers-on over martinis or appearing on a local call-in show. He might even grab a red-eye to New York—just so he could be working the ABC lobby by 8:00 A.M. "How was I last night?" he'd demand. "Wasn't I magnificent?" During the football season, Howard camped in that lobby virtually every weekday morning and evening, a habit that did wonders for ABC's work ethic. Executives would arrive very early to avoid him and leave very late for the same reason.

Most of all, Howard was funny—sometimes when he tried to be. If we sat together on airlines, he'd summon the stewardess and intone: "Young lady, would you bring this man a cocktail along with your phone number? You are about to become blessed among women. This man has stupendous sexual prowess." I can't count the number of times I felt like a piece of luggage that was too big to fit under the seat.

Howard pulled the same routine at ABC's pre-game parties. Some widget maker from Cincinnati would drag his wife over to meet Howard, and the first thing she'd hear was, "My dear, your eyes exude the mystery of the ocean depths. Can this lout standing alongside you actually be your husband? You've married far beneath yourself." The amazing thing was, the husband would always go, "Ho, ho, ho." I bet he bragged about being put down by Howard for months.

Howard was at his funniest, however, when he tried to be serious. No one could do a more hysterical parody of Howard Cosell than Howard Cosell. One of his best came during a three-way hookup on *Wide World of Sports.* I was in Lake Placid anchoring a speed-skating race, while Howard was in Havana doing a boxing bout. When the fight ended, our producer, Dennis Lewin, wanted to cut to me in Lake Placid. They were holding up the race for our coverage, and the officials were running out of patience. Suddenly, Fidel Castro walked into the boxing arena and agreed to sit for an interview. Whereupon Howard, who, it seemed to me, had always referred to Castro as "a no-good, pinko son of a bitch," glowingly announced to the camera, "In one moment, *El Comandante* will join me here at ringside."

Naturally, Lewin gave him the green light, but warned him to make it brief because we had to cut to the race. Well, Howard proceeded to gush all over Castro. It was *"Comandante"* this and *"Comandante"* that. Finally, Lewin realized we were about to lose the race.

"Wrap it up, Howard," he shouted. "Right now!"

And there on my monitor was poor Howard, turning to Fidel Castro and apologetically saying, "All right, *Comandante.* Lovely being with you. Now we have to go to speed skating, a sport that . . . uh . . . I'm sure Cubans will excel at . . . er . . . once they take it up." That convulsed the rest of us. Not surprisingly, Castro, offended at being cut short, stormed off. Howard's reaction was equally predictable. "That's it," he informed Lewin. "I'm through. I'm gone. I'm officially out of here." No one took him seriously, because he'd already quit at least a hundred times.

One of Howard's most infamous Monday-night performances involved Gordon Gravelle. He was a rookie tackle out of Alabama starting his first game with the Giants. At least that's what the Giants' press representative informed us during our pre-game briefing. What we didn't know was that, because of a communications mix-up, the guy wearing number 71 whom we thought was Gravelle was actually someone else. During the broadcast, Howard began to pick on "Gravelle" because number 71 was having a rotten game. "This man should not be in the league," he proclaimed. By the time it was over, Howard had Gravelle cut and shipped back to Alabama. Meanwhile, Gordon's wife and friends were watching, and of course they saw right away that it wasn't he. They must have been beside themselves: "Who the hell is Howard talking about?" When Gravelle heard about it himself, he went ballistic. "Cosell," he told the press, "is a pompous, senile idiot."

Of course, that's not true. (Well, maybe two-thirds not true.) What Howard was, especially when he first came to TV, was deeply insecure. He had good reason. Though the Howard I came to know so well would never acknowledge it—and probably wasn't even aware of it—anyone who looked like Ichabod Crane and spoke with a nasal Brooklyn accent didn't exactly fit the sportscaster mold. On top of that, Howard was Jewish. He'd been a target of bigots in his youth and in the military, and now he was entering a business with virtually no Jewish stars. I have a Jewish father-in-law who toughed it out as a chief petty officer in the navy during the war years of the forties, so I've learned from him a little about what it takes to overcome anti-Semitism. Though he's never complained to me about it, I really admire him for surviving all that as well as the fortitude required to do it.

Howard's genius lay in turning his liabilities into assets. He gave his voice a dramatic, staccato delivery that grabbed you by the ears. His ethnicity helped him to understand and empathize with underdogs, particularly minorities and especially Muhammad Ali. And, being Howard, he also used it to ingratiate himself. I can't recall how many times I heard him walk up to a black athlete and announce, "How-ard Co-sell, the Jew from New York." Blacks came to regard him as an honorary soul brother. Mavericks like Al Davis, the owner of the Raiders, felt such a bond with Howard that they'd slip him inside information when other owners wouldn't return his calls.

One key to understanding Howard's dark side, I believe, is that he didn't become famous until he was over fifty. All that media glare, whether it was positive or negative, came to him relatively late in life. Unlike a professional athlete, he never had to grow up with criticism of his performance. He was never told he was lousy because, say, he dropped a pass or blew a game with a late fumble. So when the arrows started coming at him from every possible source late in life, it really got to him, it really hurt. He became bitter. He became vengeful. He became paranoid. He ended up alienating virtually everyone he knew. There came a point where the only people Howard truly trusted were his immediate family.

Don and I watched it happen. It was as if Howard got up one morning to discover that the whole world had turned on him. Suddenly, the public, who he thought adored him, didn't want all that bombast and pontification anymore; they weren't amused by it anymore.

I never saw anyone take such a hammering; it was almost a lynch-mob mentality. He'd look out at a stadium and see signs and banners proclaiming everything from WILL ROGERS NEVER MET HOWARD COSELL to HOWARD IS A HEMORRHOID—and those were the printable ones. He'd pick up a paper and read that bars were raffling off tickets for the chance to throw a brick through their TV set when his face came on. He'd turn on *The Tonight Show* and listen to comics take him apart. I once watched Buddy Hackett break up Johnny by cracking, "There are two schools of thought about Howard Cosell. Some people hate him like poison, and some people just hate him regular."

Don and I also saw Howard turn on us. He began taking our teasing of him, which had always been part of the act, as a personal attack. One night Don made the mistake of ribbing him about his TV variety show, which had just been canceled. A receiver muffed a pass in the end zone, and Don said, "That guy ought to be on *Saturday Night Live with Howard Cosell*." Howard sulked the rest of the broadcast.

On another night, he got into a long sociological tribute to *Mon-*

day Night Football, how it had reshaped America's habits and all. He finally wrapped it with an Arabic proverb: "Of course there are critics. There will always be critics. The dogs may bark, but the caravan moves on." At which point Don punctured Howard's pontifical balloon with a loud *"Woof!"*

Everyone in America cracked up—except Howard.

Those were the nights I knew Roone was going to get a call. "They're doing it again," Howard would tell him. "The two jocks are after me again. They're out to get me, Roone." He said the same thing to other people at ABC. Howard came to believe that Don and I spent all our waking moments plotting against him—the "jockocracy," as he called us. The funny thing was, he'd have been devastated if he knew how little we discussed him.

I'm no psychiatrist, but I once read about something called "central position." That's the position from which a little child views the world. The child believes that the entire universe swirls around him, that everyone in it does nothing but think about him and talk about him. When his parents leave his room, life ceases to exist for them. Eventually, most people grow out of the feeling of central position. I suspect Howard may have been one of the exceptions.

Perhaps the most interesting analysis of Howard was written by David Halberstam, the Pulitzer Prize–winning journalist, in *Playboy* magazine. Halberstam wrote that he started out as a Cosell admirer, but, after years of TV exposure to him, he concluded, "In an odd way, he was like Nixon, in that his psychic needs demanded that he be more public, go further and further out on the wire, even further than his psychic strengths could really withstand. His emotional needs and the needs of his medium coincided in some terrible way . . . The Howard who emerged in that decade as 'Monday Night Football' and became more and more successful was a monster. His insecurities, which had once made him interesting and irreverent, now made him seem heavy and ponderous. The bully in him was more evident now. By the end of the decade, he had become the cartoon his enemies had much earlier drawn of him."

As difficult as Howard became, I truly felt for him because I could see what all that heat was doing to him. It finally sucked up all his energy. My most vivid memory of Howard in the booth was the night after a New York columnist really blistered him. Seconds before we were due on the air, there's Howard, exhaustedly slumped over in his chair with a burned-out cigar clutched in his fist, tobacco juice dribbling down his chin, his toupee all askew, and his headphones down around his cheekbones.

"Chet, I can't hear you," he's mumbling into his mike. "Chet, I can't hear what you're telling me."

I reached over and pushed his headphones up over his ears.

"Oh," Howard said. "*There* you are, Chet."

I don't know how he made it through that broadcast.

It's no secret that Howard and I look upon sportscasting differently. Howard took on social issues that others have shied from, and for that I respect him. Yet too often those issues didn't belong on *Monday Night Football.* Trying to solve the problem of racism between plays is a little difficult. You can't address that issue with depth and intelligence in a sports framework. If something is germane to the game—say, a player coming off drug rehab—you have to discuss it. But if you're watching the Washington Redskins, you don't need a lecture from Howard on the crime rate in the nation's capital. He may have been right, but the forum was wrong.

Howard also placed himself above the game. It started as a joke: "*I'm Monday Night Football.*" But he said it so often that, after a while, he began believing it. I had my own joke about Howard: "He wanted to do the show when the players were on strike."

Actually, I suspect that Howard felt he really didn't need the players. Which is absurd, because what has made *Monday Night Football* are all those guys who go out there and perform a degree higher than they ordinarily do on Sundays. Plus the game itself: Pro football was a shooting star in those days, and we just happened to hitch a ride. Contrary to what Howard thought, we weren't swinging that star. We were the swingees.

In 1985 Howard wrote a book called *I Never Played the Game.* It was sort of his farewell address, and it ripped almost every person and every institution he had ever worked with, including yours truly. While I didn't read the book, I read the *TV Guide* cover story that excerpted some of the nastier passages. I didn't respond then and see no reason to now; it all seems so petty. Especially in light of the last call I received from Howard. It was in 1991, shortly after he had cancer surgery and a year after the death of his lovely wife.

Emmy Cosell was the person Howard loved most and the only person whose presence made him feel less insecure. I can't recall the number of times that Don and I turned around in the booth, while Howard was off on a rant, to see Emmy quietly doing her needlepoint or reading a book. She couldn't have cared less about sports, but she was always with her husband in every sense of that term. So shortly after she died, I delivered a brief eulogy to Emmy during a Monday-night game. When Howard called to tell me about his cancer, he started off by thanking me for that.

"Howard, you don't have to thank me," I said. "It's what I felt. How you doing?"

"Well, as you probably read, I've got the Big C. But I'm going to beat it."

"I'm sure you will. And I want you to know that Kathie and I are praying for you."

"Giffer, that's so kind of you."

"Howard," I replied. "I didn't say which way we're praying."

There was a pause, then the sound of that inimitable cackle.

The last time I actually saw Howard was at a dinner for All-American college golfers that I emceed not long after that phone call. It was at a ballroom in the Waldorf-Astoria, with about three hundred sports stars and television people in the audience. As I sat on the dais, in walked an uninvited guest. It was Howard, looking terribly shrunken and frail. I had read that he was going in for more cancer surgery in a few days. God, I felt sorry for him.

I watched Howard as he began working the room. In the old days, he wouldn't have been able to move three feet without some guy grabbing him: "Howard, you've got to meet So-and-so. Come say hello!" But that night only a handful of people bothered to shake his hand. After a while, he turned and walked toward the doors. The ballroom was at the end of a long hallway, which I could see from the dais. I watched that stooped figure move slowly down that hallway, then pause and look around, as if to see if there was anyone to greet or anyone about to greet him. There wasn't.

When Howard finally vanished, memories of all the years we worked together came pouring back. The mayors' luncheons and the keys to the cities and the hordes calling his name and trying to get to him. Now he was just a shrunken-up old man walking down an empty hallway.

Howard Cosell, Don Meredith, and I took a hell of a trip. We had many laughs; we shared many great moments. The pity of it is, at this time in his life Howard should be a revered elder statesman for this industry. He should be going on shows and having fun and talking about all the things he loved to talk about. I feel nothing but compassion for him.

DON

The first thing you should know about Don Meredith is that he is not, never was, and never wanted to be "Dandy Don." That was Howard's nickname for him, but to Don it came to symbolize everything he disliked about his public image. He certainly didn't see himself as "Dandy," nor did anyone who knew him well. That big country bumpkin who warbled "The Party's Over" on Monday nights is actually one of the most intelligent creatures on the planet. There's nothing dandy about him in any sense of the word.

First of all, Don dressed like a circus barker; it was part of his free spirit. He'd show up at ABC's dinners for sponsors wearing beat-up jeans and a green-and-silver shirt with a red tie. He was a walking Christmas tree. After a while, I started lending him my old suits, slacks, and sports jackets—and anything else I didn't lock up.

Don is also incredibly well read. He might liven up a game by singing a couple of lines from Bob Dylan, but at a bar he'd be quoting Dylan Thomas. He could recite passages from some of the most esoteric works in literature. Around his house, he was always writing free verse or doing some sculpting or painting or working on a novel. But all his fans saw was good ol' Dandy, the guy who took the air out of that windbag from Brooklyn. He was typecast from the moment he first opened his mouth. Not that Don wasn't fun. Hell, he lived for fun. You never knew what game he'd invent next. One night he began interviewing an imaginary character named Harley Smydlapp. Harley was a member of the investigative firm of Smydlapp, Smydlapp & Calhoun, but he actually came from another planet. He'd been sent to earth on a fact-finding mission to find out what the hell was going on. After a few more chats with Harley, Don started getting letters addressed to him. There were people who claimed they hailed from Harley's planet.

Don performed on TV the way he played quarterback: He ad-libbed it. He was not renowned for doing his homework, before either a game or a broadcast. As he saw it, digesting too many facts would destroy his spontaneity. Everyone accepted that. I used to jokingly tell reporters that we were never concerned about what Don knew about the two teams in a given game. We just worried whether he'd show up in the right city. Don came to the booth as an observer, to enjoy the game, and, if the spirit moved him, to enhance the fun.

And did he ever. Once we covered a game between the Oilers and the Raiders in Houston that was so one-sided half the Houston fans vanished by the third quarter. It was a horribly boring game, and, naturally, Howard took that as a personal affront. He began berating the Oilers for not playing well for him. Don, meanwhile, had pulled down his cowboy hat, put up his feet, and stopped watching. He'd just written the whole thing off.

Frantically searching for something interesting, Chet Forte began sweeping his cameras around the stadium. Suddenly, he found a fan wearing an Oilers jacket sleeping all alone in the end-zone section. But just as Chet zoomed in on him, the guy woke up, spotted the camera, and thrust his middle finger skyward. He gave Monday-night America half the peace sign.

For the first time in Howard's career, he was speechless. Fortunately, Don happened to come around at exactly that moment. He glanced at his monitor, saw the obscene gesture, and quickly said, "How about that, Hahrd? They still think they're number one."

Nor was Don overly impressed by VIPs. Before a game in Baltimore in the early seventies, Howard visited the Colts locker room and spotted Vice President Spiro Agnew chatting with the team's owner. Agnew ranked just below Fidel Castro on Howard's enemies list. Nonetheless, he grabbed the vice president's arm, gushed all over him, and—without checking with our producer—dragged him up to our booth for an interview. He opened the show with it: "Hello again, everybody, Howard Cosell. Before we get to the rudimentary facts of the game, I'd like you meet a dear friend of mine, the vice president of the United States." That cracked Don and me up, because Agnew was one guy that Howard never stopped vilifying.

At the end of the interview, which all but deified the smug vice president, Howard bid his guest farewell and turned the show over to "the Danderoo." Don couldn't wait to get it. He knew that the hottest fad among people who disliked Spiro Agnew was Spiro Agnew wristwatches. "It was really nice having the vice president in the booth tonight," he told viewers. "What you probably didn't notice was that he was wearing a Howard Cosell wristwatch."

Another one of Don's virtues is loyalty, even to those who may not deserve it. In *North Dallas Forty,* Pete Gent, Don's old Cowboy teammate, wrote something that wounded him deeply. In the novel, the team's backup receiver—supposedly, Pete—is a hell-raiser into booze, uppers, and grass. His quarterback and best buddy—supposedly, Don—is into the same things. At the end of the book, the team's management calls the Gent character on the carpet for doing drugs and, basically, gets rid of him. When he comes out to the street, there's Meredith's character lolling in a big convertible. And Meredith, acting like a scared schoolboy, asks his buddy, "Did you say anything about me?"

Now, anyone who knows Don Meredith knows that's not him. He would never, ever say that line. When he read the book, he was very hurt and very angry, two highly uncharacteristic emotions. He knew that millions of people who read those words would forever attribute them to him. What made it even worse was that Don had regarded Pete as a friend.

Years later, in 1973, Don, Howard, and I were in Dallas's stadium to do a Cowboys' game. A few minutes before airtime, a security guard walked into our booth and whispered something in Don's ear. Don put down his headset and leaned over to me.

"You're not going to believe this," he said. "The police have Pete Gent locked up downstairs. They tell me I'm the only guy who can get him out."

"My God," I gasped.

"What do you think? Should we let him rot?"

"It's up to you, I guess."

"Don't say nothing about where I'm going," Don said, and he headed quickly out of the booth.

Meanwhile, Chet Forte was positioning us for our opening. Suddenly, Howard stopped waving to the crowd long enough to notice the booth was only two-thirds full. "Where's the Danderoo?" he asked.

"He had a little problem," I answered. "He'll be back in a minute."

"Chet!" shouted Howard into his mike. "I don't know where Dandy is!"

"What?" Chet exploded. And then: "Three, two, one, *you're on, Frank!"*

"Texas Stadium, Irving, Texas," I announced. "Hello again, everyone. I'm Frank Gifford. We have some, uh, late arrivals tonight . . . but it looks like a big crowd."

About five minutes into the game, Don returned and picked up his headset. "Hi, Howard, hi, Chet," he said with a grin. "I have to weewee just like everybody else."

Later that night, Don told me the real story. The police had picked up Gent in the parking lot. He was trying to climb a fence to get into the stadium, very disheveled and really messed up. When Don found him, he was locked in a kind of cage under the stadium. They'd stripped off almost all his clothes, and he was going absolutely berserk. Don quickly took over. First he vouched for Pete's character. Then he called a friend of his in stadium security and arranged for Pete to be taken to a hospital instead of to a real jail, where the cops were dying to dump him.

But before leaving, Don couldn't resist a farewell flourish. He walked over to the cage, looked at Pete through the bars, and said, "Did you say anything about me?"

A few weeks later, Don found himself in trouble over something he said on the air. During a game in Washington, he quipped that what the Redskins needed to win this one were a few plays from their First Fan: "Tricky Dick." Now, at the time, *Saturday Night Live* never called President Nixon anything but "Tricky Dick," so none of us thought this was a big deal. We were wrong. ABC got thousands of angry calls and letters from viewers and sponsors, and the papers quickly picked it up.

Though our boss, Roone Arledge, didn't ask Don to publicly apologize, he kind of implied he should say something on the air. Don really agonized. He was hardly a Nixon supporter, yet he didn't think his comment was unfair. During the ride over to the game the next week, he was still groping for something to say. Nor had he found it by the time we opened the show. He started an apology, then began hemming and hawing. Finally, he turned to me and said, "Help, Frank."

It was too tempting. "You got yourself into this," I replied. "You get yourself out." Then we both broke up and went back to the game.

As it happened, what Don eventually got out of was *Monday Night Football.* I had watched his unhappiness building. For openers, there was the pressure people were laying on him. It was much more than the pressure on Howard or me. Don liked to say, "Someday they're going to give me a job description," but he knew his job was to get laughs. It's kind of like introducing a comedian as the funniest man in the world, only instead of performing before a Catskills nightclub audience, you're doing it before 40 million Americans. You're expected to top yourself week after week after week. Always up, always ready, whether or not your dog dies or your wife's in a hospital or your dad's terminally ill.

Don finally had it with being funny. He had it with being Dandy. He couldn't walk down a street or get on a plane anymore without people coming up and saying, "Hey, Dandy, how ya doin', babe?" Then they'd wait for him to entertain them. Don got so sick of Dandy that he started talking about him in the third person. He came to hate Dandy. Mostly, he hated the fact that America thought that's all he was.

In 1974 Don signed a terrific contract with NBC. Besides broadcasting football, the network wanted him to do TV movies and prime-time specials and parts in series. Naturally, he was excited. But he wasn't over there long before he discovered a sad irony: NBC really wanted him to be Dandy Don. They put him in a movie called *Banjo Hackett,* in which he played a free-spirited cowhand who was quick with a gun and even quicker with a quip. Though Don saw right off what the NBC folks were doing, he loved one thing about that movie. Banjo Hackett constantly quoted a wise old Indian god named Kumkachie. Right off, Don started referring to "Old Kumkachie" in real life, and he's still doing it. He loves that Indian god more than Harley Smydlapp.

Not that Don was a flop at acting. He made two or three movies that were damned good, co-starring with some pretty fancy people. He did a lot of guest shots on crime shows like *Police Story* and sitcoms like *Evening Shade.* Many people have approached Don to star in a TV series, but he's never wanted to get tied down. He simply likes to express himself in all kinds of other ways.

The thing about Don, and I mean this as a compliment, is that he never wanted that last little rung, that ultimate success, if it conflicted with his own values and priorities. When he quit the Cowboys, they were on the verge of becoming a great football team. And he did it with full-time acting, too. He just walked away from it, even though he had won an Emmy and a couple of producers had major plans for him. In football and in acting, Don achieved stardom, but in my estimation he could have gained superstardom. I'm not saying that should have been his goal. He's lived his life exactly how he wanted, and that's by keeping everything in it in proper perspective. Hell, there's no way he could be a finer man or a dearer friend. As a person, Don has never been anything but a superstar.

I sure missed him when he left *Monday Night Football.* Don, his wife, Susan, and their dog, Dink, were the world's best traveling buddies. In almost every city the show went to, Susan made up a list of things for us to do. In San Francisco, we'd go on a cultural kick all day, then take the ferry to Sausalito, have dinner, and laugh all night. When Don went to NBC, we talked on the phone at least twice a week. In some ways, our relationship became even closer. Nor did Don's leave-taking affect our Nielsen numbers. I think it's pretty well documented that, contrary to the thinking of some of the egos who've graced the *MNF* booth, the show's ratings were never affected by their comings and goings. The only thing that has ever depressed the ratings, in my opinion, is a weak schedule going in or a schedule that turns out to be weak.

When Don decided to return to *Monday Night Football* in 1977, I suspect he thought he could play a different role. But everyone still wanted Dandy. One night he said to me, "Frank, I'll *never* get away from that guy." And nearly a decade after Don left the show for the last time, he still can't go anywhere in public without hearing, "Hey, Dandy!"

Today the Merediths live in Santa Fe, twin pillars of the city's cultural scene and perfect ads for happy living. We call each other regularly and exchange visits often. Dan Jenkins, who wrote *Semi-Tough,* the hilarious tale of a pair of pro-football buddies, once told Don that he modeled the novel's main characters after the two of us. Ever since, my nickname for Don has been "Billy Clyde" and his for me is "Shake." We call Susan "Barbara Jane Bookman."

One of our most memorable reunions came in 1991. The Giffords hosted three houseguests that weekend: Don, Susan, and Marla Maples. Kathie had become a confidante of Marla's and was counseling her on her much-headlined relationship with Donald Trump, who hooked up with Don and me at a golf course on Saturday morning. As I quickly realized, however, the game he was playing that day was with Don. Now, I happen to like Donald Trump: He is what he is. Needless to say, though, he's hardly Don Meredith's cup of Lipton's. He's also a needler to end all needlers—as poor Don was about to learn.

It began on the first green. Golf, of course, is a game of strict etiquette, and the worst no-no is to distract another player. Trump, who's an extraordinary athlete, had hit the ball to within a foot of the pin. As Don lined up his own ball, which was about ten feet farther away, Trump loudly said, "God, I really put that close, didn't I?" the Cowboy's ears turned pink.

From then on, Trump never shut up. After almost every drive, and he hit some long ones, he'd stand back and admiringly exclaim, "Look at that! Isn't that something, Don?" By the end of the round, Don's ears were a bright crimson.

Next we adjourned to my house for cocktails and dinner. As I fired up the barbecue, Trump got into a tennis discussion with Susan Meredith, who's an excellent player. "Remember that famous Bobby Riggs–Billie Jean King match?" he asked her. "No way did Billie Jean actually win that. Bobby decided to dump it. No woman can play with a man."

Now it was Susan's ears that were reddening. Of course, that only encouraged Trump. "I bet if I played you on Frank's court right now," he continued, "you wouldn't win a single game."

"Bet," snapped Susan.

So out they traipsed to my court. Not only did Trump beat Susan 6–0, he rubbed it in on every serve. "Coming to your forehand, Susan," he'd taunt as he tossed up the ball. "Get your forehand ready, Susan." Then he'd blast it past her and yell, "Aw, *come on, Susan!*" Meanwhile, Don was taking all this in with an expression that would frighten Godzilla.

We wound up the night with a game of eight-ball pool. Trump not only stayed on Don's case, he went one better. As Don was finishing off a nice run, I noticed something weird. Though he'd knocked in five balls in a row, there were still five on the table. While Don concentrated on another shot, I glanced over at Trump. Grinning malevolently, he was removing a ball from the pocket and sneaking it back onto the table.

When Don finally clued into what was going on, his entire face turned fuchsia. I knew he was close to solving all of Donald Trump's problems for him, or at least realigning his profile. Instead, he settled for another drink, this one a double. What self-discipline! What love for his fellow man!

Actually, Don Meredith relishes teasing almost as much as The Donald. Though he's known tragedy—the youngest of his three children was born blind and retarded—he's still incurably irrepressible. A few years ago, when I called to inform him that Kathie Lee was pregnant, his first words were, "Who is it? Tell me, and I'll get the sumbitch!"

That's pure Meredith, and so's this. When Cody was born, we appointed Don his godfather in charge of his "spiritual upbringing." Shortly afterward, Don sent Cody a painting. It shows an Indian warrior standing on a hilltop. In the background, the beautiful Santa Fe sky is dotted with white clouds, and among those clouds, if you look very carefully, you can see the face of an ancient Indian spirit. The painting came with a note: *Tell Cody to always reach for the stars—because that's where he'll find Old Kumkachie.*

More recently, when Kathie informed me that she was pregnant again, one of my first calls went to Don. After I told him of this surprising development, there was a long pause. "Sheet," he finally said. "I got the wrong sumbitch!"

The night before my own debut on *Monday Night Football* in 1971, Roone Arledge sprang a little surprise. Just in case I wasn't feeling enough pressure, he had arranged for me to do a halftime interview with the president of the United States. Thank you, Roone. Of course, this president was an old friend. When he confirmed the interview by phone, he told someone at ABC that "Frank should remember me because I used to attend parties at his apartment." Can you believe that? Who the hell's not going to remember Richard Nixon?

Though Nixon seemed even more nervous than I was, the interview went well. After discussing his upcoming trip to China and his love for football, he said something that took me aback. He said that if he had his life to live over, "I'd like to have your job."

I knew that Nixon's love of sports approached fanaticism. During his tenure at the White House, he sometimes suggested plays to Washington Redskins coach George Allen. (I still have fantasies about how George treated those directives from his commander in chief when he passed them on to the troops.) Nevertheless, I thought Nixon was joking. Twenty years later, I watched a TV interview with Nixon and heard him say that being a sports announcer "would be the greatest job in the world." Now I realize he was serious about wanting to do what I did.

Can you imagine Richard Nixon and Howard Cosell in the same booth? Just think about it.

The reviews of my first few performances were nothing to paste in a scrapbook. One critic called me "a walking mannequin." There's no question that I fluffed some calls, especially in that initial season. I didn't always match the name with the number and occasionally graduated a player from the wrong college (though in some cases, that constituted a considerable upgrade of their education). However, I would challenge any mortal being to get through three hours of the madness of *Monday Night Football* without dropping a ball or two. Take the Howard-and-Don era. Basically, my role was that of traffic cop, to move everything along. But I really was the resident psychiatrist. On any given night, almost anything could affect the mood of the two guys I worked with. I'm not putting them down, because their unpredictability made them terrific. But I never knew which Don or Howard was going to show up.

Suppose we're in Washington and Larry Brown of the Redskins has just taken a handoff. "Larry Brown over the right side," I say, and then quickly cut out. I'm waiting for either Don or Howard to jump in. Sometimes they'd both start talking. Or Howard would become so wildly gregarious that I'd be lucky to get Larry Brown down on the ground. But at other times, Howard might be sulking. Something Chet said to him or a sportswriter wrote about him has him ticked off. He might not say anything for a whole quarter.

Meanwhile, as I'm trying to call the plays, I've got bedlam going on in my ear. "Get Howard, bring Howard in on this!" Chet might be screaming. Or, "Wind those two guys down and get us out! We've got to go to another commercial! We're fucking behind!" Or, if he held down his interrupt switch too long, I'd hear everyone cussing at each other in the truck. "Take seven, take seven! Fuck you, you asshole!"

At the same time, my other ear is picking up the very tail end of something Howard is saying, usually followed by, "Isssssn't that right, Giffer?" I have no idea what he's been talking about. All I'm trying to do is get out one sentence: "Larry Brown, brought down around the twenty-one."

On some nights I walked out of that booth feeling like a survivor of Omaha Beach.

There's little question, I guess, that I'm less critical of the players than most other sportscasters are. Part of that may be due to the unique nature of *MNF*. I've always been conscious of the show's enormous audience, which brings with it tremendous responsibility. In one respect, we're totally unlike the Sunday football shows. On Sundays, the players are playing, the coaches are coaching, and the newspaper writers are covering their teams. On Monday nights, the players, coaches, and writers are watching us. So taking a gratuitous swipe at someone can do him enormous harm among those whose opinions of him count most.

I've also been a player, and that makes you view the game differently. Howard is so proud of having never played the game that he made that fact the title of one of his books. The problem is, football is not like any other sport. It's not cut-and-dried like baseball. What you see is not necessarily what happened. If a receiver went up in the air and didn't come down with the ball, Howard might knock his hands, when, in fact, the cornerback made a great defensive play. And if that same cornerback got badly beaten on the next play, that might not be his fault. The safety may have blown the coverage, and the cornerback made a hell of an effort just to get that close. So you have to know about tactics and techniques and player responsibilities. Most of all, you have to know that you don't know everything.

These days, too many sportscasters feel obliged to smash-mouth. They feel their career depends on coming up with put-downs that will make the column of a TV critic the next morning. I couldn't care less about that stuff. When I criticize a player, I try to do it within the parameters of what's deserved. Perhaps that's because I remember my kids hearing in school that their daddy muffed a crucial pass on Sunday, when maybe Charlie just overthrew me. Some other kid had heard it from his daddy, who read it in the paper over breakfast. Now magnify a bum rap like that by the reach of *Monday Night Football.* You better be absolutely dead-solid certain you're right before you blast a player before 40 million people.

Finally, I understand the physical and emotional agony players go through, because I've been down there. I know what it's like to have your frigging leg almost torn off and to feel the roots coming out of the ligaments in your knee. I know how it feels to sweat over making the team, and if you don't, how will you feed the kids? So the last thing these guys need is some rap artist up in a booth who doesn't have a clue to what it's really like. Nor do they need somebody who's forgotten what it's like because suddenly he's riding around in limousines and has gotten a big, fat contract and everyone's telling him how wonderful he is. The game doesn't need that.

To me, one of the most fascinating aspects of *Monday Night Football* is the way it's mirrored the political and sociological mood of the nation. In the early seventies, when we had Vietnam and racial turmoil and the rebellion against authority, the cast of the show reflected that.

Howard defended Muhammad Ali's refusal to get involved in Vietnam and became an instant hero to blacks and war protestors. Don would come on the air and sing a couple of lines from the Grateful Dead or Willie Nelson or Kris Kristofferson—he loved to do "Sunday Mornin' Comin' Down"—and pick up a countercultural cult following. He became the hippies' Big Daddy. The furthest Don carried that was at a game in Denver in 1973. "Welcome to the Mile-High City," he announced with a giggle. *"And I really am!"*

Chet and Roone went crazy. Of course, Don wasn't any higher than most of the people in the stadium, not to mention half the players. But that was the world of the seventies.

MNF could also bring together the most unlikely people. The weirdest scene I ever witnessed in the booth happened in 1976. The night before a game in Los Angeles, I ran into John Lennon at a cocktail party promoting the release of a Beatles collection. On impulse, I invited him on the show. He liked the idea but warned me he knew nothing about football. Meanwhile, I'd forgotten we had arranged for Ronald Reagan to come on the same show. Now it was just before halftime. I turned around, and there was Reagan with his arm around Lennon, explaining what was going on down on the field. And John looked absolutely enthralled. Here were two of the most political, ideological, and cultural opposites on the entire planet in the Monday-night booth—acting exactly like father and son!

In the eighties, the show took on a conservative tone, reflecting both the country and pro football. Discipline had returned to the game: The players cut their hair and dressed up again when they traveled on the road. My hair got shorter, and I put my tie back on. These days, we're allowed to remove our jackets only on a hot night (and it has to be hot as hell). But the biggest change was that the game became the show, rather than the other way around.

As the seasons passed, and new partners came and went, my role evolved with them. Each of the guys I worked with was totally different, and that required me to make many adjustments. My briefest, and most unforgettable, relationship was with Fred (the Hammer) Williamson. He's the former Kansas City cornerback who starred in several "blaxploitation" movies during the early seventies, earning a reputation for brutality, flash, and cockiness in both jobs. When Don split to NBC in 1974, Roone decided that Williamson would make the perfect replacement.

The Hammer is hard to dislike. He's a very intelligent, fun guy. We've had two memorable athletic encounters. With seconds remaining in a 1962 game against the Steelers, Freddy's first pro team, Tittle sent me on a desperate fly pattern from about forty yards out. Freddy was covering me man-to-man, and as we both raced into the end zone, the ball came in short. With Freddy in front of me, we both had to leap for it. But just before I launched myself, I hooked my thumb in the back of Freddy's pants. I went up like a rocket, while he found himself stuck on the pad. When I caught the ball to win the game, I really couldn't believe it. What I did was so blatant I knew I would be flagged. Freddy was just as certain, and when it didn't happen, he went ballistic.

Years later, he got revenge by annihilating me in a one-on-one basketball game at his home in L.A. The way his jumper was working that day, I'd have needed a dozen thumbs to beat him.

As a TV analyst, though, Freddy was an instant disaster. His idea of analysis was to challenge Howard with crude, heavy-handed gibes. He also thought he was still starring on the big screen. I sensed that right before his first performance, an exhibition game in Miami. As we settled into the booth, he turned to me and asked, "Where's my key light?" That's a movie term for a low spotlight that removes unflattering shadows from an actor's face. My God, with the guys who lit our booth in the early years, we were lucky if we got a flashlight.

Then I took a closer look at Freddy. He was wearing an open-neck shirt set off by a gold necklace, and hanging from the necklace was a perfect replica of . . . a penis and pair of balls.

Chet noticed it at the same moment. "Frank?" he said into my headset on my isolated key. "Would you ask Mr. Williamson to kindly remove his necklace?"

Fred Williamson was about six foot three and 220 pounds, with muscles on top of his muscles. "Tell Howard to ask him," I answered.

"Ask me what?" said Howard, overhearing me.

"Chet has something he'd like you to do."

By now Freddy had figured out what's going on. "Got a problem, Chet?" he growled.

"Uh, it's nothing, big guy," came the reply. "Have a good game."

A few weeks later, ABC paid off the Hammer's contract.

Though Freddy's replacement, Alex Karras, had more traditional tastes in jewelry, I learned early on why they called him "the Mad Duck." In one of our encounters on the football field, when Alex was an All-Pro lineman for the Detroit Lions, he shattered my noseguard with a single swat of his forearm. Alex was a great player, incredibly tough. I used to kid him that he was the only guy I ever knew who held up his sweat socks with thumbtacks.

Alex brought a bent wit to the TV booth. In his very first game, our sideline camera zeroed in on a mammoth Oakland Raider lineman removing his helmet to reveal a shaved head. "That's Otis Sistrunk," said Alex. "He's from the University of Mars." Both Otis and Alex lived off that line for years. Off the field, Alex had even more fun. In whatever city the show visited, Roone Arledge made sure that the best hotel suite was reserved for himself, just in case he wanted to do some entertaining. It didn't take us long to realize that Roone didn't travel much. He was too busy doing other things in New York. So whenever he failed to show up, which was all the time, Alex blithely checked himself into Roone's suite under Roone's name and partied all weekend.

As Alex would be first to concede, he was no student of the game. Linemen, after all, rarely see anything but the guy directly across from them. They see about two feet of the whole field. At least halfbacks get to travel around out there. Consequently, unless an Alex Karras studies a lot of game films, he really doesn't learn much about football. Of course, what always interested Alex most was acting. He just used athletics and sportscasting to get into it.

Apparently, Alex also sees himself as an author. A few years ago, he wrote a novel called *Tuesday Night Football.* It was supposed to be a spoof of you-know-what, complete with an impossibly air-headed ex-jock sportscaster named "Lance Allgood." Hmmm. That seems to require a response.

All I can say is that Alex has written one more book than he's read.

Fran Tarkenton, O. J. Simpson, and Joe Namath brought their own unique styles and insights to *MNF,* but I missed Don Meredith, and so did the show. In 1986 ABC was purchased by Cap Cities. One day the new head of our sports division, Dennis Swanson, called me into his office and delivered a shock. They had decided to go with a two-man booth. Would I agree to switch to the role of analyst? They wanted to bring in a new play-by-play man, Al Michaels.

I didn't get mad, but I was hurt. After fifteen years of handling play-by-play, suddenly being asked to give it up bruised my pride. On top of that, it was a traumatic time in my personal life. My brother had just died, my mother was seriously ill, and I was going through a tough divorce. So I told Swanson I needed to think about it.

In the meantime, I looked at other options. CBS had expressed interest in my joining its morning show in a revised format as co-host. The CBS people had seen me fill in many times for David Hartman on *Good Morning America,* and often the show's ratings not only held up but took a spurt. But what I really thought I needed was a major midcourse correction. I seriously considered packing it all in and starting a new life in Santa Fe. If it was good enough for Billy Clyde, I figured, it should be good enough for Shake.

Dennis Swanson, however, can be very persuasive. "We want you here, Frank," he said. "The ratings are slipping, and the package is losing money. We need you to help the team." That appealed to the player in me. Then he offered me a four-year contract with a whole lot of zeros. It goes without saying what that did for the poor kid in me.

As I gradually got to know Dennis, I came to admire him almost as much as his predecessor, Roone. Within the industry, he's regarded as a rough, tough, loud guy, a kind of bull in a china shop. I suspect Dennis is kind of proud of that image. Certainly, it took a hell of a lot of toughness to do his job at first. Right off, he had to confront a financial crisis unlike anything Roone ever faced. Like its counterparts at the other networks, ABC Sports was hemorrhaging money in the mid-eighties. It was TV's version of the real estate collapse. Dennis took us out of covering baseball, which was drowning us in red ink, helped turn around the ratings for *Monday Night Football,* and cleaned up our act in a lot of other areas.

In a business teeming with two-faced schemers, Dennis is one of the few executives who will stand up, tell you exactly what he thinks, and then do it. You never have to wonder what he really means or intends. Vince Lombardi was that way, too. No hesitancy whatsoever about making decisions, even if it meant taking heat. I like people like that. As for Dennis's bull-like image, I've never seen a father suffer more pain than Dennis did when his son, Eric, a student at USC, got hit by a car several years ago. It shattered his leg and gave him a terrible concussion. Since I'd undergone something similar with my own son, I was able to console Dennis. He's a very large man, but to me he looked about half his size when he sweated through that. From then on, I knew where Dennis Swanson was coming from.

My decision to stay with *Monday Night Football* turned out to be a smart one, because I've never felt more comfortable with my boothmates. Al Michaels is, in my estimation, the best play-by-play man in the business. He's really almost perfection. Al worked damned hard to get where he is, and he's still working his tail off. I admire dedication. Dan Dierdorf, who joined us a season later, is the only former lineman I've ever met who knows the entire game of football. In the beginning, working with him seemed a bit awkward, since we're both basically doing color and analysis. Gradually, we learned to complement each other. Say we're doing a Cowboys game, and Mark Tuinei makes such a great block that Troy Aikman has enough time to hit Michael Irvin, who makes a great catch. Dan will point out the block, and I'll handle the catch. It seems to work.

I'm constantly amused by how completely Al and Dan immerse themselves in sports. They both have satellite dishes at their homes so they can pick up almost any event anywhere on the planet. I'll arrive at a production meeting and hear them discussing last night's sumo wrestling match, or maybe a tractor-pulling contest. They get into such obscure minutiae that it's almost like who can top who (or, as Howard would correct me, whom). Half the time, I don't know what the hell they're talking about.

I know it was difficult for Al and Dan in the beginning, because the early years of the show haunted them. They grew up hearing about it and reading about it. Whatever they thought of Howard, Don, and me, they knew it was the biggest thing in sports television. As a matter of fact, the first game that Dan played on *Monday Night Football* was the first game I broadcast. So to them, I guess, I represented the show's past, and they were supposed to take it into the future. But nobody takes this show anywhere. It takes *you*.

People always ask, "How in hell can you keep doing this?" I'm starting to feel like a walking institution, or is it a dinosaur-in-training? Well, I do it because I still love it. Even after twenty-three years, I love the solitude of preparing for a Monday-night game, the total focus before the contest. It's like getting ready to play the Browns or the Colts all over again. And, in a way, I look on this show as my baby. I watched it grow up, I heard the press periodically write it off, I saw it bounce back and always bounce a little higher. I identify with it, and it's identified with me. How many people get to call something like that a job?

Not that the job still doesn't have its bizarre moments. One I'll never forget came in Indianapolis on Halloween a few years ago. I opened the show with my usual spiel, then we cut to a shot of the crowd. Not only was the crowd dead quiet, but every one of the sixty thousand fans in that stadium was wearing a mask of either Al, Dan, or myself. Not caricatures—these were black-and-white photographs of us someone had printed up and handed out.

I kept having the same nightmare all night. How would you like to look at twenty thousand people who look exactly like Dan Dierdorf?

CHAPTER 2

THE ROUGHNECK'S SON

Not long ago, I took a nostalgia trip to a fence. The fence was just as I remembered it, a chain-link barrier about a dozen feet tall enclosing a high school football field. The high school is in Bakersfield, California, and the football team is called the Drillers. Once I was one of them, but years before that, when still in grade school, I regularly snuck over that fence to watch the Drillers play.

Those Friday nights are as vivid to me as yesterday. I can smell the special fragrance of freshly mowed San Joaquin Valley grass mingling with the tang of popcorn. Banks of lights have turned the field into something magical, and it seems as if the whole town is passing through the gates. I'm with my older brother, Waine, and a few of his friends. We've jumped the fence because the admission is twenty-five cents—exactly twenty-five cents beyond our reach. We try to find seats, which usually proves impossible, so we run up and down the sidelines following the progress of the ball, then sit down wherever it winds up. No one bothers us.

The best part comes when the game ends. As the teams straggle off the field, we rush onto it. They've left on a single bank of lights so people can see their way out, just enough illumination for us to see each other. There's a whole gang of us now, and we're playing "tackle the man with the ball." Only it's not actually a ball, it's a rolled-up bunch of rags. I'm really good at this game, really quick, darting past these kids even though they're a few years older. Then, suddenly, *bang,* off go the last few lights. Although we can't see much of anything, we keep on playing. When I finally get home, I catch hell. There are grass stains all over me, and my shirt is torn. It doesn't matter. For a few hours, it was like stepping into a dream.

In a way, a lot of my life has been about climbing fences. My mother once figured out that by the time I started high school, we had lived in forty-seven different towns. When I mention that to friends today, they react with amazement. But to me back then, that kind of endless jumping around seemed to be the natural order of things.

My father started working in the oil fields at the age of sixteen, breaking in as a "roughneck"—the lowest job in the trade. Wherever a new field opened up, that's where my dad went. The problem was that this was the Depression, and nothing was more depressed than the California oil industry. No one was pumping oil or exploring for oil because nobody was buying oil. An oil worker's job would last anywhere from thirty to ninety days, depending on how fast the well was dug, and then he'd have to find out where else they were drilling, assuming that there was a somewhere else. So the five of us—Mom, Dad, my brother, Waine, my sister, Winona, and myself— ended up doing a *lot* of moving.

In retrospect, it seems as if we dropped in and out of half the towns and cities in the state: Hanford, Taft, Fresno, Stockton, Santa Maria, Lompoc, Watsonville, Ventura, Modesto, Wasco, San Luis Obispo, Redondo Beach, Long Beach, Huntington Beach, Hermosa Beach, San Diego, San Jose, Santa Monica. We also lived in West Texas in a place called Wink, which is about as quickly as I forgot it. When we arrived in a town, Dad would already be at the oil field, so my mom and the three of us would drive around looking for a place to stay. We'd have to find a room by that night or we'd end up sleeping in the park or the back of our car or pickup truck. Sometimes we'd move into a town and move out a couple of days later, living in trailer camps and such. Once we did a twenty-four-hour turnaround.

"We're moving to Avenal," my mom announced one night. "Your father has found a job there and rented a place for us."

So we immediately packed up and went to Avenal, and the next morning Mom enrolled the three of us in school. When I came home that afternoon, she was waiting at the door.

"We're moving to Coalinga," she said. "Your father has found a better job there."

That night we packed up again and went to Coalinga, a few miles up the road. I don't think we were there more than a week. Of course, in those days, it wasn't that difficult to leave one school and get into another. I don't remember completing a single grade in the same grammar school.

And yet the Gifford children never felt deprived because we never felt different. I've read *The Grapes of Wrath,* and I guess we were part of that scenario. We just never realized it. As a little kid, growing up in the thirties, I thought everyone lived like this. It wasn't until I was eight or nine that I started to realize there were people who lived better than we did, that there were people who stayed home. Our home was wherever the job was. Yet somehow or other, Mom and Dad always got it done. Somehow or other, we always ate, even though we ate a lot of the same things over and over. In retrospect, it's kind of amazing that the family survived. I can see now that it all came down to the character of my parents. They were *good* parents.

My father was an identical twin. He was Weldon; his brother was Sheldon. They used to joke about alternating their attendance at school. Actually, I suspect that's exactly what they did. When my dad was growing up, his parents homesteaded in a valley in central California that's probably the worst place to homestead if you're going to homestead. After things on the farm finally fell apart, Dad went off to work in the oil fields. He met my mother in Ventura— how, I don't know. Neither of my parents ever talked about things like that.

From the outset, it was a real tough go for them. But you'd never have known that if you'd met my dad. He was pure fun, a naturally gregarious person with an unbelievable number of friends. When he died, men of the "oil patch" he'd worked with and for came from all over the world to attend his funeral in Ventura. One virtue that eluded him, though, was practicality. He didn't have a clue about how to manage our finances, whatever finances there were. When I was in the fourth grade, he suddenly decided to become an entrepreneur. By some miracle, he scraped up enough bucks to buy a little service station. There should have been a red flag flying over that station, because its last half-dozen owners had gone broke. Late at night, while lying in bed, I'd overhear my parents debating whether to make this move.

"I've had enough of the oil fields," Dad would say. "This is a really great opportunity."

Mom always gave the same reply. "How are we going to live? You know we can't afford it." I must have heard "We can't afford it" a thousand times in my childhood, and most of the time, it was true. Maybe that's why a search for financial security has been one of the driving forces in my own efforts to succeed.

But, by God, Dad bought that station, and we all went to work there. It folded within six months. All we came out of it with was about a hundred radiator shields, the old-fashioned kind that kept the bugs off, which were stored in the back of the station's garage. For some reason, that collection impressed me mightily. I remember marveling: "Boy, Dad's really doing fantastic. *Look at all those radiator shields!*"

Yet even during the worst of times, even when things hit absolute bottom, my dad never lost his sense of humor. He rarely showed anger and never pain. If I had only a few words to describe him, they would be these: My dad was a very dignified man.

My mother, Lola Mae Hawkins, was much more reserved. I've only recently realized how rough she had it, what with Dad off chasing jobs and the burdens of where we were going to live and how we were going to eat falling primarily on her. The funniest thing she ever said, though it was unintentional, came out when she lay dying. It was 1986, and she was in intensive care in a Ventura hospital, all kinds of tubes and wires coming out of her. Kathie and I'd flown out to see her a couple of times. The last day we were together, Kathie decided to try to buck up her spirits.

"Mom, you don't want to die now," she whispered, leaning close to her face. "Why don't you wait around, and maybe we can have another little Gifford for you."

At that, my mother jerked herself up—wires popping from every orifice—and shouted, "What do you want to do a dumb thing like that for? What's the kid going to do—walk Frank to the Social Security office?"

Kathie and I came close to breaking up. But then, with her very next breath, Mom said something sad. "When you have a baby," she said, "you lose your love . . . you lose your life." I think my mom was tired of the life she'd lived. She was tired from raising kids, mostly alone while my dad looked for work. She was tired of always moving; she was tired of worrying. She was just exhausted by living, I think, or at least living the way she had.

Curiously, it's a lot more difficult recalling what I was like back then. One of my few early memories is of trying to ride my tricycle up a slope of dirt behind one of our houses. I was unbelievably tenacious about making that tricycle go up that slope. I'd fall over backward, wail my head off, then lift the damn thing up and start over. I'd become enraged that I couldn't do it. Finally, after weeks and weeks, I got the bike up there. Looking back now, I realize that kind of challenging experience always motivated me most. All I needed was to be told I couldn't accomplish something. They told me I was too small and too slow for pro football. They told me I was too wooden for broadcasting. And that slope was telling me the same thing: No way, Gifford. Call it dumb stubbornness, but I learned very early that if you do it hard enough and do it long enough, you damn sure can do it.

Another challenge required the kindness of a teacher to overcome. I had a noticeable lisp. Maybe it was related to my shyness around strangers; I absolutely dreaded having to meet people. Or maybe it was my dawning realization that the Gifford kids weren't dressed so well. I think I was more aware of that than my brother, whose hand-me-downs I wore. Whatever its cause, I was acutely conscious of that lisp. Enter my third-grade teacher, the unforgettable Mrs. Van Doren. She was extremely pretty, with big, *big* legs over which she wore long, tight skirts. I was looking at those legs even then. Not only did Mrs. Van Doren genuinely like me, but she'd been trained in speech therapy. She made me stay after school every day to work on what she called my "lazy tongue." I can still remember her favorite drill:

The skunk sat on a stump. / The stump thought the skunk stunk, / and the skunk thought the stump stunk.

Considering the business I'm currently in, that rhyme may have been the most important I ever learned. Thank you, Mrs. Van Doren, wherever you are.

Because the Giffords rarely settled anywhere for long, my older brother became my only real friend. He was like my dad: He picked up friends quickly, so I wound up playing with them, too. My first football field was a beach. Hermosa Beach. I played a lot of touch football there with my brother and his pals, which meant I had to constantly compete with an older crowd. When they put together the teams, I always got picked first or second. That was the first time that I realized I could do things better than others athletically, and look better doing them.

My high school in Bakersfield had more than five thousand kids, definitely the bottom of the socioeconomic ladder. Many of them were the children of farmers and oil workers. They were tough kids—black, Spanish, poor whites, kids like me. Consequently, the school enjoyed a great football tradition. The varsity was called the Drillers and the lightweights the Sand Dabs, another oil-field term. I went out for the varsity in my sophomore year. The coach took one look at my five-foot-seven, 120-pound body and relegated me to third-string end on the Sand Dabs. I stuck it out, but frankly I had lost interest in football. Even then I felt I should have been playing ahead of some of those who were starting. It was a frustration I would experience throughout most of my athletic career.

As for the academic side, I never had any interest to begin with. Anything resembling schoolwork left me instantly apathetic. I was even flunking wood shop. Probably, this had something to do with all that moving around we did. Every time I changed schools, it seemed, they were teaching a different system. I must have been given one hundred different directions to identify vowels. Math was even more confusing. Take, say, long division. At one school I'm learning to divide 4 into 160. I'm told to put down a four and carry the zero. But at the next school, they tell me not to do any carries. Virtually every school used a different approach. That affected my ability to learn, and when I lost confidence in my ability, I lost interest in learning.

By my junior year, I was cutting every other class and headed straight for expulsion. Avoiding that embarrassment required exactly the kind of creative thinking I wasn't channeling into schoolwork.

Two football pals and I came up with an ingenious scam to beat the attendance office's system. The rule was that if you missed a day in school, the attendance office stuck an "absent" slip in your file. When you returned, you had to go to the office for a readmittance slip. You filled out the slip in duplicate, and it would be stamped with a date clock; you were handed the original. To get back into each class, you had to show the slip to each teacher. The last teacher would send it back to the attendance office, where it would be filed with both the duplicate and the absent slip to confirm you were back in school.

Complicated? It was almost Kafkaesque. But it finally gave the three of us a goal in life, which was to skip school as often as we wished without any absent slips staining our records. To manage that, we simply stole the attendance office's stamp clock along with a pad of readmission slips. After swimming all day in the Kern River under the hot California sun, we'd go straight to class the next morning with slips we'd stamped ourselves. When the last teacher signed off and sent the slips to the attendance office, a girl we knew who worked there stuck them in our files—after carefully removing the absent slips. Throughout an entire semester, the only perfect grade I received was in attendance. In fact, I was attending school even when I was home sick.

The man who finally found us out ended up turning my life around. His name is Homer Beatty.

Homer looked like Central Casting's idea of a high school football coach. He was swarthily handsome, with big black eyes that drilled straight through you and a very severe, no-bullshit manner. After playing halfback at USC, he hooked up with the Hollywood Bears, a semi-pro team. That really filled us with awe. We'd say to each other, "Wow, Homer was a pro once. *He played for the Hollywood*

Bears!" Actually, he probably hadn't been as good as we thought. But that man definitely knew how to motivate.

Homer was the first to sniff out our attendance scam because he also served as the school's attendance officer. Shortly after I started my junior year, he called me into his office.

"Something's going on, Frank," he said, those black eyes locked on me like lasers. "You cannot be doing this poorly in all your classes and be earning an 'A' in attendance. I don't know exactly what you're doing, but I want it straight out, and I want it now."

Something told me it was time to come clean. "We've got our own readmittance system, Mr. Beatty," I said.

I suspect he appreciated my leveling with him, though I definitely didn't sense it at the time. "I should kick you out of school," he growled, his eyes growing even bigger and blacker. We stared at each other for what seemed like several days. "Okay," he finally said, "I'm going to give you a break. You're on probation for the rest of the year. Let's see what happens. Now get out of here."

From then on, I saw a lot of Homer Beatty. You might say that he made me his personal reclamation project. Although I sensed he sincerely cared for me, I also realized that he had mixed motives. Homer was a very ambitious coach, and because of a shocking tragedy, I had suddenly become important to his ambitions.

Myrl Hume, the Drillers' star quarterback and the most popular member of the team, had been killed in an auto accident right before the opening of that season. Since I was the only other guy Homer had who could throw the ball, he decided to start the first game with me—a lowly third-string end—in Myrl's position. I remember standing in the middle of that field waiting to return the kickoff before five thousand people, while they had a minute of silence for our late quarterback. I thought, *Holy God, what am I doing out here?*

I didn't play well, and Homer replaced me in the second half with someone who wasn't nearly as good. That only added to my humiliation. The next day, the local paper reviewed my performance. It was anything but kind. My mother, who had never seen my name in print before, got very upset. In all honesty, that story didn't bother me. I knew I had played poorly, and deep inside I knew I could play better. And in all honesty, just seeing "Frank Gifford" in a headline was an unbelievable thrill. I remember thinking, This is probably the first time the name "Gifford" has ever appeared in a newspaper.

Despite my dubious debut, Homer started me the following week, and I began to show rapid improvement. By now he was inviting me into his office on a regular basis.

"Did you ever consider doing something with your life?" he hit me with one day.

"Like what, Mr. Beatty?"

"Like going to college."

I was dumbstruck. No one I had ever known had gone to college. My dad never even made it through grammar school.

"Are you talking about Bakersfield Junior College?" I asked. That was the traditional next step for outstanding players in my high school. The Bakersfield Junior College Renegades were very big stuff around those parts.

"Uh-uh," he replied. "I'm talking about Southern Cal. If you continue to improve, and I think you will, there's a chance you could win a scholarship to USC. But never as a wood-shop major, never when you're even flunking that. Why not start taking some courses that will be acceptable for college admittance?"

Nobody said "No" to Homer Beatty, and I sure wasn't going to be the first. By the last half of my junior year, I had changed everything around. Not only did I stop cutting classes, I signed up for extra courses, along with a full load of English, math, and the like. Though making it to USC seemed an almost laughable fantasy, I gradually got caught up in it.

Athletically, Homer did me an even bigger favor. He built his offense around me. By now I was a pretty good passer and an even better running back. In order to utilize both those talents, Homer shifted us out of a T formation into a single wing. As the tailback, I'd take a direct snap from center and either throw the ball or run it. I also punted, kicked conversions, and ran back kickoffs. Suddenly, I was doing things I'd always suspected were within my capability but had never been able to bring off. Suddenly, I started to realize: I can *play*.

Of all the coaches I've had, from Jim Lee Howell to Vince Lombardi to Allie Sherman, I learned more about football from Homer Beatty than anyone else. All the great coaches are essentially great teachers. Lombardi taught high school mathematics, Homer taught phys ed. And on the field, he taught us remarkably sophisticated stuff, things none of our peers were learning. He taught us to read defenses and change a lot of plays at the line of scrimmage. He taught our offensive linemen intricate blocking techniques and how to really blow off the ball.

Most important, he taught us attitude. I learned from Homer Beatty that if you invest your heart in it and work hard enough, you can accomplish pretty much damn near anything. It sounds corny and old-fashioned, yet it's true. So many people, I've noticed, aren't willing to expend the necessary perspiration. Of course, with Homer in charge, there was no other option. When he asked us to do twenty wind sprints, we knew we were going to do twenty wind sprints. And if you couldn't, you were going to stay there until you could.

As the months passed, Homer became a sort of big brother to me. We began talking to each other man to man. We discovered we had similar backgrounds: two blue-collar children of the oil fields. He should have become a famous college coach, but, being Homer, he refused to do the necessary butt-kissing. Basically, that's what a lot of college coaches have to do: trot off to alumni dinners and ass-kiss some guy into changing his will so the university gets left a lot of money. The word got around that Homer wouldn't play that game. He'd just say, in his own way, screw you people. He was a loner, a tough guy, a Bakersfield guy. Later, as an extraordinarily successful junior-college coach, he enjoyed such respect that he started doing clinics all across the country. Hundreds of high school and college coaches would attend them. He also wrote how-to books and put out how-to films. It always blew my mind that my high school coach knew more football than anyone I've ever met.

Though Homer is still a very difficult man to get close to, we chat several times a year. Recently, some mutual friends threw him a party, and I got on the speakerphone to tease him a bit. I reminded him that he once desperately needed a quarterback and a halfback, and he sure as hell wouldn't have gotten either had I been kicked out of school for stealing an attendance clock. He chuckled. Homer's never denied his self-interest. In fact, he's joked about it himself.

If I could connect with Homer on a more mature level than most players, it may be because of the way I grew up. I'd been forced to become relatively self-sufficient relatively early. During my sopho-more year, my parents went off to the Alaskan oil fields, and I moved in with relatives. Then, toward the end of my junior year, my mom got sick and came home. Since there was nobody else to look after her—my sister was married, and my brother had left Bakersfield—I basically became her caretaker.

I never figured out what was wrong with my mom. All I knew was that she had these terrible headaches, sometimes lying in bed all day with them. I'd fix her breakfast, go off to school, then leave football practice early to do the shopping and help fix us dinner. Sometimes I'd go home right after school, check her out, then return to school to join football practice after it started. (Once Homer dropped by my house; I think he was both concerned and suspi-cious.) At night my mom and I would listen to the radio, or maybe I'd go out for a short walk. I was living with a recluse, really. This went on throughout my senior year.

Fortunately, I had a great girlfriend. *Full name:* Margaret Ann Ridgeway. *Nickname:* Midge. *Occupation:* Cheerleader. *Distin-guishing characteristics:* Petite brunette with sparkling smile, bub-bly personality, and cute little bottom.

Oh, was I in love! We'd go to night parties on cozy little beaches carved out by a river that came right off Mount Whitney. We'd build a fire, barbecue hot dogs, swim, and neck. Midge was good for me. She pushed me to study, and, best of all, she gave me my first real contact with a normal family. Her father, Bill, was a telephone lineman who came home every night, had a couple of beers, and turned on the radio while her mother made dinner. They were very involved in the school and in their church. When I'd come to take Midge out, they'd tell me exactly what time to get her back, and they were always up when we returned. I had never been exposed to that kind of stability before. In any case, Midge and I have talked to each other on and off for more than forty years. She ended up marrying a Bakersfield sheep rancher and raising two kids. Then they decided to have one more. Guess what? They got triplets.

I was also lucky enough to have a great buddy (in fact, we still talk two or three times a week). Bob Karpe was a big, smart, good-looking offensive tackle with a wide streak of con and an even wider streak of decency. I started hanging out with him during my pre-reform period when he ran for student-body president.

One morning Bob cornered me in the hallway and announced, "I'd like you to be my campaign manager." I looked at him with disbelief. "Bob," I said, "I don't go to school enough to be your campaign manager."

Unfortunately for him, Bob couldn't be talked out of it. He lost the election to a nerd. Though he was a straight-"A" student, that day Bob was so down he actually cut class. A bunch of us went swimming in the local sand pit and ragged him unmercifully: "Don't you know that the nerds always become class presidents? You never had a chance."

In our senior year, Bob and I were named co-captains of the Drillers. On weekends, we did a lot of double-dating—me with my cheerleader, him with his. Let's face it: It was fun being hee-rows. He went on to make All-America at the University of California, graduated magna cum laude, and became a California real estate mogul. I campaigned for Bob one more time, when he ran for the state senate. We lost again, but he met a guy named Ronald Reagan who later asked him to run the Ginnie Mae national mortgage association. Bob took a screwed-up operation that was losing the government hundreds of millions and completely turned it around. So maybe losing those two elections wasn't so bad. I got a great friend out of the first defeat, and a lot of people got financial security out of the second.

I'm sometimes asked if I had any boyhood heroes. Just one, and maybe he loomed so large in my life because he didn't really exist. His name was Henry Ware, the protagonist of a series of books about the settling of the West called "The Young Trailers." At the time, I was totally caught up in the outdoors. My dad would take me camping and fishing whenever he was around. So I had nothing but awe for Henry Ware, who could do wondrous things in the wilds. He made his own snowshoes with special sticklike supports jutting out of the heels. Once, just as the Indians were about to capture him atop a cliff, he raised the shoes' toes, dug in their heels, and swooshed all the way down the slope, which is, of course, impossible. But to me Henry Ware could do anything. When I was in the wilds myself, I even tried to think like Henry Ware.

Someone once said that you can still see things in this country that the Indians saw. Bob Karpe and I saw them every summer of our high school lives when we'd backpack deep into the Sierras. Besides being enormous fun, it was our way of getting into shape for the season. We'd walk maybe a hundred miles through the majestic Sierra Nevadas and fish in lakes that almost no one had ever visited, that were not even on the maps. We'd load a mule with our gear and, for a few weeks, just disappear.

Bob and I were also very competitive people. During the summer following my junior year, the two of us took a backpacking trip up the eastern slope of the Sierras to a place called Forester's Pass—the highest in the chain. It was a very grueling trek, but once we got to the top, the view was almost mystical. We could look out over a hundred miles of Sierras, all the way to Mount Whitney. That's where we headed next, to a remote watering hole called Wallace Lake. Done leisurely, it was about a two-day hike. We arrived shortly after noon and, while setting up camp, discovered we'd left one of our packs at Forester's Pass. We decided to return for it.

Now, Bob was an Eagle Scout, and I was a Scout dropout, yet we both had learned how to cover a lot of ground fast. Basically, you run a hundred paces and then walk a hundred paces. That's how we got back to Forester's Pass to retrieve the pack. But instead of resting there for the night, as any intelligent Scout would have done, we decided to race back to Wallace Lake—a good ten miles away. So off we ran, and quite quickly I lost Bob. I arrived at the lake as the sun was setting and waited for him to arrive so I could accept his concession. He staggered in about an hour later, in such terrible shape that, for the first time in my life, I sensed the presence of death. Though I tried to pour fluids into him, he shook violently all night long. I was even more shaken, if that's possible. Later, Bob told me he was convinced he was going to die. God almighty, we did a foolish thing.

Next to exploring nature, the Giffords' only other entertainment was religion. I'm not joking. In those days, if you couldn't afford the movies or drinking in bars or going to amusement parks, you went to church. We were Pentecostals, what used to be referred to as "Holy Rollers." No one entertained me more than Aimee Semple McPherson. When I first saw her, I thought I was looking at the world's most beautiful creature. We had driven to Los Angeles to see her perform before about four thousand people in her Foursquare Gospel Temple. It was like Radio City Music Hall. She wafted down the stairs in a flowing white gown, greeting the multitudes as the spotlights played off her golden hair. Aimee was the first star I ever witnessed—and I was mesmerized.

Though religion remains an important part of my life, some aspects of it once left me very confused. My mother, for example, disapproved of my dating Midge because she was Catholic. She never actually said that, but it was always implicitly there when Midge's name came up: "Well, you know, Frank, she's a *Catholic.*"

I wouldn't say my mom was a bigot, yet something in her religious upbringing wasn't quite right. I was also bothered by all the fear that came with the message. They'd tell you how loving and wonderful Jesus is, and if you accept Him as your personal Savior, the gates of heaven will open. If you don't accept him? We're going to fry your ass. As a little kid, the contradiction in that really puzzled me. What puzzled me even more was that it didn't seem to bother my parents.

In my senior year, everything came together on the football field. We won the San Joaquin Valley championship, and I made the all-conference team. One mishap, though, really shook me. During a game in Phoenix, I landed my left foot on a sprinkler head and felt my ankle give way. They had to carry me off the field. The next day the ankle blew up so badly that they sent me to a doctor in Bakersfield, who took an X ray. "Just a sprain," he told me. A couple of weeks later, I felt well enough to run forty-seven yards for a touchdown on our first play against our biggest rival. Now fast-forward to my junior year at USC. I twist the same ankle while skiing and visit the team doctor, who takes his own X ray.

"Did you ever break your ankle?" he asks after studying the results.

"Nope."

"Did you ever hurt it?"

"Yes, during a game in high school. But the X ray didn't show anything."

"Really? Well, all I know is that this ankle was fractured."

Ah, the resiliency of youth!

What made the injury so scary at the time was that a lot of colleges were suddenly looking me over. Every other day a coach would call or I'd get a letter in the mail. It seemed as though everyone was pulling me a different way. Bob Karpe was trying to sell me on the University of California at Berkeley, where he was headed on an academic scholarship. And Midge was attending a Dominican college in San Rafael, which was practically next door to Cal. Meanwhile, a Stanford alumnus who owned an oil company my dad worked for was recruiting the hell out of me for his alma mater. That was my first brush with big-time recruiting. The oilman even offered to fly me up to Palo Alto. When my dad heard about that, it finally dawned on him that there actually might be something positive to playing football.

Of course, there was another person pushing me toward his own alma mater. Yup, Homer Beatty. With his connections at USC, Homer was able to get me an usher's assignment at the 1948 Rose Bowl. I saw USC play Michigan, and Michigan annihilated them 49–0. I thought to myself, I can play for this team *now.*

As it turned out, I couldn't go to Cal, Stanford, USC, or almost anywhere else, because I hadn't taken enough of the right courses to satisfy their entrance requirements. That's when Homer suggested that, to make up the credits I was short, I spend one semester at Bakersfield Junior College. He practically guaranteed that would get me into USC and make me eligible to play for them right off. It didn't sound like a bad deal. As I said before, the Renegades ranked among the top junior-college teams in the country.

So that's what I did, and I had a very good semester. The Renegades' coach, Jack Frost, was smart enough to put in the offense that Homer had used in my senior year. Junior-college football was and is a major industry in California, producing many of the game's biggest names. In the year I played, California junior colleges hosted two other future Hall of Famers, Ollie Matson and Hugh McElhenny. We all made Junior College All-American that year, and I started getting some press raves. I didn't realize quite how raving they were until I came across some tattered scrapbooks in my mom's personal effects. This one is by a Bakersfield sports columnist whose name I will mercifully leave out:

> Frank Newton Gifford is an 18-year-old rifle expert, a sure shootin', hellzapoppin', diamond-studded, gold-lined piece of pigskin material. When he cuddles that porkhide in his little old right hand, fades back and picks out his receiver—that's when he's a shootin' fool.

Why can't they write 'em like that anymore?

Junior college also brought my first exposure to a type of harassment that would surface throughout my football career. Our team had a lot of returning World War II veterans, some tough, wild guys. Naturally, they treated the rest of us like a bunch of fuzzy-faced wimps. And since I happened to be the team's star, they treated me like total garbage. I was the "glamour boy," the "pretty boy," the hotshot who was headed for USC. While they hurt my feelings then, they were actually doing me a favor. When I ran into the same stuff later, it kind of bounced off.

I learned something else about the downside of football from a guy named Charlie Sarver. Charlie had been a tremendous halfback at my high school, and now, in his junior year at the University of California, he was leading the nation in rushing. Everyone in Bakersfield idolized him, especially we players. One weekend Bob Karpe invited me up to Berkeley to see Charlie do his stuff. The morning of the game, I hooked up with Bob and another backpacking buddy named Les Richter, who became an All-American linebacker at Cal and an All-Pro linebacker with the Rams, and went over to Charlie's dorm to pay our respects. He was sitting in this drab little room, very quiet and very bashful, and I couldn't stop staring at him. Wow, I thought, I'm in the same room with a Bakersfield god. In a couple of hours, he's going to be playing before eighty thousand people!

Charlie was sensational that afternoon. He ran all over the place. I can't remember whether Cal won or lost, but I was so proud of him. The very next Saturday—*poof!*—he tore up his knee so badly that he never played again. The whole city of Bakersfield fell apart, including me. Until that day, the possibility of a career-ending injury had never brushed my mind.

Little did I suspect it then, but my own prospects were about to take a major hit. One day a USC alumnus who had helped Homer recruit me dropped by my house. "Frank," he sorrowfully said, "there's no way USC can let you in. The Pacific Coast Conference is suddenly coming down hard on admittance policies. You're just not academically eligible." That shattered me. After all, I had studied my tail off from my junior year on and was getting excellent grades. It was if they'd changed the rules on me. I went to see Homer in a rage. "You told me this is how it's going to be," I said, "and now they're telling me it's not going to be."

Homer moved fast. He called some people at USC, gave me a glowing endorsement, and came away with a compromise proposal. I would be allowed to enroll in USC's extension division—basically, night school. That meant I couldn't participate in spring-practice football in my freshman year, but if I passed the right courses, I'd be admitted with no such strings as a sophomore.

It was a very tough decision for me, particularly since the recruiting offers were now arriving from virtually everywhere: Notre Dame, Michigan, SMU, Texas, to name a few. The most tempting package came from Arizona, which was trying to build a big-time program. Some Arizona alumni promised me a car and five hundred dollars a month. To someone like me, that seemed as mind-bending as winning a lottery. Homer heard about it and quickly telephoned.

"Look," he said, "do you want to play for Arizona or do you want to play in the Los Angeles Coliseum for the University of Southern California Trojans?"

I never could resist that voice. And by the time I decided to enroll at USC, I'd realized how incredibly far I'd traveled. The laughable fantasy that Homer Beatty had planted in my mind had somehow become a reality.

The roughneck's boy was a university man.

CHAPTER 3

TROJAN WARS

*E*ven today, more than twenty years after the late Fred Exley wrote *A Fan's Notes,* a lot of very smart people believe my life at USC conformed to how he described it in that novel. And the sentence they remember most often is this: "Frank Gifford was an All-America at USC, and I know of no way of describing this phenomenon short of equating it with being the Pope in the Vatican."

I liked and respected Fred Exley. Over the years, we shared many hours of stimulating conversation and more than a few cocktails. But in *A Fan's Notes,* at least the parts that depicted me at USC, Fred proved a better fan than note-taker. Or to put it another way: I sure hope the pope gets a lot more attention than I did then.

To begin with, USC was sort of a rich kids' playground, and I was poorer than a church mouse. When I arrived at midterm, a friend of Homer Beatty's and USC's director of alumni, Nick Pappas, rented me his converted garage across the street from the practice field. I lived there for two years. Since my scholarship paid only for tuition, not for room and board, the school gave me what they called an O&M job, which stood for Office and Maintenance. That's a fancy term for cleaning up the gym every morning and evening, mopping the locker rooms and such. It paid seventy-five dollars a month.

Under Homer's compromise, I was attending night school, not having enough credits to get into the regular undergraduate division. Pacific Coast Conference bylaws forbid such students from participating in athletics until their sophomore year. That meant I couldn't go out for spring football practice, which was crucial for anyone hoping to make an impression on the coaches. The frustration of that didn't really hit me until my first night class. I knew that USC had also recruited Hugh McElhenny, a great junior-college halfback and a friend who later became a Hall of Fame running back for the 49ers, the Vikings, and the Giants. And I knew they were also making him go the night-school route. On the first night of class, I'm sitting at a desk listening to my first roll call.

"Gifford?"

"Here."

"McElhenny? Hugh McElhenny? No Hugh McElhenny."

The next morning, I picked up a newspaper and learned that Hugh had pulled a last-minute switch to the University of Washington. A smart move on his part because I later heard that Washington gave him several hundred dollars a month along with a new car. (For the way McElhenny performed over the next three years, they should have given him an entire fleet.)

Meanwhile, the guys in the USC athletic department came up with a scheme to get around my spring-practice problem. "Look, we've got a hundred thirty players out there," they said. "Who's going to notice if we have one more?" So that's what we did. I worked out with the team all week, but never during scrimmages, when the press usually came around. Whenever a reporter popped up, I had to vanish. It was humiliating. I had left Bakersfield a Junior College All-American for a place that was treating me like an illegal alien.

As it later turned out, USC paid a price for its little scam. A Los Angeles reporter got wind of it and wrote a big story, and the Pacific Coast Conference fined the school twenty-five hundred dollars for letting an ineligible player work out. That was the first time my name made the papers while in college—as a guy who'd been hiding out from the press. Now I felt like a *notorious* illegal alien.

On top of that, I didn't have anyone to confide in at USC. I didn't know anybody really well. I was lonely and miserable. So after working in the Nevada oil fields that summer, I thought seriously about quitting school. Hell, I'd finished my freshman year virtually starving, and here I was making big dough as an oil worker. I could even afford to buy a car. But around August, I got a letter from USC's head coach, Jeff Cravath.

"For the upcoming season, we probably will use you on defense at first," he wrote. "But we will certainly include you in our plans for quarterback." That really pumped me up again. Quarterback!

What Cravath actually meant, it soon became clear, was *fourth-string* quarterback. Jeff was a very decent man—he played with USC's famous "Thundering Herd" in the thirties—but sort of from the Dark Ages. He simply didn't know what to do with a quarterback-turned-halfback who was also a good defensive back, punter, and placekicker. So he shunted me to safety and extra-point kicker, and that's where I basically languished for the next two years. It's a scenario that haunted my football career, first in high school, later even with the Giants. Though I was convinced I could run and pass better than the guys doing the running and passing, the coach saw me only on defense. I tried to swallow my frustration and focus on what he wanted me to do. With no other option—other than the unacceptable option of quitting—I learned patience.

In the Trojans' home opener against Navy, my first game at USC, our starting safety went down with an ankle injury in the first quarter. I remember sitting toward the end of the bench and hearing "Gifford!" And I thought, *What could they possibly want ME for?* When I found out, I almost freaked.

But as soon as I hit somebody, everything became very natural. It was almost like playing touch football at Hermosa Beach again, except that there were about eighty thousand people looking on. Every now and then I'd take a peek to see who was up there. I intercepted two Navy passes that day and booted six straight conversions, which, amazingly enough, was so rare back then that it set a USC record. One brilliantly imaginative writer dubbed me the "Trojan Toe."

As it turned out, my toe was about the only thing giving me any kick. Against heavily favored California, I was asked to attempt a twenty-yard field goal with less than two minutes to play and the score tied 7–7. Though I'd never tried a field goal, I made good on it. Now we're ahead 10–7 and looking at a major upset. On the very next play, a guy named Frank Brunk returned my kickoff a hundred yards for the winning touchdown. No wonder his nickname was "Merriwell." Later that season, while I was hospitalized with appendicitis, my roommate gave me a Siamese cat he'd named Brunk. Try as I might, I could never learn to like that cat.

My appendix attack nearly prevented me from going on my first big train trip, to South Bend to play Frank Leahy's undefeated Fighting Irish. I talked Cravath into it by convincing him that, while I couldn't play only ten days after my surgery, I could still kick extra points. I knew we had no shot in that game when both teams appeared on the field. Even though it was colder than a sled dog's ass, we were wearing our dainty little lightweight jerseys. The Notre Dame guys had on big wool sweatshirts with evil-looking black hoods. We never stopped shivering, and they never stopped scoring. In fact, they shut us out 39–0. I traveled fifteen hundred miles and never got into the game.

Recently, while going through my mother's scrapbooks, I came across three postcards I sent her during that 1949 road trip. Here's the entire message of each:

Postcard #1 (showing snow-covered South Bend): *It's snowing in South Bend.*

Postcard #2 (showing the Grand Canyon, which we visited on the way back): *Big, huh?*

Postcard #3 (showing our motel): *I'll see you Friday night.*

I was not what you would call loquacious.

The nicest thing about my junior year was meeting Maxine Ewart. She walked into the student union on a winter afternoon, and I decided she was the most beautiful creature I'd ever seen. Maxine had been the homecoming queen of the previous year's Rose Bowl, and I was so out of touch with the USC social scene I didn't even know it. She had green eyes and light brown hair, but what most attracted me, at least later, was her shyness. She was a beautiful, sensitive, shy woman, and I developed a major-league crush on her. It didn't even bother me that she knew zilch about football.

Maxine was an arts major smart enough to make Phi Beta Kappa. That made us a very unlikely couple, because, academically, I was just getting by. I was fascinated by all the things she knew and could do, especially her talent as an artist. As for her, I suspect she was amused by me more than anything else.

Soon after we started going together, Maxine said, "Why don't you sit in on my 'Man and Civilization' course? Dr. Caldwell is teaching it, and he's great." So I went with her, and it opened up a whole new world. I became interested in the things that interested Maxine. That spring I started to take courses, such as "Money and Banking," for reasons other than to remain eligible for football. All of a sudden, I began learning about things I had no idea existed. The gross national product. The federal discount rate. The money markets and how they affected the national and international economies. I also discovered there was something inside books other than pictures and football plays and gobbled up as much as I could. I was a big, cavernous hole just waiting to be filled.

During those last three semesters, I learned more academically than I had in all my previous fifteen years of school. I also discovered what I didn't know, like how to read properly and how to approach a subject in an organized way. No one in the countless schools I'd attended had ever taught me that. Eventually, I wound up winning USC's combined prize for academics and athletics, called the Trojan Diamond Award. I'm as proud of that as of anything I've ever accomplished.

I was also motivated by a sense of embarrassment. Maxine's father was a doctor who was married to a very elegant lady, and they lived in a fashionable area of Long Beach. For the first time, as the saying goes, I recognized the difference between me and thee. Not that I was some raunchy, Harley-riding idiot. I simply had a lot of rough edges. To rectify that, I started loading myself up with public-speaking courses—and not merely for Maxine. Despite all of Mrs. Van Doren's efforts in grade school, I was extremely self-conscious about my lisp. I don't know if I actually still had one, but I sure thought so, especially before I had to make a presentation in class. Looking back now, it probably all stemmed from my basic insecurity. In the back of my mind, I worried whether I was really good enough to jump from the wrong side of the tracks to the right side. Those doubts bothered me for the longest time.

On the field, my junior year brought more of the same damned thing: still stuck on defense, still convinced I should be playing offense. I did, though, get one shot at quarterback. Against Washington State, our starter went down, and his backup couldn't get it done. We were down 20–0 at halftime when I went in at quarterback, threw two touchdown passes, ran for a third, and salvaged a 20–20 tie. I also missed the extra point that would have made me Hero Number 1. The next week, they put me back on defense. I was not pleased.

Then, in the season's second-to-last game, something truly incredible happened. We were playing Notre Dame, which this time was visiting us. Because I'd twisted my knee the previous week, I wasn't playing. With less than two minutes to go, we owned a 9–7 lead and were facing fourth and long down near our goal line. What we needed now was a long punt to lock up the upset. Since I'd had nothing to do at practices that week, I'd filled the time with some punting, doing it way over on the sidelines and with my good leg. One of our assistant coaches, a former Eagles kicker named Joe Muha, had been working with me. I was just fooling around, but Jeff must have been watching me. Suddenly, he barked, "Gifford! Go in and get it out of there." I couldn't believe what I was hearing—I'd never punted in a USC game before. I hadn't even warmed up.

The play unwound like a slow-motion dream. The ball came back, I got it in my hands, held it, and dropped it just the way Muha had taught me. Miraculously, it sailed over the Notre Dame safety's head and went out of bounds on their 27, a distance of roughly seventy-five yards. There were nearly a hundred thousand people in the Coliseum, and suddenly you could hear them breathing. Then came this incredible roar, because everyone knew the game was over. And I'm standing there wondering, *Who the hell kicked that thing?*

That was a major moment in my life, because it changed my view of myself. Before that, coaches had taken a chance on me only in bizarre situations—sort of, well, we don't have anybody else, so here, Gifford, you do it. Now someone who had other options had trusted me to reach way beyond my limits. And for the first time, I

discovered there really were no limits. How I kicked that ball continues to mystify me. Yet on other occasions, in totally different circumstances, I've done almost the same thing. Athletically, it
happened to me over and over. I would make a play at a key moment
that, to spectators, seemed electrifyingly fast. But to me it had unfolded in almost surrealistic slow motion. Athletes call that sort of
thing "the zone," the period of performance when time seems to
stand still.

That kick also seemed to create a bond between myself and Jeff
Cravath. He knew his job was on the line that season, which ended
up a disaster. After being favored to take the conference title and go
to the Rose Bowl, we won exactly three games. So in placing his faith
in an unproved punter, Jeff put his security in even greater jeopardy.

Toward the end of our final game, a 21–0 loss to UCLA, he called
me over to his side. It was a wet December day in the vast Coliseum,
and a flock of seagulls was circling above us. "See those buzzards,
son?" Jeff said. "They're after me." Then he winked and gave me a
big hug. The very next morning, they announced his firing. I felt
mixed emotions. I'll never understand why Jeff Cravath gambled so
much on me, any more than I understand why he didn't use me on
offense to begin with.

USC's new head coach, Jess Hill, turned around my college
career. Jess had been both a track coach and a track star, and, while
he had also played football for USC, he hadn't been close to the game
for years. He was so open about that deficiency that, shortly after
being hired, he called me into his office and, in effect, asked me what
he should do. Needless to say, I was dumbstruck. But what Jess
finally decided upon made me ecstatic. Just like Homer Beatty at
Bakersfield High, he switched us from the T formation to a combination of the wing T and the single wing and built his attack around
me at tailback. Besides continuing to play defensive back, I ran and
passed and blocked—and we won our first seven games. Life was
wonderful.

One of those victories brought my first exposure to hate mail.
Against Oregon State, a heavy favorite, I threw a touchdown pass
that won the game and knocked them out of Rose Bowl contention.
The Oregon State coach claimed that the pass had been thrown
illegally ahead of the line of scrimmage. That just wasn't so, as our

game film proved. I'd gotten upended just as I threw the ball, and, from a rear angle only, it looked as though I were past the line. Unfortunately, a photo taken from that angle ran in all the Oregon papers. I couldn't believe the viciousness of my mail. You'd have thought I was Count Dracula. Hell, I was just a dumb jock who'd been lucky enough to get a pass off while up in the air. As much as I hate the instant-replay rule, where was it when I needed it?

USC's unexpected success made our annual confrontation with California even more significant. The Bears had won thirty-nine straight and were ranked number one in the nation. Since my old buddies Bob Karpe and Les Richter both played for Cal, this was also a chance to even a score. The previous summer, the three of us had gone backpacking over California's Sierra Nevadas, and they'd razzed me unmercifully for two weeks about my choice of college. By then they'd both been to two Rose Bowls and made All-America, Bob at offensive tackle and Les at linebacker. To them I was just another Humpty-Dumpty with a losing team.

"You sure picked the right school, Frank," Les would chuckle as we whipped up a high mountain lake with our fly rods.

"At least it's a private school," I shot back. "Not one of those state-run factories like Cal. I guess some people were born to go first class." (Forty years later, we're still trading the exact same gibes.)

The game was a sellout, eighty-thousand-plus packing Berkeley's Strawberry Canyon on a scorching afternoon. By halftime, Cal had a 14–0 lead. But oddly, we had a sense they were just hanging on. Our team was in great shape, one of the benefits of working under a track coach like Jess Hill. He may not have known a lot about football, but he'd run us ragged from the moment we arrived at camp that summer.

At halftime, in the locker room, I did something I had never done before. I felt so confident that we were in control that I stormed around the room, whacking guys on the head and shouting things like, "These babies aren't so tough! We can kick their ass!" Maybe all those speech lessons were finally kicking in.

In any case, on the first play from scrimmage in the second half, I went sixty-nine yards for a TD. Best of all, I did it over Les Richter. It was a sweep to the right side, and as Les closed in on me near the sideline, I faked to the outside and broke to the inside, and my guard, Elmer Wilhoite, wiped Les out. Later, on a pass-option play with the score 14–7, Les came at me with his arms upraised. So I flipped the ball sidearm, and my receiver, Dean Schneider, scored the tying TD. Toward the end of the game, I ran it in from the 2 to wrap up the upset, 21–14. We were all in another zone that day. It was almost like playing in a Hollywood football movie, where the good guys pull it out just before the gun. I kept waiting for someone to yell, "That's a wrap!"

The California game also taught me something about a certain type of journalism. *Life* magazine had decided to do a big cover story on the nation's top team. *Life* reporters spent an entire week on Cal's campus, treating us as if we didn't exist. So when we ruined their story, they got ticked off, and then they got even. Their article accused Pat Cannamela, our All-American linebacker, of intentionally maiming Cal's All-American running back, Johnny Olszewski.

Pat Cannamela was what some people would call ugly, though inside he was beautiful. He was short and squatty, with sloping shoulders and an enormous bulbous nose. But put him in a uniform, and he turned into a cannon. He was an awesome and deadly tackler, and every time Olszewski took the ball that day, Pat ate him alive. Since Johnny was Cal's golden boy, their notoriously "ugly" all-male rooting section really got on Pat. They kept chanting, "Forty-two, back to the zoo . . . Forty-two, back to the zoo." Olszewski finally limped off the field.

A few days later, *Life* went after Pat worse than the fans. They portrayed him as an almost animallike creature, the very embodiment of football brutality. They took a lovely, decent kid and turned him into an ogre. Journalistically, they would have been far better served by spending a little more time on the USC campus.

That story haunted Pat for the rest of his life. Weeks later, he was still receiving death threats. And the following year, when he tried to play in the NFL, people kept mentioning what they'd read about him in *Life*. Pat never made it big in pro football. And while he'd never let you know how emotionally shattered he was by the viciousness of the *Life* piece, we all sensed his pain. After his shot at the pros, Pat settled into civilian life and, within a few years, became manager of a Wal-Mart-type department store. One morning he arrived early to find some robbers holding hostages. They asked him for the key to the safe. When Pat resisted, they shot and killed him. It's true that life can be cruel—and *Life* even crueler.

Years later, I visited Pat's hometown of New London, Connecticut, for the renaming of his high school football field in his honor. While there, I met many members of his family. They were so much like him, wonderful, warm, decent people who deserved much more in life. As did Pat Cannamela.

For me, the Cal upset brought a much more pleasant journalistic shock. *Collier's* magazine called to say it wanted to photograph me as running back for its All-America team, which at the time was *the* All-America team. Suddenly, I became hot copy. Everyone seemed to want an interview, the wire services, newspapers, even radio stations. Never had I been asked so many personal questions. They wanted to know everything from the size of my calf muscles to the name of my girlfriend. It was all very unsettling, particularly to someone who'd only recently overcome a lisp.

But the biggest surprise came during the Christmas holidays. Maxine informed me that she was pregnant. While I was deeply in love with her, I was unbelievably shocked. But I knew there was only one thing to do: We were married on January 13 at a place in Las Vegas called the Hitching Post. I had forty-seven dollars to my name. But that night I tossed a quarter into a slot machine, and we hit a $130 jackpot. It seemed a great omen. The next morning, we drove to Bakersfield to tell my mother; Dad was working in Alaska. My mom got very upset. In fact, she went up like a skyrocket. "How can you do that to me?" she kept saying. It wasn't whom I was marrying, because Mom liked Maxine. It was that she thought I could walk on water, and she figured marriage would inhibit me from taking the first step. Though I got angry at her, I secretly respected her for at least showing how she felt.

That same day we drove to Long Beach to inform Maxine's parents. They couldn't have been more understanding. Then we rented a little apartment near USC, slapped on some paint, and moved in. Our son arrived in June. We named him Jeff, after my fired coach, Jeff Cravath. By now we'd adopted the standard social ploy and had told all our friends that we'd gotten married the previous summer. Everyone seemed to accept it, even when Maxine started getting big. Of course, I'm sure there were some secret snickers.

When something like that happens to the football hero and the homecoming queen, there's bound to be a lot of gossipy babble.

As for me, I never looked back. Don Meredith likes to say, "When you come to a fork in the road, take the one least traveled." Believe me, this was a road I never expected to travel. But once I started down that road, I never shot a glance at the rearview mirror. I've never done that in football or in broadcasting or in my personal life. Thankfully, the road always seemed to get better.

My toughest adjustment to fatherhood was financial. I mean, we didn't have anything, and nobody was going to help us. While Maxine's father had been a fine practicing physician, he'd been an invalid for years and a drain on the family's resources. I needed a job, and the best bet seemed to be in pro football. The Chicago Bears and Washington Redskins had already sent pre-draft inquiries: "Are you interested in playing for us this fall?" was the way they both put it. But the team I hoped to be drafted by was the Los Angeles Rams, largely because of their proximity to the movie industry. Having already worked as an extra and bit player in several films (more about this later), I entertained fantasies of a big-time acting career, or at least some easy off-season work.

To my disappointment, the Rams drafted Vanderbilt quarterback Bill Wade as their number-one pick, and the Giants selected me. I later learned that Wellington Mara, the Giants' personnel boss, had been in the stands at Yankee Stadium when we stomped on Army a few weeks earlier. It was a horrible day—snow, sleet, rain, you name it—yet I had a good one, rushing for more than 150 yards, passing, receiving, and kicking conversions. (Wellington wasn't the only future colleague watching me that afternoon. Army's backfield was under the charge of an assistant coach named Vince Lombardi.)

As my contract negotiations with the Giants quickly made clear, my versatility was as much a curse as a blessing. Take my final season at USC. I rushed for nearly 900 yards, completed 32 of 61 pass attempts, caught 11 passes for 178 yards, made 3 interceptions, kicked 26 extra points and 2 field goals. In other words, I was a Frank-of-all-trades. Unfortunately, pro teams, even back when some players played both offense and defense, were not impressed by college hotshots who could do a lot of things. They favored specialization. One man, one job.

On the other hand, the Giants were trying to reconstruct a team saddled with a bunch of aging, broken-down veterans. Since they'd drafted Kyle Rote from SMU the year before, they didn't need another young halfback. So if I hadn't proved I could also play defense, the Giants probably wouldn't have wanted me at all.

Today a running back who's a number-one draft choice can expect a multiyear, million-dollar contract. The Giants offered me exactly $7,500. It goes without saying that we didn't have agents then. I was disappointed enough by their offer to seek out Mel Hein, a USC assistant coach and former Hall of Fame linebacker and center with the Giants. I asked him, "Is *that* all number-one picks make?"

Mel shook his head. "If you hold out," he said, "you'll probably get another five hundred dollars."

Hell, I thought, why bother with pro football? Not only did I have a baby on the way, but my brother-in-law in Bakersfield had already asked me to go into the building business with him. One night Arnold Eddie, USC's alumni director, invited me to the home of a friend in Hollywood Hills. "He may be able to help you," he said.

The friend turned out to be a representative for the Edmonton Eskimos in the Canadian Football League. After dinner, our host ushered Maxine and me into the library. He opened an envelope on a desk, removed a stack of hundred-dollar bills, and counted out about twenty of them on the table. "Take these with you," he said, "and if you sign to play for Edmonton, I'll guarantee you twelve thousand dollars for the season."

I'd never seen a hundred-dollar bill before. Plus his timing was perfect: Just that afternoon, we'd had to borrow a couple of bucks because my check from my school job wasn't due until the next day. In any case, I turned him down. It was an agonizing decision, but if I was going to play pro ball, I wanted to play in the NFL and the United States—not in Canada. A couple of my USC teammates had gone up there and just disappeared. It still happens.

Even so, I wasn't so dumb as not to recognize contract leverage. I told Mel Hein about the Edmonton offer, he told Wellington Mara, and a few days later Well gave me a call.

"We're prepared to offer you eight thousand dollars a year," he said.

"Well, my problem is I need some money right now. Maxine's

about to have our baby, and I don't have enough to pay the doctor's bill."

"How much do you need?"

"About two hundred dollars, I think."

"Okay, let's make it eight thousand dollars on the contract, and I'll send you a check for two-fifty tomorrow. We'll call it a signing bonus."

"Done deal," I said, feeling like Howard Hughes.

Actually, I never did sign that contract. In fact, it was the first of a whole series of Giants contracts I never bothered to sign. That's how close Well Mara and I became. We'd arrive at a salary agreement, then simply trust each other to keep it. I never had a single doubt about that trust.

Although I left USC with a job in the pros and a new baby, I didn't get my degree, at least not then. USC would not accept my academic credits from Bakersfield Junior College, which left me twelve units shy. So later, during my off-seasons with the Giants, I commuted one night a week between Bakersfield and USC, finally earning my B.A. in 1956. There was no way that degree was going to escape me.

My final thrill as a collegian came on an August day at Chicago's Soldier Field. Until 1977, a team of college all-stars annually played the reigning NFL champion, which that year was the Rams. Though I got stuck on defense again, I made an interception that led to our only touchdown. That was my first encounter with pro rules. The interception was a leaping one around our 10-yard line. Tumbling to the ground, I stayed there a second before realizing that the pros allow you to get up and run if you can. I did, and got to midfield.

Right then I decided I liked this game.

CHAPTER 4

HOLLYWOOD DETOURS

*T*wenty movies? Or was it thirty? I really can't remember how many I appeared in, just as my parts in those films were mercifully forgotten by everyone else. My "Hollywood career" began and ended with the 1950s, during which I rose to a highly exalted level. Call it talking stuntman.

A college buddy opened the door for me. USC has always served as a sort of farm team for the movie industry, with graduates of its film school becoming directors and producers, then recruiting undergraduates as bit players and extras. My own recruiter was an unforgettable character, a Phi Sigma Kappa fraternity brother and former Bakersfield High School Driller who played fullback on the USC football team. Johnny Rosetto was our movie-star guy. He had the looks of a Sly Stallone and the con of a Bruce Willis. Johnny was an *operator*.

For some reason, he took a liking to me, even though, at the time, I was a total nobody. "Hey, kid," he'd say on a Friday night. "You got anything to wear?" Hell, I owned exactly one jacket. Johnny, on the other hand, was Mr. Flash. He even set off his shiny silver jackets with cuff links—I'd never seen a cuff link before.

On Friday nights, we bounced along the Sunset Strip, hitting the industry hangouts like Ciro's and Frascati's. The maître d's greeted Johnny as if he were the hottest thing on the screen: "Hey, John, you're lookin' good, John, got the best table for you, John." I later learned he was passing out football tickets to them. Johnny took me to Hollywood parties where the smell of marijuana was as strong as the scent of Chanel. As he worked the room, it became obvious that a lot of women wanted him, and I'm talking about some major stars. I was so shy then. I'd just stand in a corner and ask myself, Why can't *you* be like that?

Thanks to Johnny's connections, I started getting jobs as a movie extra, scheduling my classes around them. If you wanted to work the next day, you began phoning the studios after 3:00 P.M. They'd say, "No work, call later." Or maybe, "Work coming up, call back." Or they'd put you on hold, then return and ask, "Frank Gifford, are you available at ten o'clock tomorrow to play a soldier at Warner Brothers? Two days' work, maybe three. Could you go five?"

Damn right I could. The pay was only $18.75 a day, but to someone with nothing that looked like big bucks. And if you happened to land what they called a "silent bit"—if Henry Fonda turned to you and said, "What do you think?" and you simply shrugged—then you'd get two hundred dollars. The key was to work with an assistant director who was an alumnus of USC. He'd almost always jockey you into shots with the movie's principals.

If a studio made a football film, I was sure to be in it, and there were a lot of them then. My first real score was *That's My Boy* with Dean Martin and Jerry Lewis. I did all the kicking for Jerry, who wins the Big Game with a last-minute field goal. Jerry ran out on the field, then they cut to a long shot of me lining up in the backfield and trying to look like him, about as easy as Joe Namath impersonating Woody Allen. Next, someone snapped the ball, you saw Jerry charging forward, and I booted it through the uprights. I had always thought that Jerry Lewis was a very funny guy. But the Jerry I met wasn't funny at all; he was almost severe. The funny one turned out to be Dean Martin. While Jerry constantly fretted about how he was doing, Dean couldn't have cared less. He kept everyone in stitches, perhaps, I sensed, because he kept himself just this side of inso- briety.

My most heartbreaking setback was *Saturday's Hero,* a realistic football drama starring John Derek. I was absolutely convinced I was going to land the part of Clayhorne, the end who breaks down and cries near the film's climax. A speaking part like that would have meant eight hundred dollars a week for several weeks, not to men- tion membership in the Screen Actors Guild. I and my roommate, Al Baldock, who later became a very successful college coach, audi- tioned for the role together—and the son of a gun beat me out. As a matter of fact, virtually the entire USC team wound up with parts in *Saturday's Hero.* But not me, and I was crushed.

I finally got my hard-to-get SAG card in 1953, again with the help of those old school ties. Two USC alumni (both All-American foot- ball players) named Jesse Hibbs and Aaron Rosenberg were directing and producing a Tony Curtis football film called *The All American.* Why not, they asked themselves, get a real All-American to coach Tony? So they called me up and said, "Would you agree to make Tony look like a quarterback?"

Their timing couldn't have been better. Following my rookie season with the Giants, Maxine and I had gone skiing in Sun Valley, where she suffered a grisly spiral fracture of the leg. They screwed the leg together and gave her a cast all the way to her hip. Conse- quently, I had to put on an apron and take care of Jeff, then eight months old. I learned a lot about fathering, but, frankly, it also drove me crazy. So the offer to be a technical consultant on *The All American* gave me an excuse to turn Jeff over to Maxine's mother. For some reason, that delighted Maxine even more than it did me.

I expected Tony Curtis to be a conceited hotshot. At the time, he and John Derek were Hollywood's reigning Mr. Beautifuls. Instead, I liked him the instant I met him. I learned that his real name was Bernie Schwartz and that he hailed from the Bronx, not far from Yankee Stadium. He was so compulsively enthusiastic that he in- sisted we start our lessons that afternoon. I saw right away that Tony was a good athlete, not very big but extremely quick. For six weeks, he worked his tail off until his ball handling was believable for a small-college quarterback.

One supporting actor, though, kept falling over his cleats. So Rosenberg, seized with inspiration, decided to give his part to me. That's how I got to play Stanley Pomeroy, a fraternity-type Goody Two-shoes: The shoes, naturally, were white bucks. Stanley's primary function was to try to straighten out Tony's character, a mixed-up kid from the coal mines. In one scene, I put my arm around his shoulder pads and said, "You've *got* to get hold of yourself." I really couldn't blame the guy for knocking Stanley into the swimming pool, a scene we shot at the pond outside the USC library.

I took a lot of ribbing after *The All American* came out. Several of the Giants insisted on calling me "Stan (The Man) Pomeroy." Some of our opposing teams took it up, too, with choice side remarks.

The most enjoyable aspect of all this was the week I moved in with Tony and his wife, Janet Leigh. It was part of our deal. During the most intensive period of shooting, when we were working almost round-the-clock, I needed to be as close to the studio as his home was. They struck me as a terrific couple. Janet regularly dropped by the studio back lot where I was teaching Tony how to imitate a quarterback, rooting us on like every guy's fantasy of the perfect cheerleader. They were also the proud parents of a baby daughter. One night, while I was holding this lovely little creature, she peed all over my lap. Her name, of course, was Jamie Lee Curtis. Someday, I vowed, I would tell her about that.

Over the years, Tony and I have kept in touch. In fact, two of his paintings hang in my Manhattan apartment. Our most memorable reunion occurred after a hard-fought Giants victory in 1956. I'd finally played my way out of my reputation as a California glamour boy, a rap that had brought me nothing but grief from my tough southern teammates. They'd finally accepted me as a regular guy.

So here we were in the locker room, celebrating after this very tough win, when the security guard came in and told me, "Some flashy asshole wants to see you." A moment later, there's Tony, flanked by two bodyguards and wearing a silk suit that literally glowed. The locker room became deathly still. All eyes were on Tony. He walked over, wrapped his arms around my shoulders—and gave me a big, moist kiss.

Though *The All American* was a box-office winner, the speaking parts inexplicably stopped coming. For a while, my most strenuous Hollywood activity consisted of lifting starlets. Whenever a clean-cut gridiron type was needed for a publicity shot with a bosomy bimbo wearing an oversized helmet and an undersized sweater, the studios sent for me. The photo caption would read, "Frank Gifford of the New York Giants holds up Mamie Van Doren, appearing in the soon-to-be-released motion picture blah-blah-blah." Mind you, I never complained.

As for stunt work, *Sign of the Pagan* was about it. I fell off a lot of walls in that one, sometimes as a pagan, sometimes as a Roman soldier. Jack Palance played Attila the Hun, and he turned out to be one weird dude. He wouldn't have anything to do with anyone; he just sat in a corner and brooded. In one scene, he was supposed to rough up Rita Gam, who was cast as a slave girl. Jack, presumably a fervent believer in the Method approach to acting, got so deeply into his character that he freaked everyone out with his almost scary intensity. He dragged Rita toward a smoldering campfire and held her close to the hot coals. We couldn't believe what we were seeing. A couple of us leaped in and grabbed him before any damage was done. Jack didn't seem too pleased. Later, I thought I was going to be fired for that.

Meanwhile, my own attitude toward acting had shifted. In college, making movies, no matter how tiny my part, seemed a lark. But after my second year of pro football, I started to think seriously about acting as a career.

It wasn't the flash of Hollywood. I'd been around that stuff from the time I went to USC. I was looking for some financial security beyond football. With the Giants, I saw careers end in a split second; knees blew out right in front of me. And all of a sudden, I've got one kid, then three (Kyle and Vicki). I had known what it was like to live in the back of a pickup. I sure didn't want that for them. But what in hell was I going to do when football was over? I wasn't trained professionally for anything. Acting represented a chance to shoot some craps and, just maybe, roll for a big one.

I went about it very practically. During the season, I took acting classes under Wynn Handman, a very talented guy who still runs the Wynn Handman Studio in New York. I took those classes two nights a week for about three years. Not only did I get to know an entirely different type of person, but it gave me a little more personal confidence.

Sometimes we'd work on scenes from films and famous plays. I once played Biff in *Death of a Salesman.* Other times we'd have to improvise in front of the class. Wynn would give you a scenario— say, you're a farm kid just arrived in the big city and trying to convince a pretty girl you're a smooth guy. Then he'd pick some girl from the class, and the two of you would create a five-minute scene. I became so immersed in it all that it actually lessened the pressure I was feeling on the football field.

Later, during the off-seasons, I studied in Hollywood under an actor named Jeff Corey, who was teaching drama because he'd been blacklisted during the McCarthy witch-hunt. People who were working on a film would come in and have Jeff help them with their parts. Sometimes they'd perform in front of the class, which was great for me. I'm basically not an outgoing person and never have been. This was really the first time that I was able to perform before an audience without being self-conscious or inhibited. In other words, it was easier to play a role than to play myself. For that reason, I enjoyed studying acting as much as anything I've ever done.

It took a TV game show to give "my career" a much-needed boost. In 1956 I was voted the Most Valuable Player in the NFL, an honor that got me invited on *What's My Line?* as the "mystery guest." I must confess I was feeling quite famous at the time. Well, I came embarrassingly close to breaking the show's record for stumping the panelists. What made it even worse was that this was *before* they started wearing blindfolds. Jayne Meadows finally guessed my identity, and then John Daly, the host, said, "Right, it's Frank Gifford, halfback of the New York Giants." To which Jayne responded, "Half back, whole back, I'd like to be on that back."

(Years later, I got a chance to get off a similar line. One night, while I and some friends were standing at the bar of the Racquet Club in Miami, Eva Gabor came running into the room. Apparently, a burglar had just robbed her suite, punched her in the face, and tied up her husband. Eva ran straight up to me and screamed, "Don't just stand there, you halfwit. Call the police! I've been robbed!" And I said, "Lady, I'm not a halfwit. I'm a half*back*." A week later, Eva told the story on Johnny Carson's show, and Johnny broke up.)

In any case, TV reception must have been exceptionally good on the night of my *What's My Line?* appearance, because my phone rang all the next day. Among the calls were offers of screen tests from Twentieth Century–Fox, Warner Bros., and three independent movie producers. I was bowled over.

The Twentieth Century test turned out to be what they called a "personality profile." They plunked me before a camera, then had me turn to the right and to the left and look over each shoulder while they asked dumb questions. "Did you ever have the mumps, Frank? What's your favorite vegetable, Frank?" All the while, I'm supposed to be exuding an irresistible magnetism.

In a screen test for Warner Bros., I had to reenact a scene from a John Wayne classic called *Hondo.* It was a long, heartrending speech in which the Duke tells this purty little gal about his family gettin' killed by Injuns. Then he climbs on his horse and rides off. Unfortunately, the studio didn't want to pay for a horse for me. So, when I finished talking, I had to pick up my saddle and walk out of the shot—trying to look as if my horse was hitched just off-camera.

While sweating out the test results, and always in need of money, I took an off-season job guaranteed to prepare me for the movie business. I sold manure. Its official name was anhydrous ammonia, a chemical fertilizer. But no matter how upscale I portrayed my off-season profession, my friends insisted on calling me a manure peddler. I sold it to Bakersfield farmers for a company called Agri Serve. I'd get into my company car, with FRANK GIFFORD, AGRI SERVE painted on the side, and drive out to the farms. All of the owners knew me because I'd grown up there and gone to high school with many of them and their kids. I'd come bumping across their fields, pull up at the house, knock on the door, and say, "How you doin' this morning? Need any shit?"

By now I'd hooked up with a genuine Hollywood agent. Bob Raison specialized in collecting what he called "the young Turks," the supposed male stars of tomorrow. Besides myself, Bob's agency represented a strange character named Dennis Hopper, whom he referred to as "the next James Dean," and a UCLA basketball player named Clint Eastwood.

Bob had heard that Warner Bros. was interested in signing me, and he was looking for a long-term deal. He knew I wanted eventually to get out of football. In the meantime, he dragged me around to the auditions. I even tried out for the role of Tarzan. I'd been modeling bathing suits in Jantzen ads, which apparently caught the eye of a producer who was doing a *Tarzan* remake. For my audition, I had to come into a room wearing nothing but a loincloth and twirl around in front of this producer and his assistants. But the really embarrassing part was explaining to the sports press back in New York why I didn't get the role. I eventually came up with three different lines:

"I don't look good in trees."

"I'm allergic to chimps."

"I wanted to see Jane before I committed to anything."

At last, the Warner Bros. deal got done. On a beautiful February morning in 1958, I signed a seven-year contract. Presumably, the studio would arrange my schedule so I could play at least one more season with the Giants. In any case, I was ecstatic. Wow, I said to myself, you're on your way to stardom! I rented a nice house in Studio City, moved in with my family, and waited for it all to happen. And absolutely nothing did.

I'd call in every morning and ask, "Do you need me? No?" Click. Back I'd go to wearing out my tennis racket. Meanwhile, they're paying me $450 a week. Finally, they asked me to work with Howard Hawks, who was casting a John Wayne film called *Rio Bravo.* They wanted me to help screen-test the people trying out for roles. Obviously, you couldn't ask the Duke to come in and do that. But I regarded the offer as an omen. I'd won my Warners contract with the help of a John Wayne movie. Maybe now I'd end up with a part in one.

It turned out to be the most boring two weeks of my life. In the mornings, I sat outside Hawks's office and watched his secretary take calls. I'd say, "I think I'll go get some coffee," and she'd snap, "You better not. Mr. Hawks wants to talk with you." The morning would pass and then lunch and then the entire afternoon, and still no word from Howard. Finally, he called me in and introduced me to an unknown named Angie Dickinson. "Frank will be working with you on your test," he said. So I did a scene with Angie, who'd never been in a movie before, and she got a big part. Later, Angie became a good friend of Kathie's and mine. I never fail to remind her to whom she owes her start in films. She doesn't care about that—as long as I don't remind her of the year.

I also got a chance to work with another famous director, George Cukor. Texaco was looking for a TV spokesman for its commercials on NBC's about-to-premiere *The Huntley-Brinkley Report.* "This could be enormous," Bob Raison told me. "This show will reach tens of millions!"

So I taped a Texaco commercial as my audition, and George Cukor, who was a friend of Bob's, helped me with it. I'll never forget that scene. Here's this directorial genius with a Hungarian accent pacing back and forth behind the camera and shouting at me, "Motivation! If you're going to sell anything, you have to feel it. You have to care for it. You have to really love what you're doing, and *that has to show!*" And here I am in a Texaco uniform pumping gas.

Anyway, I finished second to George Fenneman, the announcer on Groucho Marx's *You Bet Your Life.* He did those Texaco spots for more than ten years. Just George, Chet, David, and the rest of America.

Finally, Warner Bros. gave me bit parts in a couple of James Garner war movies. The first, *Darby's Rangers,* was about a commando unit's exploits in Italy. I had one line and a lot of stunt work. The line was, "Can you get us out of here, sir?" I made a bundle, though, on the stunts. They paid me a $500 bonus for rolling in front of a moving tank, $250 for a hand-to-hand fight, and $250 for tumbling down a hill after blowing up a pillbox. The director, William Wellman, was a very macho guy who just loved all that stuff. And half the actors in the movie couldn't walk with boots on, so there was a heavy demand for a stuntman. Wellman had me roll in front of that enemy tank over and over. I can't remember which of us got more excited, him for the action or me for the five hundred dollars I earned for each roll.

In the other Jim Garner film, *Up Periscope,* I got blown away on the deck of a submarine by a Zero coming out of the sunset. After it strafed me, I executed a spectacular nosedive down the conning tower. This time they gave me three lines. They were spoken from a bed in the sick bay, where my shipmates had carried my horribly shot-up body. Garner, who played the captain, dropped by and said, "Don't worry, kid. Everything's going to be okay." And I replied, "Don't *you* worry, Skipper. Just complete our mission. I know that's what my folks back home would want." Then I let out some wild moans and died. I loved that little speech so much I called Wynn Handman, my old New York drama coach, for some help with it. I practiced it endlessly and was enormously proud when I delivered it well.

On the night *Up Periscope* came out, I eagerly took my family and some friends to see it. My big scene was very believable, especially the moans. The only hitch was that they'd cut all my lines.

About this time I started wondering where my movie career was headed. The press must have been wondering, too, because one morning I picked up a newspaper and read an assessment of my progress by a Warner Bros. executive named Solly Baiano. "For someone who has done very little dramatic work," Solly said, "Frank Gifford is outstanding in talent. Naturally, he needs training and experience. However, he's loaded with personality and shows great promise." Even someone as naive as I was could translate that: We're keeping Gifford's name on file, but don't expect to see it in lights.

A few weeks later, at a Hollywood party, I ran into a USC buddy who worked in the Warners publicity department. "What happened to my movie career?" I asked him. After checking the room, he motioned me into a corner.

"It's your eyes, Frank," he said.

"What?"

"They're too small."

"What?"

"Jack Warner, the head of the studio, refers to you as 'the football player with the little eyes.' And Jack's convinced that no actor can make it in movies without big eyes."

That was enough to send me to the Warners executive who'd originally recruited me. He silently heard out my complaints. Then he put down his cigar and gave me his most sincere look. "You don't understand, Frank," he said. "We now see you as a television star. We have major plans for you in our new TV division." I resisted the urge to ask the obvious question. Had Jack Warner suddenly decided that little eyes look bigger on a small screen? Anyway, the studio had started turning out some hit series, shows like *Maverick* and *Chey-enne.* If they saw me as a TV star, who was I to argue?

That's how I got involved in *Public Enemy,* one of America's first experiments in recycling. *Public Enemy* was going to be, according to Warner Bros., the next cop-show blockbuster. But to save money on the pilot episode, the studio got the bright idea of taking the long shots from *White Heat,* an old Warners mob movie with Jimmy Cagney and Edmond O'Brien, and intercutting them with close-ups from the new stories in *Public Enemy.* I played O'Brien's character, a heroic undercover detective. The long shots showed O'Brien, the close-ups showed me wearing a matching suit and trying to copy his movements. There wasn't any acting involved, just impersonation.

Now the studio had to sell the pilot to a network. While it tried to do that, the 1958 football season began looming closer. All of a sudden, it was late spring, and I was in a big jam. Though I really wanted to play another season, Warner Bros. insisted that I be available throughout the fall to shoot the series. Meanwhile, the Giants were getting ready to open training camp, and the newspapers were starting to run headlines like WILL GIFFORD GO ON TO TV GLORY? I even got a call from Charlie Conerly. "Am I going to need a new roommate?" he asked, which I knew was the closest Charlie could come to saying he'd miss me.

Finally, I went to see the head of the studio's TV department, an immaculately groomed guy who happened to be Jack Warner's son-in-law. He had this little platform behind his desk, so when he stood up, he looked taller than he was.

"Isn't there some way for me to play football and still do *Public Enemy?*" I asked him.

"Absolutely not," he snapped. "Look, this series is going to go big. The pilot is getting a fabulous reaction. Besides, we've got a heavy investment in you. And as far as we're concerned, you work only for us. Just look in your contract."

I raced over to see my agent. "Is what he said true?" I asked. Bob nodded. "Your contract precludes you from doing anything else," he sadly said. "If you don't perform, they could sue you for the cost of the pilot plus damages."

Dear God, I thought, *what have I gotten myself into?* I was really shaken. I had never even heard of a major-league lawsuit, much less been threatened with one. In desperation, I called a close friend named Jack Landry. Jack was both a passionate Giants fan and a big-deal vice president in charge of advertising for Philip Morris. I figured he might have some dope on how the selling of *Public Enemy* was going.

"Jack, I got a real dilemma here," I said.

"Yeah, I know," he replied. "I've been reading the papers."

"Have you heard anything about my pilot?"

Jack burst into hysterical laughter. "I *saw* your pilot," he finally said. "Believe me, Frank, deciding whether to give up football for this thing is not a problem you're going to have to face."

He was right, of course. Nobody bought *Public Enemy.* In fact, the pilot ended up getting recycled into another Warner Bros. series, *Bourbon Street Beat.* You got it: *White Heat* was chopped up into *Public Enemy,* which was chopped up into *Bourbon Street Beat,* which survived all of one season. Jimmy Cagney may still be spinning in his grave.

Even though Warner Bros. and I agreed to divorce soon afterward, I got one more shot at a TV series in 1959. CBS, having grown tired of paying the Hollywood studios to make their shows, began producing them themselves. I was working for CBS on the radio side, so when the network came up with the idea for a series called *Turnpike,* they thought of me. *Turnpike* was the saga of the New Jersey State Police, and I was to play another undercover agent. It turned out to be one of the all-time fiascos. The day we arrived in New York to shoot the thing, the producer moved into the Plaza and went on a two-week bender. Meanwhile, the head writer plunged into a wild fling with a model. We could never find either of them. While I was waiting around, I talked the casting director into hiring Charlie Conerly and Alex Webster to play state troopers. "What the hell," he said with a shrug. "At least they're used to wearing a uniform."

Suddenly, CBS got wind of what was happening and informed the producer, "You have three more days to finish the pilot." He instantly sobered up, arrived on the set, and told us how we were going to meet this deadline. "We'll just kill everyone off," he said. So that's what we did. We blew all the bad guys away, every rotten one of them, packed up, and went home. Needless to say, nothing happened to that pilot, either.

Cut to a summer evening in 1987. Marty Davis, the chairman of Paramount and a longtime buddy, had invited me to attend a screening of his new film, *The Untouchables,* at Paramount's headquarters in Manhattan. I should have guessed something was up when I ran into my son Kyle at the elevator bank. We got off on the same floor, walked into the screening room, and there were many of my dearest friends. I figured it was some kind of surprise party for me, though I didn't have a clue to what the occasion might be. Anyway, after I said my hellos, we all got comfortable, the lights went down, and the show started.

There, to my mortification, was *Turnpike.* Or rather parts of *Turnpike,* which Marty Davis had devilishly spliced into an old TV episode of *The Untouchables,* complete with a Walter Winchell voice-over. The audience howled when my scowling face first popped up. It was a mug shot, identified by Winchell as "William Youngfellow, full-blooded Cherokee." By the time it was all over, the room was in hysterics. My only consolation was that the writing was even worse than my acting. In the last scene, I gazed down at a dead mobster, whom I'd just pumped full of lead, as his stunned flunky came running over.

FLUNKY: Tony can't be dead. He was just becoming a big man.
ME: Maybe. Depends on his last thoughts.
AUDIENCE: *HUH?*

To this day, I still can't decide what that line was supposed to mean.

Years before Marty's little joke, of course, the truth had finally sunk in. I wasn't going to become a Clint Eastwood, or even a Chuck Connors. In a way, though, that may have been a blessing. In retrospect, I'm thankful as hell that I didn't get a TV series. Most of them last only a couple of years, then you're hunting for work again. My TV series has run for twenty-three years.

All those acting lessons weren't a total waste, however. I finally put them to good use on, of all places, a theater stage. In 1985 Susan Meredith, Don's wife, was looking around for some celebrities to do a benefit performance for a Santa Fe theater group she was connected with. One night, while Don and I were popping a few beers at their house, we started imitating the two guys in *The Odd Couple.* Susan broke up—and that's how I wound up on a Santa Fe stage playing Felix Unger to Don Meredith's Oscar Madison.

I loved doing *The Odd Couple.* We sold out all 530 seats every night for two weeks, and, for once, my reviews were good. My best review came from a *Good Morning America* reporter named Kathie Lee. Who could be more objective? Don and I both invited a lot of our friends for opening night, and, surprisingly, many of them showed up. As a matter of fact, when I peeked out from behind the curtain, I saw Bob Lilly and Bobby Layne settling into their front-row seats, evil grins on their faces. For the first time, I knew the meaning of stage fright.

I also finally understood what my drama coaches meant about getting inside a role. I became Felix Unger, and I couldn't let go of him. After having dinner at the Merediths', I'd clean the table and do the dishes. It drove Don nuts, especially when I began tidying up after him. Pretty soon we were sounding like our characters. We'd be driving home, and one of us would be sulking about something the other did wrong onstage, and the conversation would go:

"All right, where did I screw up this time?"

"It's all right. Don't worry about it, man."

"Come on now, out with it."

"Okay, you asked for it. In the second act you forgot to . . ."

Onstage, we got our biggest laughs trying to cover up our goofs. In one scene, an enraged Oscar is supposed to order Felix out of his apartment after storming off to gather up his suitcases. On this night, Don flawlessly delivered his "Get out of my life" speech—but forgot to go get my bags first. Now he's standing there glaring at me, wondering why I'm not leaving. And I'm staring at him, wondering how to wiggle out of this. I could hear the audience beginning to whisper. Finally, I blurted out, "If someone had gotten my luggage, I'd be gone by now." Don cracked up, and so did everyone else.

In another scene, I'm supposed to clear the table of the dinner dishes except for one plate. A bit later, after Felix and Oscar get into a huge spat, I pick up the plate and threaten to throw it as Don devilishly goads me on. One night I mistakenly cleared the table of every dish. Don and I were halfway through our squabble when we both realized there was no plate. As my big moment crept closer, my sweat flow increased. But when it arrived, Don was ready. "If you hadn't taken all the plates," he shouted, "you could have thrown one!" This time the audience freaked.

The Odd Couple was so much fun that I started asking myself, "Why can't I do this the rest of my life?" Of course, Hollywood had already told me why. But once the acting bug bites you, I guess, it's impossible to cure the itch. Let's just say this: If the theater ever needs me, I'm ready.

Oh, by the way, I finally got to confront Jamie Lee Curtis about that little incident, and it's as fitting an epitaph for my movie career as any. It was at a party for her ABC sitcom a couple of years ago.

"I have a long-standing grievance with you," I told her.

"Really?" she replied. "What's that?"

"When you were a baby, you peed on me."

Jamie Lee didn't bat an eyelash. "Look at it this way, Frank," she said. "There are guys around today who'd pay me a fortune to do that."

CHAPTER 5

WHO NEEDS THIS GAME?

*I*t strains belief today, but when I broke into professional football in 1952, it was the ugly duckling of sports. It ranked just a notch above wrestling. Major-league baseball and college football owned the fans, and we, with almost no TV exposure, played in obscurity. At some games, fewer than ten thousand people showed up. I even played in an NFL championship game that had five thousand unsold seats.

After those first few seasons ended and I made my annual return home to Bakersfield, friends would often ask, "Where've you been?"

"In New York."

"Really?" they'd say. "Doing what?"

The Giants had it especially tough because they were competing against three baseball powerhouses. In my rookie year, the Yankees were coming off a sweep of the last four World Series, the Dodgers were National League champs, and the Giants were still reveling in their "Miracle of Coogan's Bluff." As the song says, the town belonged to "Willie, Mickey, and the Duke." As for press coverage, not one of New York's eight newspapers had anyone permanently assigned to the football Giants. The writers who did cover us were second-stringers moonlighting between baseball seasons. Most of them couldn't wait for spring training, when they'd hustle to Florida and freeload off the baseball teams.

The Giants operated like the small family business they were. Timothy J. Mara (T.J.), a professional bookmaker when bookmaking was an honorable profession, purchased the franchise in 1925 for the then-considerable sum of $2,500. As the years passed, Tim's oldest son, Jack, took over the business side, and his other son, Wellington, functioned as personnel manager and talent scout. Later, Jack's young son, Timmy, worked as the team's secretary. They were a wonderful Irish family, and, over the years they became family to me. I came to look on T.J. as a kind of distant grandfather, Jack as a favorite uncle, Well as a surrogate father, and Timmy as both brother and best friend.

Unfortunately, my relations with my first Giant field boss were a lot less warm. Steve Owen, the team's head coach since 1931, was a fat, snarly Oklahoman who dipped snuff—the juice would dribble onto his dirty rubber jacket—and stuck rigidly to his "old ways" of doing things. He wouldn't even fly in an airplane. We had to take trains to all our games, even the ones on the West Coast. We dragged ourselves across the country so many times we felt like Lewis and Clark.

Because Steve either didn't understand the offensive game or couldn't care less about it, his best players could always be found on defense. In fact, his defense was so good and his offense so bad that he'd win or lose a lot of games by a single TD or a couple of field goals. As for handling people, Steve believed in intimidation. You know, yell at 'em, insult 'em, and they'll play better. As far as I'm concerned, that's ridiculous. Or at least it never made me play any better. I also don't think Steve felt anyone other than a southerner could play the game, especially not a hotshot rookie from the state of weirdos, California. Everything I did in training camp seemed to irritate him.

One day, as I was making an end run in a practice scrimmage, what seemed like a ton of flesh crashed down on me. So many guys clobbered me that I thought they'd come off the bench just to take a whack. John Canady, a grizzled southern linebacker who'd almost torn my head off, was grinning as he got up. So was Steve Owen. "This is a mighty tough league, son," he drawled.

I always suspected that Steve had instructed the offensive line not to block for me. I guess he thought I needed to be hammered down to size. Though I couldn't believe he'd be that petty, it didn't really anger me. Who knows, maybe it was good for me. I knew I'd never get hit any harder.

Meanwhile, I ran into definite resentment from some of my teammates. It didn't surprise me. The Giants had a lot of crusty old veterans, not only from the football wars but the Big One. Now here comes this number-one draft pick from La-La Land who's married to a former *Argosy* centerfold (the magazine "discovered" Maxine in her senior year at USC). I knew they perceived me as a media-made glamour boy, all glitz and no substance.

During practices, I'd get a thumb in the eye here, an elbow in the ribs there. Or if I missed a block, I'd hear, "You dumb f———!" They also had their little cliques, and I didn't belong to any of them. I knew they were all going out for the traditional few beers before dinner, and I was never invited. It wouldn't have taken much for one of them to say, "Hey, rook, let's get a cold one." Still, I understood their attitude. And once I got over the hurt, I learned from it. Later, when I found myself on the other side of the coin, I tried to be especially kind to rookies.

What made that first training camp—the site was Gustavus Adolphus College in St. Peter, Minnesota—even tougher was missing my two-month-old son, Jeff. I was homesick as well as lonesome. During my spare time, I'd read novels—believe it or not, I got deep into Ayn Rand—or hang around with Timmy Mara, the owner's sixteen-year-old grandson. He was such an outgoing, happy kid, always laughing and obviously enjoying life in every way. Timmy and I played a lot of Ping-Pong and spent hours talking. We really got to know each other. It was the start of a friendship I've never stopped treasuring.

From the outset of camp, I knew that my chief rival for running back was Kyle Rote, whom the Giants had drafted the season before. Kyle had been an incredible halfback at SMU, but he'd torn up his left knee in his rookie year and was coming off postsurgery rehab. Since Kyle couldn't work out without the knee flaring up, I took over his position. I had some good exhibition games, scoring a couple of touchdowns on runs and receptions. Kyle barely even suited up, so I assumed I had a lock on the starting job.

The Giants opened my rookie season against the Dallas Texans at the Cotton Bowl. Just before we left the locker room, Steve Owen waddled over to me, snuff juice oozing down his lower lip. "I guess you know we're gonna start Kyle today," he said.

That was it: no explanation, no nothing. *You asshole,* I thought. How could they even think of starting that cripple ahead of me? My brain churned with fantasies of storming off, packing it all in, and heading back to La-La Land.

On the first play from scrimmage that day, Kyle bolted sixty-five yards for a touchdown. It was a simple sweep to the right, and he planted his good knee, cut back inside, and shot by everybody. My jaw dropped. I'd never seen anyone accelerate like that, especially on only one leg. Of course, the Cotton Bowl, where Kyle had played his collegiate glory days at SMU, went nuts. Kyle ended up having a spectacular game that day, catching passes like Ray Berry and slipping tacklers like Gale Sayers. I was awestruck.

From then on, they stuck me on defense almost all of the time. Aside from a few fill-ins for Kyle when his knee acted up, I played cornerback and handled kickoffs, and, needless to say, quietly seethed. It was USC all over again: I wanted to run the football, and I knew that I could, but here I was back on defense.

The Giants of 1952 were an aging team desperately trying to rebuild. Though we finished the season at 7 and 5, we were clearly headed south. The most shocking evidence of that came against the Pittsburgh Steelers. During practice that week, I'd pulled a groin muscle, and, despite my protests, the team doctor—a wonderful old Irishman named Francis Sweeny—told me not to make the trip to Pittsburgh. Charlie Conerly, our quarterback, was also out with a shoulder injury that week, which left the job to his backup, a rookie named Fred Benners.

When I turned on the TV that Sunday, I felt miserable about not being there. But what really broke my heart was seeing Benners get knocked out of the game in the first quarter. Since I was our third-string quarterback—kind of our oh-shit-we've-got-no-one-else dire-emergency quarterback—I'd have gone in for Benners had I been there. Instead, they tapped Tom Landry, who had briefly played single-wing tailback in college, as I had. As I watched Tom on my old Motorola warming up on the sidelines, my misery became total.

"Look at that, look at that," I kept moaning to Maxine. "How could this happen? That would have been *me* down there!"

Well, I've never seen one team get the crap kicked out of them the way the Giants did that day. Poor Tom tried, but virtually every time he dropped back, the Steelers ripped through our pitiful line and snowed him under. By the third quarter, my armchair felt amazingly snug and secure. By the end of the game, a record-breaking 63–7 massacre, I was raising a glass to my astonishing good fortune. I felt like an airline passenger who missed the flight that crashed on takeoff.

I went to the Pro Bowl that year as a defensive back, but as far as I was concerned, I hadn't performed all that well. About that time I started undergoing a kind of confidence crisis. I began to seriously question whether I could play pro football. I agonized over whether I really had the tools, and, if I did, I would ever be allowed to use them.

To begin with, the competition was much stiffer in those days. There were only twelve pro teams, which employed fewer than five hundred players. Today we have twenty-eight franchises using more than three times that number. So while the players may be better today, there was less room for us back then. You had to be truly outstanding to make it.

After much agonizing, I decided that my best hope lay in concentrating on only one position. In practices, they had me working half the time at cornerback and the other half at running back, just in case Kyle's knee went out. That was not only frustrating, but the preparation during the week—working at both positions—was exhausting. So I went to Steve Owen with what I thought was a great idea: "Steve, this isn't working. I think we'd all be a lot better off if I just focused on playing defense."

Steve took out his ubiquitous can of Copenhagen and once again mesmerized me as he loaded his mouth with a fistful of snuff. He stared at me, the juice starting its familiar downward course. I watched it blend with yesterday's snuff stains on his warm-up jacket. Then he just grunted—and I went back to working both ways.

·   ·   ·

In 1953 the wheels came off. The Giants won only three games, and I, disgusted with virtually everything that was happening on the field, almost packed it in as a football player.

It was depressing enough to get hammered on the field each week: We ended up scoring fewer points than any team in the league. But the whole organization seemed to be falling apart, from the players, whose morale was miserable, to the head coach, who'd totally lost touch with the players, to the owners, who were having major money problems. In fact, the press was speculating that the Mara family might lose control of the club. Attendance at the Polo Grounds was averaging fewer than twenty thousand a game, and we weren't all that certain of our paychecks.

Not that we were living all that well to begin with. Players today look at me with disbelief when I describe our equipment conditions back then. For example, I don't ever remember getting a new game jersey. If you ripped up yours on Sunday, the next Sunday you'd find it hanging in the locker with patches on it. Same with the pants. They might look great from a distance, but up close they looked as though they'd belonged to Jim Thorpe. And if you wore out your shoes, *you* bought a new pair.

As that disastrous season progressed, our morale was about as miserable as our won-lost record. There was a lot of bitching and grumbling, and several of our key players started talking about jumping to the Canadian Football League, which lacked the prestige of the NFL but often paid more for American players. (The CFL rules, however, allowed only a limited number of Americans per team.) The Canadians had already cut a secret deal with our best defensive player, an enormously gifted tackle named Arnie Wein-meister. They must have thrown in a recruiting bonus, because Arnie tried to convince several of us to join him.

My problem was the exact opposite of the year before. I had started the season as a defensive back, but when Kyle Rote went down with an injury, I wound up going both ways in a world of two-way football. I don't remember ever coming out of any of that season's last five games. I played halfback, cornerback, kicked off, and ran back kickoffs and punts. And when you do that with a bad team, it's hard to describe the physical beating you take. Somehow

I survived it, but as exhausted as I was, I don't know how I got out of that year without getting hurt.

The worst part was knowing that my skills were being diluted along with my energy. On a typical Giants drive, I'd carry the ball four or five times and maybe catch a couple of passes. When we punted, and we did that a lot, I'd be in on the coverage. Then, as a cornerback, I'd have to go man to man against some well-rested, speedy-assed wide receiver. After the other team punted, or more than likely kicked off, I'd run the ball back. On the next play, I'd make an end run, pick up a couple of yards, get the shit kicked out of me, or fumble. In which case, it was back to playing defense. Then the cycle would start all over again. Once again I'm staring at that racehorse, my tongue's hanging out and he's licking his chops because he knows I'm totally wiped. You can imagine what happened on the next pass.

The guy who really suffered, however, was poor Charlie Conerly. Charlie was a brilliant quarterback, but in those early years he had pitiful support. We had no really talented receivers, and some of our offensive linemen were barely bigger than he was. Typically, the press and the fans assumed the quarterback was responsible for everything wrong with the team. Charlie became the focal point for an incredible amount of anger, almost all of it unfair.

The only fight I ever had as an adult was over Charlie. After one defeat toward the end of the season, a couple of guys waited an hour or so outside our locker room just to heckle him. I never have, and never will, understand people like that. They're like the ghouls who hang around a car crash.

As Charlie and I walked out, one of the idiots started on him. Charlie kept walking. Since I was a few steps behind, the guy turned to me and said something about "your motherfucking quarterback." By then I was so tired I couldn't think rationally. And to see somebody wait so long to insult someone who'd already taken an unbelievable pounding on the field that day was more than I could handle. So I laid him out. Actually, I hit him with a kind of open-handed slap, but he dropped like a rock.

His buddy looked down at him all curled up on the ground and started shouting, "Look at what Gifford did! Look at what Gifford did!" And I'm standing there thinking, Did I just do that? It was almost surreal to me. The guy finally came around, but I felt awful about it for the longest time.

We wound up that miserable season against Detroit, which went on to win the NFL championship. The week before, Cleveland had annihilated us 62–10. It was like witnessing a track meet. Here I was trying to cover a great receiver like Dante Lavelli man for man while a quarterback like Otto Graham waited in the pocket with enough time to eat a steak dinner. Dante would zoom by me, and Otto would lay it right in there. I think they beat me for three touchdowns that day. It was all literally a blur.

In our final game in Detroit, I played both ways once again. A lot of us who had hung in that year, despite all the crap flying around the team, were very proud of that game. We had the Lions, the defending NFL champs, down 14–13 in the closing minutes. They went on to beat us and take the NFL title once again. But the Bobby Laynes, Doak Walkers, and Cloyce Boxes knew on that day they'd been in a battle. Even with that satisfaction, I'd personally never been as exhausted and depressed as I was sitting in the locker room. I was a muddy, bloody mess. All I wanted to do was get my ass out of there.

As I sat peeling off my uniform, I saw a tall, silver-haired man in an elegant gray suit and black homburg striding toward me. It was the Giants' owner, old T.J. himself. We rarely saw him around, but here he was with his head held up high on the final day of a disastrous season. He came over to me, shook my hand, and said something like, "We thank you." As he did that, I noticed him slip an envelope onto the shelf in my locker. Then he was gone. Later, when I opened the envelope, I discovered that it contained five hundred-dollar bills. It doesn't sound like much now, and I don't know why T.J. did it or whether he ever did it for anyone else. But I was very moved—and I also needed the money.

Later that night, my wife, Maxine, my eighteen-month-old son, Jeff, and I flew home to Bakersfield on the red-eye. The moment the plane took off, my depression returned. It was a midnight flight on an old TWA prop Constellation, which pitched and tossed its way eleven hours across the nation.

Somewhere over Colorado, I suppose, I turned my aching body

to Maxine and said, "Pro football isn't what I thought it was going to be. We can't beat anyone, nobody's coming to the games, I'm getting my ass killed, and I'm not making enough money to support us. Hell, I can make more than the eight thousand a year they're paying me hammering nails with my brother-in-law. Who needs this game?" Before she could reply, little Jeff turned his head around, let out a loud groan, and vomited all over me. It was the perfect ending to my season: All that had been missing was to be covered with barf.

"What I'm trying to say," I continued as I wiped myself off, "is that I don't ever want to play this game again. Ever." And I meant it. I seriously considered giving it all up. In the off-season, I decided, I would look for a *real* job with some real security.

THE GENIUS AND THE GUNSLINGER

During my first couple of years in the NFL, there were no superstars. Only national television can create superstars, and in those days television was barely local. The game did, however, have its legends—two of whom were especially fascinating to me. One was a coach, the other a quarterback.

Throughout the 1950s, Paul Brown was to pro football what Balanchine became to the ballet. Not only did he coach the Cleveland Browns, which bear his name, to seven championships, but he invented much of what we take for granted today. He invented playbooks and training camps, college scouting and game films. You name it in pro football, and it had a Paul Brown spin.

My only encounter with Paul on the same side of the field was at the 1953 Pro Bowl in Los Angeles. I had played both ways against the Browns that year, getting beaten on two touchdown passes but also throwing an eighty-three-yard one myself. Now here we were in the Pro Bowl, he as coach of the Eastern Conference team and me named to his defensive unit. On the first day of practice, Paul sought me out on the sidelines. He was wearing his signature brown hat— he was bald and quite vain about it—a brown sports jacket, and balloonish brown slacks. "Frank," he said, "I think we're going to use you a lot on offense Sunday. So maybe you better concentrate there."

My first reaction was, *God, he's talking to me!* Paul always acted like a legend, which meant he was Mr. Aloof. The idea of playing on offense for him seemed even more astonishing. He already had most of his own guys on offense, including All-Pros Ray Renfro and Dub Jones at running back.

In any case, Paul worked me at halfback for the rest of the week. Then, on the Friday before the game, as we were returning to our hotel in our bus, he hit me with a real shocker:

"Would you ever think of leaving New York?"

I gave him a disbelieving look.

"Seriously, Frank," he said. "How would you like to be a Brown?"

After what I had been through that year? Would I ever! Besides, I was awed by how Paul Brown ran his team, how incredibly organized the players were. They were programmed to perfection. Even working with him for those few days showed me that his understanding of the game approached genius. So I became enormously excited. I said to myself, "Do you believe this? Paul Brown really likes me! I think he wants to trade for me!"

On Sunday, Pro Bowl day, Paul called out his starting offensive lineup, and I wasn't on it. Instead, I was assigned to the kickoff team. I did that, and nothing else, all day. Forty years later, I can still feel the humiliation. This was my hometown, my college, and my stadium. My mom was there and many of my friends.

At the end of the game, which we lost, I found myself standing next to Paul on the sideline. I couldn't resist turning to him and saying, "You know something? I couldn't have hurt you today. I can't believe you didn't play me." He never flinched or said a word. And as he walked away, I felt enormous hurt and anger. I also thought, *What a no-class thing to do!*

I'm sure Paul was playing mind games with me that week. He was already working on next season, and he suspected the Browns might see a lot of me. I believe he wanted me to think I was nothing. Later, when the Giants under new leadership began to beat the Browns, I had some good games against them. Playing halfback, by the way.

Despite all that, I never lost my respect for Paul Brown. Among other innovations, he was the first coach to signal plays from the sidelines. In fact, he called all the Browns' plays by shuttling his guards. In 1956 he went so far as to put a radio receiver inside the helmet of George Ratterman, the Browns' quarterback. During the exhibition season, Paul began transmitting the plays to George through a hand mike. There was no rule against it. In fact, according to the press, it was going to revolutionize football.

The Browns opened the regular season against the Giants. That year we'd picked up a quarterback the Browns had released on the last cut named Gene Filipski. So he knew their offense cold. Meanwhile, someone on Tom Landry's staff had figured out how to eavesdrop on the FM band that Paul was transmitting on. Thorough as always, Paul had followed the letter of the law and officially reserved the band with the FCC.

As the game started, Filipski put on a headset tuned to the band and stationed himself next to Landry on the sideline. When the Browns went into their first offensive huddle, Filipski heard Paul's voice calling the play for Ratterman: "L split, twenty-five dive."

"Jimmy Brown over the right side," Filipski informed Tom, who had the perfect defensive alignment signaled to Andy Robustelli. Andy immediately called that defense for everyone in our own huddle.

Poor Jimmy took the ball and was instantly nailed behind the line of scrimmage. It was brutal: The Browns ended the first half with minus yardage. I could imagine what they were saying in the locker room. "This is the greatest defensive team we've ever played! They're killing everything we do!" Unfortunately, Paul's transmitter broke down in the second half, and they ended up beating us by a field goal. But at least it was his last foray into electronic communication.

When Art Modell bought the Browns in 1961, Paul lost his absolute control over the team. He had run everything, top to bottom, which was why his system had worked. Art Modell is a hands-on guy, and the relationship with Paul Brown lasted only two years. Paul retired after the '62 season with the remarkable won-lost record of 167–53. Like a lot of people, retirement was not his thing, and he was back in the game in the late sixties as co-owner and head coach of the Cincinnati Bengals. Three years later, he had his expansion team in the play-offs. Paul coached the Bengals for eight years, a period that witnessed a tremendous sociological change in America. The players were changing, and Paul wasn't. They were coming out of college with long hair and free spirits. Disciplinarians were out.

Paul could be mean, I guess, and he could be cruel. But as I wrote to him in a letter after his retirement, the game will never be the same without that commanding figure stalking the sideline in that brown fedora. He meant so much to it. He also got off a line so right it's still being quoted.

The Bengals were down by 17 points, and some little, spindly-assed wide receiver caught a pass a three-year-old couldn't miss in the end zone. He jumped up and down like a friggin' hero, waving the ball and giving the crowd the "We're number one" sign. I still shudder when I see that today: some little fart dancing in the end zone while his big, bloodied offensive linemen (or a well-hammered quarterback) who made it possible are totally ignored.

Paul Brown's reaction when it first happened to him became an instant classic. He met the receiver as he strutted off the field with a gaze that could penetrate steel. "Son," he said, "why don't you act like you've been there before?"

Bobby Layne was as legendary for his wild flamboyance as Paul Brown was for his stiff-backed militarism. On and off the field, Bobby did it *all*.

As the quarterback for Detroit during most of the fifties, this swashbuckling, blond-haired Texan led the Lions to four division titles and three NFL championships. Bobby wasn't a classic passer, and he didn't have the great numbers, but God was he tough. He just refused to let you beat him. He'd stand in that pocket until his receiver got open, knowing full well he was about to be creamed. And he took some terrible beatings. Yet when the league made face masks mandatory, Bobby asked for and got one of the few exemptions. "Face masks are bullshit," he said. "A real man doesn't wear one." In today's world, it's hard to imagine that anyone would be that brave and/or stupid. But then Bobby was one of a kind.

I think his Lions teammates feared Bobby as much as they loved him. If a guy missed a block and had been consistently screwing up, Bobby'd chew his ass right on the field. If he felt some guy wasn't giving 100 percent, he'd call him out of the huddle and go right in his face, shaking his finger and raving at him while everyone in the stadium looked on. Yet he was just as likely to seek out the guy after the game, throw an arm around him, and say, "Let's go drink some whiskey."

Bobby drank a lot of whiskey. Many nights—after a game, before a game, or just during the week—he'd hire a band, get two or three cabs, and lead them around to different bars. He always took the drivers in with him. When Bobby walked into a bar, the whole place lit up. Pretty soon he'd have people laughing or dancing or brawling. It was like a John Ford western, with everyone tearing up the saloon and Bobby paying for the destruction. Bobby generated fun wherever he went, and no one enjoyed him more than his wife, Carol. "If I believed in reincarnation," she once said, "I'd want to come back as Bobby's cabdriver."

After Bobby got traded to the Steelers in 1958, he and I hooked up in a Pro Bowl. He was closing out his career now, so Norm Van Brocklin of the Eagles was named our team's starting quarterback and Bobby his backup. Since he knew he probably wouldn't play that Sunday (not that it made a difference), Bobby partied all week. I don't think he ever went to bed. He only showed up for a couple of practices, his eyeballs hanging down to his shoulders. He just stood on the sidelines, coughing and barfing and planning another wild night.

On Friday night before the Pro Bowl, Van Brocklin came down with a terrible flu and was hospitalized. On Saturday, after an all-points bulletin had been sent out, Bobby showed up in the middle of practice, looked about, and said in that whiskey voice of his, "Where's Norman? What's wrong with Norman?"

Somebody muttered, "He's in the hospital."

"Oh, shit," groaned Bobby. "You mean I gotta play?"

He cast his bleary eyes around and spotted me. "Frank, we're in a lot of trouble, ain't we?"

"Uh-uh," I said. "*You're* in a lot of trouble."

By game time, Bobby had laryngitis as well as a five-day hangover. I heard he'd been out singing all the previous night. He hadn't changed a single party plan. There were about eighty thousand people in the Los Angeles Coliseum, and I suspect all of them knew our offensive plays better than Bobby did.

On our first third down, he stuck his head in the huddle and croaked, "What y'all got?"

It was hot, and I could smell the whiskey coming out of him. "Well, Bobby," I suggested, "let's go balance right and I'll run a IX with a wide post. If I'm not there, hit the flare back."

"All right, on three, let's go!" he shouted.

Before Bobby could even get his arm back, he got hit. They hit him all day. Man, it was brutal. The three best guys in our offensive line had come down with late-season injuries and hadn't shown up. By the fourth quarter, Bobby was damned near dead. Still, he never gave up. He was still scratching and clawing at the bitter end, throwing pass after pass and getting hammered every other play. We lost the game, but Bobby almost got killed.

As the years passed, I occasionally ran into him at golf tournaments. He'd always say, "Come on, Frank, let's go drink some whiskey." Bobby was proud of his drinking. I think he looked on it as another challenge. Lots of guys tried to stay with him over the years, but they'd fall by the wayside, and he'd pick up somebody else. It was as if they were running a sprint, and he was running a marathon. The marathon finally got him at the age of fifty-nine. Although Bobby's obituary said cardiac arrest, I heard he'd been suffering from liver problems for a long time. Some people said that he'd killed himself with booze, that he died way too young. Maybe so, but he sure gave life a hell of a shot. I know of no one in football who lived more of life or made so many others enjoy their own lives.

Once Bobby was asked who he'd like to be if he could be anybody in the world. "Nobody else," Bobby replied. "There's no place I've ever been where I would have had any fun unless I'd been along."

Needless to say, I didn't decide to hang up my helmet after the debacle of 1953. The only job I'd found during the off-season, as I continued my classes at USC, was working as an extra and doing bit parts in movies. As the weeks passed, pro football seemed a lot more alluring. The bad memories had faded; the Giants had hired a new coaching staff and even come up with my first raise. I was now a ten-thousand-dollar man! Nevertheless, when I reported to training camp in Salem, Oregon, I brought along no illusions. I expected more of the same—more of the two-way grind and more losing football.

When I arrived at our camp at Willamette College, toting my suitcases, I noticed a burly figure standing by the entrance to the dormitory where we would spend the next six torturous weeks. I didn't have a clue who he was. He spotted me, walked over, and stuck out his hand. "Hiya," he said. "I'm Vince Lombardi." Then he uttered three words that changed the rest of my life:

"You're my halfback."

What had happened was that the Giants had finally joined the modern era. They'd fired Steve Owen, an extremely tough decision for the passionately loyal Maras, and elevated Jim Lee Howell, a crusty ex-marine captain who had served as an assistant coach, to replace him. Jim Lee was the beneficiary of two brilliant moves by Wellington Mara. First Well brought in Lombardi, his former Fordham classmate who had been coaching the backfield at West Point, to handle our offense. Next he asked Tom Landry, our All-Pro safety, to take total charge of the defense as a player-coach. The New York Giants, and Frank Gifford in particular, were about to be reborn.

Do you believe in genies? Unlike Aladdin's, my genie had three different names: Homer Beatty, Jess Hill, and Vince Lombardi. Yet each one granted me the same wish when I most needed it. Just as Homer in high school and Jess in college rescued me from the defense and built their offense around me, so did Vince in the pros. They could have all sprung from the same magic lamp.

Lombardi believed that the left halfback position—now my permanent home—was the key to a successful offense, the point of attack. That attack would basically hinge on three plays: the 49 and 28 power sweeps, in which I took a handoff from Charlie Conerly and followed two pulling guards around end; and the halfback option, the same play except that I either passed the ball or ran it.

As I later learned, Vince had watched from the sidelines when I helped USC wipe out Army—playing halfback out of the single wing—and I suspect he filed that away. In any case, my versatility, which had been a curse under Steve Owen, perfectly° fit Vince's concept of offense. I could run, I could pass, I could catch passes, and I could block. Vince believed that a versatile offense keyed around a versatile player could be as effective in the pros as it was in college. Most other pro coaches disagreed. They wanted running backs to be running backs, receivers to be receivers, and quarterbacks to do all the passing.

In effect, my pro career began that season. After the first eight games, I'd posted an average gain per rush of 5.6 yards, the highest in the conference. What really turned me on, though, was passing the ball in Vince's option play. Ever since Bakersfield High, I'd been a frustrated quarterback. All of a sudden, I found myself averaging a touchdown every four throws. Of course, the way the option play worked, I threw the ball only when I saw a man open. Otherwise, I ran it. But that didn't dilute the emotional charge. There were Sundays when I felt like Bobby Layne without the hangover.

Charlie Conerly was having even more fun. Before training camp, he'd announced his retirement from football. Six long seasons of battering and boos had finally gotten to him. Determined to change Charlie's mind, Jim Lee went down to his little hometown of Clarksdale, Mississippi, and offered him a salary boost. Charlie just shrugged. Then Jim Lee got to him by promising to find some linemen to protect him and maybe a decent end or two. In any event, Charlie was on his way back.

It was Lombardi, however, who rejuvenated our rapidly aging quarterback. For the first time in Charlie's pro career, he had a coach who was all offense and who gave him a running game that kept the other team sufficiently off balance to allow a passing game to succeed. With that new philosophy and protection up front, Charlie threw twenty touchdown passes in 1954 (a twelve-game season, by the way)—exactly seventeen more than the previous season.

Tom Landry, meanwhile, was beginning to refine his defense that would eventually become *the* defense. He took Steve Owen's 6-4-1 "umbrella" of 1950 and gradually turned it into his own 4-3-4. He had four linemen to contain the run and pressure the passer. His three linebackers filled specific holes against the run and had exact assignments against the pass. His four defensive backs covered wide receivers and backs working deep out of the offensive backfield in a precise manner that the game had never known before.

In defensive strategy, Tom went far beyond Paul Brown. And in my estimation, defense is what wins football games. The offense gets the hosannas and the genuflections and all that crap. But the defense wins it—and Tom Landry was an absolute master of the science of defense.

I think we could have won our conference title in the first year of our new regime. We'd gotten rid of all our locker-room lawyers and kept the guys who truly wanted to play. We were actually leading the conference when, in the season's ninth game, *bang*, Kyle and I were injured on the same play. I was carrying the ball off right tackle on a 47 power and Kyle was blocking from his flanker position. Somehow we collided and, in the pileup, my right knee whacked him in the head.

Kyle missed the next two games with a bad concussion. I ripped the ligaments in my knee and was finished for the year. Since Kyle was our leading receiver at the time, and I was our leading rusher, that basically wiped out the Giants' offense. We lost three of our last four games, and once again the Browns took the title.

The second I felt my knee go, I thought, *God, my career's over.* The knee was incredibly loose and flappy. I'd never been seriously hurt before, so it really shook me. They put my knee in a splint, took me to the hospital, iced it down, and kept me there almost a week.

That put me in a tough position when they named me to the Pro Bowl. The bottom half of my right leg still felt as though it were about to fall off. The knee joint was still loose. Finally, I called Well Mara and told him of my fears. He advised me to skip the Pro Bowl. The thing was, I desperately needed the dough. They gave you five hundred dollars just for showing up, and I was getting ready to build a house in Bakersfield for my family. So I ended up going to the game and kind of limping through it.

For the next nine years of my career, I never played one game without being aware of my right knee. There were certain things I couldn't do anymore, like plant the knee a certain way. I just knew that sucker was about to blow out. On the other hand, today they would have probably operated on me, and I might not have played nine more years. I think they cut altogether too quickly today. There are many talented orthopedic surgeons, but in my opinion surgery is often used as a device to get a high-priced player back into action quickly. Often, the irreversible damage doesn't manifest itself until years after the athlete returns. In the modern world of sports, this happens in every game at every level, from high school to the pros.

Fortunately, Doc Sweeny, our grizzled little team physician, believed in time, nature, and good scotch whiskey—a formula that worked for me. Here's to you, Doc.

Right from his first day on the job, Jim Lee Howell functioned as more of a figurehead than a head coach. He was a six-foot-six Arkansas farmer with a huge head, a big shock of white hair, and a booming voice. He wore his pants so high they looked as if they were buttoned under his armpits. Somehow, that made him seem even more intimidating. Rookies were terrified of him.

But Jim Lee knew little or nothing about the tactics of pro football, and I think he realized it. So he delegated virtually all his authority. In fact, he let Lombardi and Landry run the team. And to his credit, Jim Lee didn't get in the way. We used to kid about it among ourselves. Basically, our head coach's role was to decide whether we'd leave for Cleveland at three in the afternoon or four, call the roll as we got on the bus, and rule whether we'd kick off or receive.

Convinced that discipline made winning teams as well as tough marines, Jim Lee personally took curfew check in training camp. Every night at eleven you'd hear this big, bulky guy lumbering down the hallways, rapping on doors to see if you were in your bed. Sometimes he'd just open the door: Privacy was not one of his priorities. Or so Harland Svare, one of our linebackers, and Don Heinrich, a quarterback, discovered one summer evening in 1957. Harland and Don were training-camp roommates, living right next door to Charlie and me. That night, shortly after the two retired to their bunks, Harland's bad back began acting up. "It's just killing me," he kept complaining to Don. "I'm never going to get any sleep. C'mon, Don. Why don't you just pop my back?"

So Heinrich, who was as naked as Svare, dragged himself out of bed and stood behind his roommate in the middle of the darkened room. Then he wrapped both arms snugly around Harland's chest and began lifting him up and down . . . up and down . . . to pop his lower back. Unfortunately, Jim Lee chose that moment to open the door. There, nakedly exposed in the light from the hall, were two of his biggest stars doing what appeared to be you-know-what.

Poor Jim Lee. He quietly closed the door and shuffled back down the hallway. He never uttered a single word. In fact, to this day he's never said a word about that scene.

But he also never took another bed check.

As for my own relations with Jim Lee, maybe the warden in *Cool Hand Luke* said it best: "What we have here is a failure to communicate." Or maybe Jim Lee simply disliked me. Now I'm not someone who's paranoid about people, but I know a lot of them haven't liked me, and I sensed right off that Jim Lee was one of them. He was on my case all the time. Perhaps it was because I'd done some magazine layouts, had worked in the movies, and was starting to do TV commercials. All this drove him bananas. Though I never let any of that interfere with football, I suspect he thought I did.

I'll never forget the time I did a Rapid Shave commercial at our training camp in Vermont. The camera crew and I were in the college gymnasium about ten minutes before practice was to start. I knew we could finish shooting in time, but I also knew that Jim Lee was likely to make sure.

"I gotta get my ass on the field," I warned them as I lathered up one more time. "Jim Lee is going to come in here any minute and raise holy hell."

The words had barely left my mouth when Jim Lee stormed into the gym. First he let out an enormous roar, kind of like the new occupant of a bear trap. Then he bellowed, "What are you doing, Fraaank? *DO YOU WANT TO BE A FOOTBALL PLAYER OR A MOVIE ACTOR?*"

Man, did he scare those fancy little TV guys. They took one look at this six-foot-six purple-faced ex-marine, grabbed their equipment, and their asses were gone. Suddenly, I was standing there all alone, soap dripping down my chin. I couldn't help laughing. Even Jim Lee cracked a smile. A very small smile.

We had another confrontation, though, that wasn't at all funny. In the opening game of the 1957 season, the year after we'd won the NFL championship, I missed a block on a Brown defensive end. He hammered our running back, Alex Webster, so hard he coughed up the ball. I felt awful about it, and on Monday, as we were looking at the game films, Jim Lee took me apart. He made it sound as if I'd lost the freaking football game. It was obvious he was just trying to humiliate me in front of the entire team.

"We have some of these California hotshots," he said, "who've gotten so big during the off-season they're not a part of the team anymore. They've just got their minds on being movie stars."

He was still going on and on when I walked out of the meeting. I was pissed off and hurt, and I was fighting back tears. As the league's Most Valuable Player, I'd helped bring the Giants a championship the year before. Maybe I was wrong to feel that way. Maybe I was too thin-skinned. But I'd never given a coach any reason to attack me like that, missed block or no missed block, and for a long time it hurt. I never had a comfortable moment around Jim Lee Howell after that day.

By the 1955 season, the Giants' front office had transformed the team. Only nine men remained from the 1953 squad: Rosey Brown and Dick Yelvington, offensive tackles; Bill Austin and Jack Stroud, offensive guards; Ray Wietecha, center; Em Tunnell, safety; Charlie, Kyle, and myself. The Giants had drafted fullback Mel Triplett, defensive back Jimmy Patton, quarterback Don Heinrich, and defensive tackle Rosey Grier, a 290-pound, fun-loving monster from Penn State. And in an especially brilliant move, they'd lured halfback Alex Webster away from the Canadian Football League, where he'd been MVP in 1954. For the Maras, the signing of Webster was sweet revenge for the loss of Arnie Weinmeister in Canada's own raid on them. Never arouse the Irish.

I'd also witnessed a transformation in Vince Lombardi. For all his commanding presence, the Lombardi who took over our offense in 1954 was unsure of himself in the pros. His blustery personality and college-inspired strategy turned off a lot of our team's veterans. Vince didn't come to the Giants as a genius. His true genius was to adjust and absorb. He challenged each and every one of his offensive players to be the best he could be. And he gave each of us the tactics and strategy to make it happen.

After serving his apprenticeship, Vince swiftly turned himself into the best offensive coach in the game. By now he knew his players and what they could do. And we'd come to know him. His enthusiasm was incredibly infectious. He couldn't wait to get out on the field and practice. He was just bubbling with new things he wanted to do, things I'm sure he would not have even recognized the year before. And, God, did he love to see those things work. You'd trot to the sidelines after scoring a touchdown, and all you saw were his huge, glowing teeth. They'd practically blind you. And you were as happy for him as he was for you. Vince inspired you to do things you wouldn't have even tried under someone else.

Though the Giants got off to a miserable start in 1955, losing our first three games, we pulled off a great stretch run, going unbeaten in our last five games. We finished against the two best teams in football, the Browns and the Lions. Not only did we tie the Browns, which was miraculous enough, but we went on to whip the Lions—the first time in a decade the Giants had accomplished that feat.

While we didn't make it to the championship game, we could feel our confidence blossom. We realized that we could really play football, that we could beat some great teams. As a collection of individuals, we had suddenly come together. It was as if everybody grew up at once. Now we were ready to take on the world.

The New York Giants were about to turn a page and write a hell of a success story.

CHAPTER 6

SOME GIANTS AMONG MEN

Beginning in 1956, the New York Giants won six division titles in eight seasons. I'm occasionally asked what made that team so exceptional. It certainly wasn't one individual. As much as I'm fond of Wellington Mara, who handled all the drafting in those days, it wasn't his genius or anyone else's genius that turned the Giants from losers into champions.

If there's a single explanation, it may be the way the team members meshed both on and off the field. There was incredible togetherness. You don't see that anymore. These days players scatter into the suburbs as soon as they finish showering. In our day, we couldn't afford the suburbs, not on salaries of ten thousand dollars a year. So partly out of economic necessity, we hung out together. We ate at places like Jack's Delicatessen on Manhattan's West Side, and a lot of us lived in the same hotel, the Concourse Plaza in the Bronx. On Monday nights, we'd do New York as a group. Nothing fancy—as I said, we weren't making any money. But we'd hit some places and really get to know each other. That closeness paid off on the field. We understood each others' talents and personalities so well that we could anticipate almost every move. We also knew we could suggest things to each other without anyone getting huffy. Sometimes our huddle sounded like a town meeting.

What made our togetherness so surprising was that we were a collection of very different individuals, and none more so than the two guys who took the snaps:

"OLD CHOLLY"

When I first set eyes on Charlie Conerly, I thought, *My God, he's got to be a coach. No son of a bitch that old could be playing football.* Charlie had gray hair and a gnarly, banged-up nose, and he spoke with a kind of wheeze. His facial expression suggested that he was either entering or emerging from a deep slumber. It was August of 1952, and I had just joined the Giants, who were in Milwaukee playing an exhibition game. Charlie had been quarterbacking the team for four years and, though I didn't know it that day, he was only thirty-one.

During the pre-game warm-ups, I was still shaking my head about this old goat when he threw me my first pass as a New York Giant. Right then, I realized he was something special. He had this beautiful, graceful motion and an amazingly soft touch. As I discovered later, Charlie's touch perfectly reflected his personality. Not slow, just S-L-O-W. He never wanted to rush anything. He never said a word or took a step he didn't have to.

Tennessee Williams could have created Charlie. He came off a dirt-poor farm in Clarksdale, Mississippi, made All-America at Ole Miss, and spent four years with the marines shooting at Japanese in the Pacific. He probably should have died, because he was in the worst of the fighting on Guam, Iwo Jima, and Tarawa. Half his division was annihilated. He didn't open up about that for a long time. Finally, when we started sharing a few beers, he told me some hair-raising stories, like seeing the guy next to him get blown away. Then he'd shrug, take a swig, and give me that little who-gives-a-shit smile.

Charlie needed all his stoicism and guts to survive as a Giant. In 1952 the team started unraveling, and to the fans, its quarterback became the symbol of its ineptitude. Plagued by a porous offensive line and slow receivers who couldn't get open, Charlie took a horrendous pounding: He had cuts and welts all over his body. I watched him play an entire half-season with a separated shoulder in his passing arm, probably the most painful injury you can get. In one game, we had to call consecutive time-outs—the only time I ever recall that happening—while the team doctor desperately tried to stanch the bleeding in Charlie's broken nose. It looked as though he'd gone through a windshield. I don't know how he finished half those games.

Throughout all this, Charlie was hearing boos and jeers from people who didn't know anything about football. And, at the time, damned few did, including the sports press. I've never seen an athlete suffer more abuse. He and his wife, Perian, couldn't even go to a restaurant without hearing it. They became virtual prisoners in their apartment.

Yet Charlie never complained or pointed a finger. He'd look around the huddle and see Humpty-Dumpties who wouldn't have made a college team. I could almost hear him thinking, *Shoot, about all I've got is Giff, and he ain't much.* But he kept it totally to himself. In a game against Philadelphia, I watched Charlie get creamed over and over by the same Eagles end. Each time, the tackle who was supposed to block him came back to the huddle with his head down. Charlie never said a word to him. He just kept calling pass plays, even though he knew the Eagles end was going to hammer him again.

For me, one of the best things about 1954 was becoming Charlie's roommate. It was the start of a lifelong friendship, although, in terms of conversation, a bit one-sided. There'd be entire days when he simply didn't talk. He'd just sit there puffing Lucky Strikes and popping his ankle joint—*pop, pop, pop.* Sometimes it would keep me awake at night. I'd have to yell, "Charlie, would you please shut that friggin' ankle up?"

It was the same during postgame interviews, which he loathed. About all the writers got were his two favorite expressions: "Yep" and "Nope." Occasionally, he'd surrender a whole sentence. Some reporter would say, "Tell me about your great game against Pittsburgh." And Charlie would shrug and say, "Yeah, Giff made a good catch."

Aside from his family, it was almost as if Charlie didn't really give a damn about anything. He wasn't even that interested in football: He only did it for a living. You could never tell from the expression on his face whether he'd just tossed a fifty-yard touchdown or been intercepted. I've always suspected that Charlie's emotional reserve was shaped by the horrors he witnessed in the war. It taught him to act as if you don't care because everything you care about could vanish in a flash, including yourself. A few of us, however, saw through Charlie's act. We knew he was a sensitive, thoughtful man who desperately hated to fail.

Until Charlie hung up his helmet in 1961, he and I were inseparable. We were a most unlikely twosome. By this time, I had something going every minute: clothing endorsements, TV commercials, talk shows, acting school, you name it. Charlie was a classic Deep South country boy. Yet he loved going with me to Toots Shor's and Eddie Condon's and Mike Manuche's and P. J. Clarke's and the "21" Club. Toots became so fascinated by Charlie that he'd never let him leave the place. One day, I introduced him to Jack Landry, my advertising friend who had just created a new, western-flavored campaign for Philip Morris. Jack took one look at Charlie and hired him to be a "Marlboro Man."

In one sense, New York must have seemed like another planet to Charlie. He and Perian, a wonderfully warm lady, represent everything good about the South; they're kind, thoughtful, genteel people. But they were raised in a racist society. It's the only way they knew, the only way their parents knew. So it had to be a shock to suddenly leave the South and encounter a world in which blacks and whites shared everything, whether a subway seat or a shower room. Typically, Charlie couldn't have been more gracious, even though he took a lot of needling from our black players, particularly Rosey Grier. For some reason, Charlie always liked to take the front seat of the team bus. Rosey would get on, see him sitting there, and loudly say, "Back of the bus for me once more, right, Charlie?" Charlie would chuckle and reply, "Get your ass back there!"

Although Charlie was the league's Most Valuable Player in 1959, he never made the Hall of Fame. I consider that a gross injustice because there's no question he belongs. The sportswriters who elect players to the Hall have always given too much weight to statistics, championships, and Super Bowl wins and not enough to talent and circumstances.

First Charlie lost all that time to the war. He had to transform himself from a single-wing quarterback to a T-formation quarterback. And not until the age of thirty-three, when Vince Lombardi arrived, did he finally get a football coach who understood something about offense. But Charlie's biggest handicap lay at the other end of his passes. During his entire career, he never had an outstanding receiver. Look at the quarterbacks who are in the Hall of Fame. Not one of them would've gotten there without the help of a great pass catcher. Bob Waterfield had Elroy Hirsch, Bobby Layne had Cloyce Box, Otto Graham had Mac Speedie, Sonny Jurgensen had Bobby Mitchell. Johnny Unitas had *two* receivers who made the Hall of Fame: Lenny Moore and Ray Berry.

Whom did Charlie Conerly have to throw to? He had me and Kyle Rote, which was like throwing to teacups. I was what they call today a "possession receiver," which means you're slower than sludge. If they had put Charlie with the Baltimore Colts, he'd be in the Hall of Fame, not Johnny Unitas. Johnny couldn't do some of the things Charlie could do. When Charlie had a good team, he won big with it. When he didn't, he made the best of it. He may have lacked the numbers, but he was one of the great quarterbacks of all time.

When the Giants got Y. A. Tittle from San Francisco in 1961, Charlie was forty years old and at the end of the road. As Y.A. took over the starting job, Charlie didn't argue and he didn't sulk. He stayed ready, poring over his playbook at night as if he were our only quarterback. But he was such a proud competitor that he began reverting to the old recluse, rarely leaving his apartment.

Then came the season's next-to-last game. The Giants were playing the Eagles, who were tied with them for first place in the conference. Midway through the second quarter, it became clear that Y.A. wasn't getting it done. With the Giants down 10–7, Allie Sherman sent in Charlie. He threw three touchdown passes to bring off a 28–24 victory. That night I dragged him to P. J. Clarke's, New York's "in" spot, and it was just like old times. The place was packed with writers and athletes and fans. When Charlie walked in, everyone in P.J.'s rose up and applauded him. It was his final standing "O," and I never saw him wear a smile so big.

Charlie still lives in Clarksdale, Mississippi. I talk to him every now and then, which was about our quota when we roomed together. During one of those chats, Charlie repeated what he'd told me as a player: "My only hope is that my monies and my life run out at the same time." Once again, it made me laugh. As I hung up, I swear I could hear his ankle pop.

"Y.A."

My personal nickname for Yelberton Abraham Tittle was "Colonel Slick." That was strictly for the shine on his dome, because Y.A. probably was the most unslick character ever to wear a Giants uniform. His most embarrassing moment came during his college career at LSU. Playing against Ole Miss, Y.A. intercepted a pass and, as he was chugging toward the end zone, his pants came down before forty thousand howling spectators—including his future wife, Annette. Maybe she saw something in this already balding quarterback that showed the promise of greatness.

As a Giant, Y.A. was as gullible as he was guileless. If you told him the George Washington Bridge stretched all the way to Connecticut, he'd slap his noggin and say, "Really? Dadgummit, *that's* a bridge!" Yet this jug-eared bumpkin from the Texas boonies totally captured the heart of the nation's most sophisticated city. Though it only lasted four years, Y.A. and New York had one hell of a love affair.

In his first three years with the Giants, Tittle took them to the Eastern Conference title three times. Yet during his nine years in San Francisco, even though he always played well, the 49ers never finished first. In 1960 coach Red Hickey lost faith in Y.A. He decided to switch to a shotgun offense, which required the quarterback to run. Since Y.A. ran like Dame May Whitty, he became expendable, and with Charlie Conerly turning forty, the Giants wanted him. Y.A.

agonized over whether to accept the trade or retire. He was thirty-five, he had a successful insurance company going, and, most of all, his pride was deeply bruised.

Y.A. and I had become friendly during a couple of Pro Bowls. One day I picked up the phone and heard that squeaky, high-speed voice. This was a few months into the season I sat out, but he knew I was still close to my old team. Y.A. fussed like a little old lady, and this time he was fussing about the state of the Giants. "How good is the offensive line? Does Alex Webster have anything left? Is Allie Sherman my kind of coach?" Finally, I laid out what to me was the bottom line. "I bet that the Forty-niners go into a game hoping to win," I said. "The difference is that the Giants always expect to win. Hell, we're stunned when we get beat." Years later, Y.A. told the press that's what sold him more than anything else. He wanted to play with people whose competitiveness matched his own.

At first, Y.A. found himself a lonely Giant. Charlie had a lot of close friends on that team. Even I was a little ticked off at Y.A. for supplanting him. When the players finished a practice and headed for the local tavern, he'd never be asked to go along. As he later confided to me, he used to hang around our hotel lobby when we were on the road, hoping for a spontaneous dinner invitation from the players passing through. Once he followed a group of them to a restaurant and pretended he was looking for a nonexistent friend until someone asked him to join them.

Gradually, however, the team accepted Y.A. as its leader. For a supposedly over-the-hill castoff, he had an amazingly strong arm; he could zip that sucker like a bullet, and extremely accurately, even going deep. But it was his enthusiasm that won everyone over. In contrast to Charlie, he'd come on like a cheerleader in the huddle. Charlie had commanded the same respect with a different style. He'd lazily drawl, "Flanker right. L zig in. And I guess, well, we'd better run a IX on the right. Okay, Giff?" I'd nod, he'd say "On three," and we'd break the huddle.

Y.A. preferred pep talks. "All right, let's go, guys. This is it now. Flanker right, L zig in, IX right. I'm going to look for the man under. And gimme some time to get it off. Come on, chief, pick up that dog. He's been getting to me. Okay, now, keep 'em out of here. If we blow this one, we've blown the whole damned thing. On three. *Let's go now!*"

He was the same during the week, especially when we watched films of our upcoming opponent. "Look at that sucker," Y.A. would chortle, pointing at a cornerback. "If we go play-action, he's going to bite on it every time. He's going to be right at the line of scrimmage. Oooh, I can't wait to get his ass!" I suspect he lay awake nights until the day of the game, drooling with the anticipation of beating that poor unsuspecting cornerback.

Occasionally, Y.A. turned the same intensity on a teammate, though never out of meanness. It wasn't that he minded getting flattened if a guy blew a block. He minded missing the touchdown pass.

Once, a rookie halfback named Bob Gaiters took a handoff from Tittle, danced around a bit as his hole opened and closed, and was decked for a loss. Y.A. flopped down beside Gaiters, hammered the ground with his fist, and screamed, "Bobby, Bobby, dadgummit! You gotta hit it, you gotta hit it! Bobby, you hit that hole!" The rookie looked up at him and stammered, "Y-y-yes, sir."

It didn't take long for Y.A. to become the toast of New York. My God, that old country boy had a time: It was his football team and his city. Whenever he scored with his beloved "bomb," a word that entered New York's sports vocabulary when he arrived, the stadium would rock with chants of "Y.A., Y.A., Y.A.!" At the last game of his first year, they held "Y. A. Tittle Day" and gave him a yacht. He began endorsing products, making TV commercials, and appearing on magazine covers. Ed Sullivan ordered his dancers to come up with a "Tittle Polka." Strangers cheered him at restaurants, and little boys and girls knocked on his door to pledge their support. Before his 1963 championship game with the Bears, the nuns at the parochial school Y.A.'s kids were attending sent word they were saying the rosary for him—and he wasn't even Catholic.

Y.A.'s reaction to all this was pure awe. "Can you believe what's going on, Giff?" he asked me. "Every time I turn around, they're giving me something. I come in, look in my locker, there's a bag. The next day, another bag. They want me to go here and they want me to go there. Wow!"

For all Y.A.'s bumpkin ways, I suspect the city saw in him a reflection of itself. He was somebody who had come from somewhere else, who'd been gotten rid of, and a lot of New Yorkers can identify with that. He was a genuine character, and New York worships characters. If he threw an interception, he'd storm to the sideline, rip off his helmet, and drop-kick it twenty feet. "Dadgummit, how'd I do that?" he'd wail. And that old bald head would be shining between those jug ears: It looked like a convertible with both doors open.

Y.A. radiated exuberance. Once, when the Giants' defense picked off a pass, he got so excited he raced down the sideline without remembering to remove the telephone headset connecting him with our spotter atop the stadium. It nearly garroted him. When close to the goal line, he loved to run the bootleg. Actually, he waddled the bootleg. If he scored, he'd gleefully toss the ball in the air, skip a few steps, trip over his feet, fall down, and bounce back up with a grin that would've lit up the heart of Scrooge.

With Y.A., we knew we were never out of a football game. He was the Come-from-Behind Kid. Irwin Shaw, as passionate a Giants fan as he was a wonderful writer, described Y.A. best in *Esquire:* "He almost always seems in desperate trouble, and almost always seems to get out of it at the last fateful moment. . . . It's the Alamo every Sunday, with Davy Crockett sighting down his long rifle with the powder running out."

Y.A.'s greatest game came against the Redskins in 1962. After trailing 7–0 in the first quarter, he threw for seven touchdowns, which tied the record set by Sid Luckman of the Chicago Bears two decades earlier. The amazing thing was, Y.A. didn't want to pass for that seventh score, much less go for a record-breaking eighth one. In the huddle, we told him, "Throw the damned ball, Y.A." But it didn't seem right to him to run up the score. "I just can't do that," he explained.

Y.A.'s finest year was 1963. Over a fourteen-game season, he tossed an astonishing thirty-six touchdown passes, completed more than 60 percent of his attempts, and was named the NFL's MVP. The only disappointment was losing to the Bears in the championship game, a team I'm sure we could have beaten if Y.A. hadn't gotten hurt. On our first possession, he passed us straight down Wrigley

Field. Bang, bang, bang. Then he hit me for a fourteen-yard touch-down, and I thought, *Man, we are going to blow these people out of here.* But just as Y.A. released the ball, Chicago linebacker Larry Morris smashed into his left knee, tearing the ligaments and knock-ing him out of the game. Y.A. had never felt anything like it. "It's going to fall off, it's going to fall off!" he kept screaming.

They took him to the locker room and shot him up with Novo-cain, and he came back for the second half. But he was playing on sheer guts. Nothing can block that kind of pain. He couldn't set up, he couldn't drop straight back, he couldn't maneuver at all. Even so, we almost pulled it out. Late in the last quarter, we were down only 4 points. By then it was about 10 degrees, and I noticed that the infield dirt was covered with ice in the deep right corner of the Bears' end zone. I gave the cornerback my best out-move and ran straight for that spot, knowing he wasn't going to be with me and praying I could stay upright. Y.A. overthrew me by maybe half a yard. I can't remember which of us was more disappointed.

Less than a year later, after one of the greatest seasons a quarter-back ever had, Y.A.'s bubble burst. A famous newspaper photo said it all. It was snapped just after Tittle was savagely blindsided by Pittsburgh end John Baker, crushing his rib cartilage, gashing his forehead, and knocking his helmet off. It shows Y.A. on his knees, his bald head exposed, blood streaming down his cheek as he strug-gled for breath.

Though that was only the second game of the season, for the Giants and their quarterback the season was already over. Allie Sherman had swept out his aging stars in virtually one swoop, but their replacements didn't jell, especially on defense. We fell to last place. As for Y.A., he just wasn't the same after that rib hit. On top of that, his eyesight suddenly went. The swiftness of its deteriora-tion stunned him. In the last game of both our careers, against the Browns on a dark afternoon at Yankee Stadium, I ran a deep square-out on their cornerback and got open. But Y.A. held the ball a fraction too long, and the cornerback recovered, picking off the pass for a TD.

When I came to the sidelines, Y.A. followed me. "I didn't see him, I didn't see him," he moaned. "My God, Giff, I can't see any-thing!"

A few weeks later, I picked up a New York paper and read two big sports stories. Y.A. had announced his retirement before a jammed press conference at Mamma Leone's. "I don't want to come back and be a mediocre football player again," he explained. "I was one last fall." On the same day, there was another press conference at Toots Shor's. The New York Jets unveiled their young new quarterback, a guy with a gorgeous head of hair named Joe Namath. Talk about the passing of torches.

After retirement, Y.A. and Annette turned into insatiable world travelers. There were sightings of them from Monte Carlo to the Orient. Yet I knew how sad his leave-taking had been for him. Retirement is tough enough for superstars, because you start taking that big stage for granted. It was doubly tough for Y.A., whose career took off like a rocket and came down almost as quickly. Years later, we talked about it.

"Put yourself with me," he said. "Every year you're struggling. Then all of a sudden your unbelievable dreams come true. You're playing winning ball in front of sixty-two thousand people in the House That Ruth Built, and you're on *The Ed Sullivan Show,* and you're being called to endorse products and make commercials, and just as suddenly"—he snapped his fingers—"you're thirty-eight, you're an old man, and the door closes."

Y.A. turned silent. Then a grin slowly spread from ear to ear. "You know," he said, "for twenty-seven years, every time the center gave me the ball, I chuckled. *Dadgummit,* I thought, *I've got hold of it again!*"

KYLE

I first became aware of Kyle Rote on a Saturday afternoon in 1949. When I hitched a ride from USC home to Bakersfield, the driver tuned the car radio to the Southern Methodist–Notre Dame game. Kyle, who was subbing for the injured Doak Walker, had an unbelievable day. SMU came in a 28-point underdog and went away just a few points shy of winning, almost entirely because of him. As I later read, he scored all three of their touchdowns, ran for 115 yards, passed for 146 yards, and punted five times for a 48-yard average.

I think Texans voted it the greatest athletic achievement in the first half of the twentieth century.

I met Kyle three years later at my first training camp in Minnesota. I was a lowly rookie, and he was the team's star runner. Since I knew we would eventually be competing for his halfback job, my imagination had built him into some kind of super being. And there he was riding a bicycle around the field, rehabbing a knee from off-season surgery. This legendary guy on a tiny bicycle! He came over and introduced himself with a big, genuine smile. He seemed so open. The other thing that struck me was that he had an odd body, at least for an All-American. He had a little pot gut and a tiny bubble ass and almost no muscle definition anywhere. I couldn't help thinking, What a funny-looking guy to be Kyle Rote.

Kyle was one of the few Giants to be nice to me during my rookie year, and we've remained friends ever since. I even named one of my sons after him. Athletically, I've never seen anyone who could do so many things so well. Upon graduating from SMU, he had the choice of playing pro football or pro baseball or becoming a professional golfer. But after opting for football, he ran into a bad break that affected his entire life.

In the summer before his rookie season, during a workout in Arkansas for a meaningless exhibition game, Kyle stepped in a gopher hole and tore up his knee. Some surgeon down in Texas operated on it. Whether the knee was really bad or the guy just botched things, it was never any good again. Then, a couple of years later, he tore up his other knee. He literally limped through all eleven seasons of his pro career.

Even with all that, Kyle went to the Pro Bowl four times, though as a wide receiver rather than a running back. He was a thinking man's receiver, the first I ever met who understood the entire workings of the defense. He also managed to develop amazing moves. He would spin defensive backs around like tops. He would just destroy them. Kyle was absolutely the best I've ever seen at getting a defensive back to start shifting his body weight one way, then make his break in the instant before the back could recover. But his biggest value to the team was his unselfishness. He shared everything he knew with everybody, including myself, a rookie who was after his job.

Due to his kindness and humor, Kyle became the major catalyst for the camaraderie of the Giants. He had great relationships, not only with the rookies but with the veterans, those crusty southern guys who gave me so much grief. Frankly, I was a bit jealous of his relationship with them all. I don't know of anyone who ever disliked him.

In a sad way, though, Kyle's life reflected his athletic versatility. He was a victim of his own talents. Most people spend all their energies developing a single skill. Kyle could do anything he wanted to do, so he never fully focused on one thing. He taught himself to play the piano; he wrote fiction and poems and beautiful songs. In training camp, his room was always a shambles. There'd be an unfinished poem over here and half a movie script over there, and, under a pile of stuff, the tape recorder for his radio show. He'd start off all these projects at once. Sometimes he'd complete them, sometimes he wouldn't.

It was the same with Kyle's business career; he always had a lot of things going, and he usually lost what he invested. Once, during a drive around his hometown of San Antonio, he noticed how dirty the alleys looked. So he formed the Alley Cleanup Service. He wound up with a couple of pickups and a pile of bills. We ragged him a lot about the Alley Cleanup Service, and he laughed as hard as anyone. Kyle has had some tough going—health, marital, and financial problems—but he's always retained his sense of humor. I think of him as an artist who never found his brush, or maybe never knew where to dip it. I also think of him every time I look at a poem that hangs in a frame in my home. Kyle wrote it for Kathie and me when we were married.

Your Marriage

Treat it with a whisper
Grace it with a rose
Take notice of each leaf
And of each twig that grows

And listen to each note
That comes from great songs

For "greatness" bound together,
Needs everlasting thongs

Then, should the flame waver,
(No matter how low)
To feed the failing light
A soft breeze will blow.

SAM

In the summer of 1956, a third-round draft choice named Robert E. Lee (Sam) Huff decided to quit the Giants' training camp in Winooski, Vermont. Sam was a very disheartened rookie. Though he'd been a fine offensive lineman at West Virginia, it seemed clear to him he wasn't big enough to make the pros. So, along with an equally discouraged punter named Don Chandler, he snuck out of camp one night and drove to the airport in Burlington. Since their plane was delayed, they drifted into the waiting room. Just as the plane landed, a station wagon roared up, and out charged Vince Lombardi. "Hold on!" he bellowed at them. "You may not make this ball club, but you're sure as hell not quitting on me." And back to camp he delivered them.

Actually, the man who saved Sam Huff was Tom Landry, our defensive coach. Tom's 4–3 defense was becoming a dominant part of our football team, and he sensed that Sam's quickness, toughness, and intelligence added up to an ideal middle linebacker—the key person in Tom's alignment. But it was the four guys up front who really made the middle linebacker in a complex but brilliant overall scheme. It was Dick Modzelewski, Jim Katcavage, Andy Robustelli, and Rosey Grier who kept the offensive blockers away from Sam. They kept him clean and free. Tom Landry created Sam Huff, as he created all his middle linebackers. Sam, I suspect, would be first to acknowledge that. (On second thought, maybe not.)

The second-best thing to happen to Sam was a CBS documentary called *The Violent World of Sam Huff.* It was the first network documentary on professional football, and overnight it made Sam a household name. Before that, most fans didn't even think about defense. All the stars came from the offense. But shortly after the show aired, we started hearing a new crowd chant at Yankee Stadium: "DEE-fense! DEE-fense! DEE-fense!" And then they'd chant, "Huff! Huff! Huff!"

Sam was a genius at playing that crowd. He quickly developed great dramatic flair, jawing in the face of a running back he'd just stopped, patting Rosey's and Andy's butts right before the snap of the ball. We also kidded him unmercifully about his penchant for being so slow to get up from a pileup. We all knew that the last guy to emerge from the pile would be the one the announcer identified as the tackler. "Brown tackled by Huff, number seventy," Bob Sheppard's legendary baritone would once again reverberate through Yankee Stadium. Meanwhile, Jimmy Patton, who'd almost killed himself coming up from his safety position to nail the ball carrier, would be wondering, Who the hell did *I* just hit?

Number 70 had another theatrical trick. If Sam found himself rolling on the ground after an open-field tackle—at which he excelled—he might take one extra roll for the crowd. This, too, did not go unnoticed by his teammates. Let him miss a tackle in training camp, and he knew he was going to hear, "Huff! Huff! Huff!"

Sam grew up even poorer than I did, so I both identify with and admire how far he's traveled. And no matter how much heat we gave him, we all recognized that Sam was a great linebacker who gave 100 percent on every play. When Allie Sherman traded Sam to Washington at the end of the 1963 season, he took enormous criticism. A lot of it came from Sam himself, who's been bitter about the trade ever since. But Sam was always an enormously hard worker, and it's paid off. He went on to become a top executive with Marriott, getting a lot of sports teams to stay at Marriott hotels. He really worked at it. He didn't just pick up the phone and call a Wellington Mara. He traveled around, going into Kansas City to see Lamar Hunt or to Dallas to talk to Tex Schramm. He's done a hell of a job for Marriott.

As much as I like Sam, we've had a couple of confrontations. Though a lot of b.s. has been shoveled about the rivalry between our offensive and defensive units, it did exist. As the Giants emerged as a great football team in the late fifties, the defense, and Sam in particular, came to resent the offense. Since I was the focal point of the offense, they resented me most. Yet only once did things get hot.

The day before our 1958 championship game with the Colts, we met in the training room to vote on who got what in share money. That year Jack Kemp had been active on our roster and had also played in a few games. In my opinion, and that of several others on the offensive unit, Jack was part of the team and deserved a full share: then about four thousand dollars. Sam and most of the defense wanted to give him exactly nothing, which I found outrageous. Sam was always a little close with a buck. You might call him the Jack Benny of football. But giving Kemp a decent share wouldn't have cost anyone more than a hundred or so dollars. The real problem, I felt, was resentment of the offense.

We had a very intense debate. I told the defense guys I couldn't believe how incredibly cheap they were being about a guy who was part of our team. I didn't win, but I kept all my teeth, and Jack wound up with something. Although I don't know how much, it was more than he would've received had I kept my mouth shut. Years later, over dinner during a ski vacation in Vail, Jack told me that he had heard about the great debate. He made me feel good all over again when he confided what that money meant to him: He and his wife, Joanne, used it for a down payment on their very first home.

Jack, of course, went on to an All-Pro career with Buffalo and San Diego and has served in Congress as well as in the president's cabinet as secretary of housing and urban development. Should he ever fulfill his own ambition to capture the White House, I can already hear Sam's first words to him at that first Gridiron Club dinner: "Hi, Mr. President! Remember that time Gifford wanted to cut you out, and I voted you in?"

Another go-round I had with Sam was much more fun. To celebrate the twentieth anniversary of *Monday Night Football,* ABC tossed a big luncheon in Washington. Since Sam was doing Redskin games on radio, he was invited. Toward the end of the luncheon, I stood up on the dais, took over the microphone, and invited questions from the audience. Sam was always one to see an opportunity. "Come on, Frank, why don't you level with these people?" he said with a big grin but only half jokingly. "The guys who are playing this game today aren't nearly as tough as we were. We'd play hurt, we'd play in any kind of weather, and you never heard us complain."

"C'mon, Sam," I replied, "the guys playing this game today are so much bigger, so much faster, so much tougher, and so much smarter than we ever were. No way we could last five minutes with them. Sam, it's all over. You're finished. Why don't you just take off your leather helmet and relax?"

That brought down the house. Even Sam started to laugh. And, just maybe, it taught him a lesson.

Never try to blitz the guy with the mike.

"BIG RED"

When Alex Webster showed up at our training camp in 1955, we were expecting some kind of superman. He had just come off two tremendous seasons with the Montreal Alouettes, setting a bunch of rushing records and getting named the Canadian League's Most Valuable Player. Then he appeared on our field. I took one look at him and said, "You gotta be kiddin'." He was all hunched over, with a caved-in chest and slew feet. His walk was a cross between a shuffle and a stumble. Running his first drills, he looked even worse. He was so slow getting to the holes that people started snickering.

A few days later, we had our first scrimmage. Talk about metamorphoses. Suddenly, Alex was making these slashing cuts, breaking off blocks better than anyone I'd ever seen. He was so strong at 230-plus pounds that it was impossible to arm-tackle him. People either bounced off him or he ran over them. Alex was one of those very few guys meant to play, not practice. Every time he got the ball, he turned into a grinding machine. When he finally hung it up after ten years, he had gained more yardage than any Giant in history.

Alex had another claim to immortality: He was the only player I ever saw smoking during games. He'd scrunch over on the sideline and surreptitiously blow the smoke into his helmet. On a cold day, it looked as if he were defrosting it. And if a bar had been available, he probably would have grabbed a drink and bought one for the house.

Alex grew up a blue-collar kid in Kearny, New Jersey, one of the toughest towns in any state. A couple of times he took me to some of the joints he hung out in. Believe me, I wouldn't have gone into them without the entire team behind me. But Big Red wasn't a guy you messed with: He had a hot temper and a right hand that could take your head off. He learned to fight to survive, I suppose. One night, when we were at a favorite watering hole in Manhattan, a big guy came over and began giving me the usual four-letter-filled hassle. I've always tried to ignore those things and have been relatively successful. But on this night our intruder was way out of line. While I was trying to placate him, Alex stepped around me and told him to cool it. At that point, the guy did an extremely stupid thing. He pushed Alex, or at least started to.

Alex's punch traveled about six inches. *Splat!* Before they carted the victim off, I saw a lot of blood. It was a very messy moment, though I doubt Alex noticed. All he noticed was that my glass was empty. "How about another, Frank?" he said.

On another occasion, though, Big Red let me down. It was during a 1959 pre-season game against Detroit, when I was trying out at quarterback, a dream I'd nurtured ever since Bakersfield High. I'd had a pretty decent first half. With the score tied 7–7, and seconds left in the half, I threw an apparent touchdown to Alex down the sideline. It hit him right in the hands. And he, an amazingly good receiver, dropped the damned thing. At halftime Jim Lee asked me to go back to playing halfback, thereby ending my noble experiment. For thirty-five years, I've been reminding Alex that he's the only reason I didn't make it as a Giants quarterback. And for thirty-five years, he's always responded with a big laugh.

Alex put in five years as head coach of the Giants, and he's still one of the franchise's most beloved alumni. Today he owns a restaurant and bar in Jupiter, Florida, naturally called Big Red's. As a matter of fact, it's the biggest restaurant and bar in town. One thing's for sure: Alex will never have to hire a bouncer.

"LITTLE RO"

Rosie Brown was a twenty-seventh-round draft pick from Morgan State—and that says something about the integration of pro football. Over the years, the NFL has gotten a bum rap for not having more black players during the forties and fifties. Just look at the number of blacks who were then competing in big-time college programs. There were none in the racially restricted Southeast and Southwest conferences, and damned few playing anywhere else. What the NCAA was feeding to the NFL was almost exclusively white players. Like Rosie Brown, the blacks had to go to black schools, the Jackson States and Morgan States. And, sadly, those schools could turn out only so many black stars, although they turned out some great ones. It wasn't right, but it certainly wasn't the NFL's fault.

The full integration of college football, of course, changed all that. Yet there's a less obvious factor. What helped liberate black players was the emergence of sports as mass entertainment. Before that, most of the blacks you'd see at Toots Shor's were black comedians. Then, all of a sudden, the TV networks began showcasing blacks as great athletes as well as entertainers. Suddenly, professional sports could no longer ignore the Rosie Browns of the world.

As far as I'm concerned, Rosie was the best offensive tackle ever to play. We knew the moment we saw him that this was one of the great physical specimens, eventually rounding out at about six feet five and 270 pounds. But nobody imagined his incredible athletic ability. Rosie was so fast he could have played running back and would have made a great tight end. He was like the linemen today, only two generations earlier and without the pharmaceuticals.

Rosie and I teamed up on one of Lombardi's most effective plays, the 48 option. It was a quick pitch to me, and I either ran the ball around the left end or threw it, depending on what the defensive cornerback did. If he came up, then Rosie would wipe him out, and I'd toss the ball to the split end. If he covered the receiver, then Rosie would seal to the inside, and I'd run. Rosie just loved to annihilate those little cornerbacks. There'd be nothing but grease spots left of them when he got up. In the huddle, he'd practically froth every time they called the 48 option. I liked that play, too. It gave me my longest career run from scrimmage, eighty-nine yards. On that one, Rosie creamed the cornerback, got up to chase after me, and wiped out another defensive back nearly forty yards downfield.

Perhaps because Rosie was so talented, some of the clowns we played against gave him a real racist initiation. He'd hear, "You black motherf———" and a lot worse. When he'd come back to the huddle, I'd be as embarrassed as he was.

"Everything okay, Ro?" I'd ask.

"Okay, bro," he'd say with a shrug.

Rosie was as popular with the thinking sports set as he was with his teammates. He hung with us at Toots Shor's, always ordering Chivas Regal on the rocks. "Rosie, where did you learn to drink Chivas?" we'd ask him. "I'm learning now," he'd reply.

In his thirteen remarkable years with the Giants, Rosie never took himself out of a game, even though he sometimes was totally torn up. He paid the price for it, too. After he became a scout for the Giants (a job he still holds), an old knee injury developed into phlebitis, and he nearly died during a knee implant. Apparently, the doctor butchered things so badly they almost had to amputate his leg. Rosie ended up winning a malpractice suit, with the Giants paying all his legal bills. He also got into an auto accident on the George Washington Bridge that severed his jugular. This time he nearly bled to death. Yet for as long as I've known him, he's always been ready to laugh. He has a wonderful laugh, a great, rolling guffaw. Rosie Brown is a class act.

"BIG RO"

If Rosey Grier had ever managed to control his weight, and if he'd ever been able to get angry, he'd have easily made the Hall of Fame. Even so, he was damned good. He arrived in 1955 from Penn State, the most massive defensive tackle I'd ever seen. The Giants didn't own a scale capable of weighing him. The one we had only went up to 300 pounds, so Rosey would always maintain he weighed 301.

Jim Lee Howell had a big thing about conditioning, especially running. He ran us so much we felt as if we were training for the Olympics. Naturally, that almost killed Rosey, though you wouldn't know it from his demeanor. He was a totally fun guy. All the coaches would be so serious about getting him in shape, and he'd just whoop and laugh and do hilarious imitations of Jim Lee. After a while, they gave up on him. When you think about it, Rosey probably was right. How far does a defensive tackle have to sprint?

Rosey had lots of quirks, yet his geniality made us forgive them. He brought an electric guitar to our training camp at Saint Michael's

College in Vermont, hooked it up to a set of speakers in the dormitory, and strummed that son of a bitch until it drove us nuts. Before games, he'd spread out a makeshift mattress of towels in front of his locker and lie down on it. We'd have to step over or around him. And we quickly learned never to stand behind Rosey in the chow line. He often left his plate and took the platter.

As a football player, Rosey was tough but never mean. He was not Big Daddy Lipscomb, who was absolutely vicious. Big Daddy would run sideline to sideline trying to break somebody's back. Rosey would make the same great tackle but seemingly try not to hurt the guy. The irony is that he accidentally knocked one player completely out of football. He was a young rookie receiver for the Pittsburgh Steelers named Lowell Perry. After Perry made a long reception against us, Rosey caught up with him near the sideline. His grinding tackle was as sickening to hear as to watch. They carried Perry off with a fractured pelvis and a dislocated hip, and he never put on a uniform again. That really shook Rosey. He brooded about it for years.

Most players, I've noticed, live their lives the way they play the game. Rosey Grier lived and played in a very spiritual way. During training camps, I'd find him reading his Bible in his room. We'd have long talks about spiritual things. I'd tell him about my parents being Holy Rollers and how dazzled I was by Aimee Semple McPherson, and he'd go, "Ho, ho, ho, ho, ho." Rosey was one of the few guys on the defense who liked me. I made him laugh, he made me laugh, and we shared some moments I truly treasure.

In 1963, Allie Sherman traded Rosey to the Rams, where he finished his career. Los Angeles was the perfect city for him. He took up needlepoint and started doing a bunch of talk shows. Imagine an agent going to a talk-show booker and saying, "I've got a six-foot-six, three-hundred-fifty-pound former All-Pro tackle who does needlepoint." They couldn't resist him. But that was only the fun side of Rosey. He worked as a consultant to the mayor of L.A., going into the ghettos to talk to kids and to nursing homes to cheer up old people. The last time I heard from him, he was a minister with an ecumenical group. Which is what I always suspected he'd become. Whenever the Giants gang-tackled a ball carrier, Sam Huff would be trying to kill him, and Rosey Grier would be praying for him.

"EM"

Emlen Tunnell literally walked into the game of pro football. One day in 1948, he arrived uninvited at the Giants' old offices on West Forty-second Street and asked for a tryout. Nobody knew who he was. Though Em had been a running back at Iowa, he hadn't played as a senior because of an eye problem. On the day he strolled in, T. J. Mara, the Giants' owner and founder, was reposing in his usual chair in one of the tiny offices on West Forty-second Street that housed everyone who ran the team. When Em arrived, T.J. instantly spotted something special about him. Em got his tryout. From then on, few days went by without T.J., who knew little about football, inquiring, "How's Emlen Tunnell doing?"

He did just fine. Not only was Em the first black to play for the Giants, but he set sixteen team records, as well as a league record for most punt returns. Em was so low-keyed you thought he was about to nod off every time you said hello to him. I don't think he ever broke a walk outside of a stadium. But put him under a punt or a kickoff, and he'd turn electric. I first saw him play the day after USC's upset of Army at Yankee Stadium, the one at which Wellington Mara decided to draft me. The Giants were playing the old New York Yankees, and Em returned a kickoff nearly a hundred yards for a TD. (On the next play, Buddy Young of the Yankees returned the Giants' kickoff almost as far for his own TD. That had never happened before in an NFL game.)

Em's real passion was storytelling. After dinner during training camps, we'd often sit outside and listen to him spin tales and philosophize. "That Jim Lee sure makes us run a lot," he'd say, dragging deeply on a cigarette, and then off he'd go on a meandering rumination about running. You never quite knew what he was getting to, if he was getting to anything. It was "The World as Em Saw It," and everybody loved him for it.

We had a lot of great times, especially at Em's favorite spot in Harlem, the Red Rooster. Like everywhere else Em went, his big "Hello" and even bigger smile charmed everyone. Later, T.J. made him the first black assistant coach in the league. But not long after being inducted into the Hall of Fame, Em died of a heart attack. He was only fifty years old.

"SWEDE"

As a player, Harland Svare didn't have a muscle in his body, but he possessed remarkable intensity and great intelligence. He became known as a smart linebacker, and to be a smart linebacker in Tom Landry's defense you had to be *very* smart. We got him from the Rams, where he eventually returned as head coach. Today, among other things, he works for a San Diego exercise guru, flying around the country teaching golfers and other athletes how to avoid back problems. I run across him all the time, and he's still a dear friend, a wonderful, quiet man with a bizarre sense of humor.

Quite frankly, Harland wasn't cut out to be a head coach—and I mean that as a compliment. You might say he didn't have the ingredients for it. In certain situations peculiar only to this game, he'd be far too compassionate. For instance, when he had to cut the roster to forty-seven players, he might keep the running back who had a family to feed and cut the better running back. As admirable as that sounds, it's a mistake for a head coach. It certainly wouldn't be one that a lot of head coaches might make. They would feel the same compassion but know that it was better for everyone overall to keep the better player.

Swede was too good a guy to be a great head coach.

I remember some Giants for their quirks. Jim Katcavage giggled all the time, so we called him "Road Runner." But line him up and aim him, and he'd kill himself getting to the target. Though he didn't have Andy Robustelli's skills, he was much more aggressive. Jim was always in a hurry, primarily because he commuted between Yankee Stadium and his home in Philadelphia. He always had to be the first to have his ankles taped, the first onto the bus, and the first off. After a game, he'd race out of the showers and into his clothes. "There goes the commuter," we'd say, and then he was gone.

Cliff Livingston, a linebacker and defensive back, was always angry on the field and never angry off it. He was the first player I'd encountered who totally psyched himself up. He'd hunch over in the locker room, his eyes turning huge and spacey, and we'd look at him and say, "Uh-oh, Cliff's gone again." Then he'd go out on the field and become a kamikaze. He didn't give a damn about what was in front of him. When the other team formed the V on kickoff returns, Cliff would hurl his body into the wedge like a missile. He just loved to destroy. His body or theirs, it really didn't matter.

After our '56 championship, a TV quiz show called *Name That Tune* picked Cliff as a contestant. I could see why. He was a big, good-looking bachelor with blond hair and a lantern jaw, a classic California beachboy. Cliff knew less about music than any creature on the planet. He was so psyched up before games I doubt whether he ever heard the national anthem. But somehow—and I'm making no formal charge—he stayed on *Name That Tune* for weeks. They'd ask him to identify some obscure song, and he'd screw up his face, go hmmmmm, and pop out with it. We knew damned well he didn't know anything about that song. Cliff also became a Giants legend for shooting an arrow out of the Manhattan Hotel. Who knows why? He had a bow, he had an arrow, and I guess it seemed the natural thing to do.

For sheer flakiness, though, Joe Don Looney retired the trophy. The last time I read about Joe Don, he'd gotten arrested in Texas for keeping a whole storehouse of automatic weapons. But back in 1964, he was the Giants' first-round draft pick. The coaches had high hopes: He was a six-one, 220-pound fullback who could do the 100 in 9.8. Right before we were leaving for an exhibition game, Joe Don pulled a groin muscle.

"We'd like you to make the trip with us anyway," Allie Sherman told him.

"I'm not going," Joe Don said.

"Why not?"

"Because I can't play."

"You don't understand," Allie patiently went on. "We *want* you to go. You're part of the team."

"If I can't play, I'm not part of the team," Joe Don replied just as patiently. "And if I'm not part of the team, I shouldn't make the trip."

Allie pondered that logic for a long moment. Then, shaking his head, he walked slowly away.

On another occasion, they caught Joe Don coming back to the dorm at midnight, an hour after curfew.

"I'm sorry, but I've got to fine you," said Allie.

"How can you do that?" he demanded.

"Because you're an hour late."

Joe Don had a ready answer. "The night before," he said, "I was in bed an hour early. So now we're even."

I've never met a more independent spirit. Joe Don wouldn't follow his blockers in scrimmages because he preferred to make his own holes. He wouldn't throw his dirty socks into the bin marked DIRTY SOCKS because he didn't like signs telling him what to do. He wouldn't go to the trainer for an injury because, he explained, he knew more about his body than any trainer. He was so complete an enigma that Allie finally asked Tittle and me to have a chat with him. "See if you can get him in sync with the team," he pleaded.

When we entered Joe Don's room, he was lying on his bed listening to music. Y.A. flopped down on the other bed and told Joe Don how well he understood the problems of a rookie. Then, never short on words, Y.A. launched into a story about his own rookie problems: his insecurity learning a new offense in San Francisco, his loneliness coming to a strange city like New York, and so on. He got so caught up in this heartrending tale that he went on for fifteen minutes. If I hadn't heard it before, I'd have been riveted.

At last he ran down. Joe Don sat up, gave him a long, sympathetic look, and said, "Y.A., that must have been *really* tough. . . . Anything I can do for you?"

CHAPTER 7

A DREAM SEASON

*F*or a lot of famous people, 1956 was a very good year. President Eisenhower won reelection in a landslide. Grace Kelly married a prince, and Arthur Miller a movie queen. Oscars went to Mike Todd for *Around the World in 80 Days,* Yul Brynner for *The King and I,* and Ingrid Bergman for *Anastasia.* In boxing, Floyd Patterson became heavyweight champion by knocking out Archie Moore. Don Larsen pitched the only perfect game in World Series history. And Mickey Mantle captured both the American League's Most Valuable Player award and the elusive Triple Crown, leading the majors in homers, RBIs, and batting average.

As for me, 1956 will always be a magical year. Not only did the league's players elect me the NFL's Most Valuable Player, but the New York Giants—the lowly, downtrodden, hapless Giants—won it all.

Fittingly, we opened the season in a beautiful new home. The Maras had moved the team from the dilapidated Polo Grounds, which was destined to become a housing project, to Yankee Stadium. The first thing I did was check out those monuments in center field, especially Babe Ruth's. After all, it was the House He Built. Then I went looking for my locker, which they told me was Mickey Mantle's.

That struck me as weirdly appropriate. Though I'd never met Mickey, in a way we'd crossed paths. It was during a spring football practice at USC, which was conducted adjacent to the baseball field, though a long way from the diamond. One afternoon, as we crouched in the huddle, a baseball came out of nowhere, whacked me in the leg, and bounced on. One of us tossed it back with a few disdainful expletives. To us, all baseball players were a little weird.

As practice ended, and we trooped toward the locker room, someone asked an onlooker what was going on over at the baseball field.

"USC is playing an exhibition game with the Yankees," he replied.

"Really? Who threw that ball over here?"

"No one threw it. Some guy named Mickey Mantle hit it over there."

Years later, I told Mickey the story. After we stopped laughing, we got to thinking about things we shared. Here were two poor kids from the boonies—Bakersfield, California, and Commerce, Oklahoma—he the MVP in baseball and I the MVP in football, sharing the same locker in the most famous ballpark ever built. As they say, only in America.

I disliked just one thing about Yankee Stadium: The field wasn't level. If a football team was moving from the outfield toward the infield, which was elevated for drainage, the players were moving uphill. It was probably a difference of only a few inches, but, in my mind, it looked and felt like Mount Everest. On the other hand, it provided me with the perfect cop-out. Once, after I got tackled from behind after a long gain, I shamelessly told the press, "If I'd been running downhill rather than up, he never would have caught me." I was only half kidding.

I went into the 1956 season in the greatest shape of my life. In the past, I'd just counted on my body to maintain itself. But I had decided to give this season my best shot. Almost directly after the final game in '55, I started working out and really driving myself. A friend of mine from a wealthy Bakersfield family, David McFadden, had a backyard the size of a football field, and I did wind sprints there five days a week. I just ran my ass off, and then I ran some more.

Jim Lee Howell was right about running: It's the best thing a football player can do. Not only because it's great for conditioning, but because that's what you *have* to do. You have to be able to run. At practices, whenever I caught a pass, I'd sprint fifty or sixty yards with it. Or if they flipped me a pitchout, I'd take it the length of the field. That just wasn't done.

My mental transformation was probably even more important. In the past, I'd played only with my legs. I had an incomplete map of the game in my head. It seems to me that there are three stages in the evolution of a ball carrier. In high school, he learns where the play is going. In college, he learns who is blocking for him. In the pros, he learns what the defense is doing. A good player will visualize a play while he is running it and where everybody on the field is going to be, or at least supposed to be. His reaction is so fast it seems instinctive, but it comes from a highly developed sense of awareness. And the only way that awareness can be cultivated is to study films, work, study, and work again.

Whatever the reason, things began happening for me that hadn't happened before. In fact, good things were happening to all the Giants. We started beating teams easily, and with an intensity I'd never seen. About halfway through the season, with us near the top of the division, Lombardi opened a practice by calling our offensive team together on the field.

I can still see him. It was a cold fall day, and what looked like frost was coming out of his mouth and his head was rocking back and forth and his alligator teeth were flashing and his feet, which seemed as big as paddles, were tapping away.

"Gentlemen," Vince said. "I can smell something. *Oh, I can smell something!*"

We knew exactly what he was talking about. What Vince was smelling was the realization that we might win the whole damn thing.

For openers, Tom Landry's defensive unit had suddenly jelled. All it had needed was a few new parts. In 1956 they came in the form of Sam Huff at middle linebacker and Andy Robustelli, Jim Katcavage and Dick Modzelewski on the line. The first two became Hall of Famers, the last two All-Pros. Though we were no powerhouse on offense, our defense was the best in the game.

That year also marked the start of the much-publicized rivalry between the offense and defense. While it never got mean, it did get intense. Probably, the defense's unprecedented fame had something to do with that rivalry. Never in the history of football had fans gone to a stadium primarily to root for a "DEE-fense." Suddenly, everyone knew who Andy Robustelli was and that he had a wife and three kids and lived in Connecticut. Suddenly, the fact that Jim Katcavage commuted from Philadelphia became a big story. Sam Huff even made the cover of *Time* magazine. The rivalry also extended to Lombardi and Landry, who, as the proud architects of their two units, in a sense created it. It's hard to imagine two more different personalities than Vince, a gregarious, volatile Italian, and Tom, a shy, reserved Texan. The one trait they shared was a fierce competitiveness, especially with each other.

Since the defense was on the field a *lot,* they developed an attitude toward the offense: "We're the ones who win games, not you guys." If they made one of their famous goal-line stands, we'd hear about it all week. Or if they recovered a fumble, Sam might walk by me as I started onto the field and say, "See if you can hold 'em for a while."

Not that we didn't do some needling, too. I discovered that the quickest way to get under Huff's skin was to tell him, "You know, Sam, I've played defense and I've played offense, so I know on which side of the ball they pay the big bucks." That would drive him frigging bonkers. As I said earlier, Sam's respect for the dollar approached reverence. Yet even if not all of us recognized that the internal rivalry was good for this particular team, as far as I'm concerned, it did make the players play better and the coaches coach better.

While the Giants' offense wasn't capable of blowing anyone away, we compensated by playing smart. We were a uniquely intelligent collection of guys, a true thinking team.

Everyone on offense was involved in the game. If you had a play—a pass or a run—you thought would work, you didn't just sit on it. You let it out. And the guy who really made our democratic way of doing things possible was Charlie Conerly. I've never met a quarterback with less of an ego. Charlie called all his own plays and was the kind of quarterback who wanted information brought back to the huddle. He knew that no quarterback can see everything going on downfield. He respected his guys and made each of them part of the play-calling process.

When Charlie called a play in the huddle, at times it was almost by committee. If he called a pass, I might say, "I'll run a circle on it. It'll hold the middle linebacker." Then Kyle might shake his head and say, "Down and in won't work this time. I'll take it down and out." While that was going on, Rosie Brown and Ray Wietecha might be suggesting altered blocking assignments. All of this would take a matter of four or five seconds. And while it might sound confusing, it was really quite simple and effective.

Because Charlie and I were such good friends, even rooming together, we became so close that our communications were almost coded. If I noticed that a defensive back had been crowding me on a down-and-in move, I'd say to him as we returned to the huddle, "Charlie, give me a Brown right, IX left, only this time I'll Z it out." Basically, that meant I would run straight down, fake to the inside, and then break it back out as Charlie released the ball.

Usually, Charlie trusted me, which made me try a hell of a lot harder to make sure the play worked. But sometimes he might wave off my advice—or even say, "Shut up." I knew he didn't mean anything by it. He just had something else he wanted to run.

Charlie also had other ways of communicating. Suppose, as we went up to the line of scrimmage, one of us read a blitz coming and wanted Charlie to change the play by calling an automatic. Of course, the way this was expressed was a bit blunter: "Shit, Charlie, blitz. Let's get the fuck out of it!" If Charlie began tapping his left foot as he bent over the center, we knew he agreed. He would repeat the snap number, which was our clue that a new play was coming, and then give us the numerical change. For instance: "Three [snap number], forty-nine [new play], hut, hut, *hut!*" Then we'd run the new play—a 49 sweep.

Kyle, too, liked to use foot signals at the line of scrimmage. If he noticed a change in the defense and decided to tell Charlie he wanted to change his pass route, he might drop his right foot back instead of his left as he went into his stance. If Charlie didn't want Kyle to switch, he'd scrape his left foot. Those two guys took the foot in football seriously.

As unusual as all this tactical ad-libbing was back then, today it would be totally unthinkable. Most teams send in all the plays from the bench and allow their quarterbacks minimal parameters for change. Charlie was unique in recognizing who could make a contribution and who was just talking. On any team, there are receivers who are "always open" and backs who can "get six if you just give me the ball." On Charlie's team, we had none of that.

No one was a bigger beneficiary of the new, improved Giants than yours truly. With the help of Charlie's arm and Vince's brain and the muscle and speed of some overachieving linemen, I finished the season as the league's fifth-leading rusher and third-best pass-catcher. Nobody before, I was told, had ever ranked in the top five in both categories.

Early on a frigid December morning, the sound of a phone jolted me awake in my bedroom at Manhattan's Excelsior Hotel. It was Murray Olderman, a veteran New York sportswriter.

"Morning, Giff. The vote is in on the Jim Thorpe Trophy," he told me.

"Huh?" I said, still groggy from sleep.

"You know, for the Most Valuable Player in the NFL. The players around the league have just voted for you."

Boy, did that ever clear my head! Then, after the euphoria had subsided, I started thinking about who really deserved that MVP award. In all honesty, Rosie Brown should have gotten it. But the Rosie Browns of the world never do. The General Pattons always get the glory, while the guy lying in the mud of the foxhole goes home as just another statistic.

They presented me with the trophy at halftime during a nationally televised game (then a big deal) in Baltimore. That night I took the train back to New York with the trophy in a large box with a string around it. Maxine and I were supposed to attend a cocktail party on Central Park West and, since the train was late, I called her to say I'd meet her there. So up I walked to this fancy apartment house—pro football's reigning hotshot proudly bearing his trophy—and the British doorman stopped me cold.

"Sir?" he said, eyeing my by-now-bedraggled box.

"Apartment fourteen-D, please."

"Deliveries are at the side," he sniffed.

"You don't understand. I'm Frank Gifford of the New—"

"Deliveries are at the side!"

"Yes, sir," I mumbled, and around to the side I slunk.

Winning the MVP award completely changed my life. Virtually everything good that's happened to my career started at that moment. Up until then, I'd never, ever totally believed in my ability. I'd heard so many people tell me, "You can't." In high school, they said I was too small to make the varsity. In college, they said I couldn't pass well enough to play quarterback, so they made me a defensive back again. In the pros, they said I was too slow to be a runner, so they put me on defense. Even when I achieved something, there was always someone saying "But . . ." Now there were no more buts, and even in my mind few doubts remained.

The award also tossed me into a very bright spotlight. All of a sudden, wherever I went, people were after me. I must have signed a thousand autographs in one week. As they say in Hollywood, I'd been discovered. *What's My Line?* wanted me as a mystery guest. Jantzen wanted me to endorse its sportswear. Jackie Gleason wanted me to play golf. Ed Sullivan wanted me to take a bow from his audience. Ed would even seek me out on Sunday nights at Toots Shor's. "Hel-lew, Frank," he'd say with that mortician's expression. "Riiiillly big game."

It was like waking up one morning to find your most impossible fantasy come to life. All of a sudden, in a city where Mickey Mantle was a god and the memory of Joe DiMaggio even more sacred, there was an awareness of another sport, another player, another team. And I was the player, and the Giants were the team. Heady stuff— and I loved it.

Attendance rocketed. Suddenly, we were averaging crowds of forty-five thousand a home game, about twenty thousand more than had ever showed up at the Polo Grounds. The year 1956 marked the start of a passionate love affair between New York and the Giants, and one that turned into a great marriage. New York fans recognized what was happening with the team before the sportswriters did. Hell, most of them were more sophisticated than the writers, at least about football. We became the hot ticket, our games The Place to Be. Socialites, politicians, CEOs, ad-agency honchos, the network biggies, newspaper columnists, even priests—they all embraced the Giants. In a way, our fans became a part of the team. They were wonderful. New Yorkers just worship winners. They did then, they do now, and they always will. Of course, they shoot losers.

Vince Lombardi told the press that my best performance of that season was against the Redskins, who were pressing us for the division lead. I read later that I had a hand in all four of our touchdowns, scoring three of them and passing for another. The weird thing is, I can remember almost nothing about that game except that it unwound exactly like a dream. A beautiful dream, the kind in which everything you do turns out perfectly.

I'd tell Charlie in the huddle, "Give me a play-action thirty-six slant from the Brown formation. That bozo's playing run every time. I'll take it on a fly." And damned if the linebacker didn't bite exactly as I thought he would, giving Charlie plenty of time to hit me down the sideline after the fake run. The most dreamlike moment came on a busted pass play late in the game. Charlie, seeing that I was blanketed in the Redskins' end zone, tried to throw the ball away by firing it over my head. But for once he didn't fire it hard enough. Somehow I reached up and hauled it in for a touchdown.

"I made you look good, you old fart," I said to Charlie on the sideline. But I was also giving him a big hug. I think I had as much fun helping people finally realize how great Charlie was as I did living out my own dream season.

After clinching our division title with an 8-3-1 record, we prepared to meet the Chicago Bears for the championship. But something almost as momentous as that game happened on the day before we played it. The National Football League Players Association was officially announced at a New York press conference. We finally had a union!

Actually, the Association had been secretly formed three years earlier, and I was one of its founding members. It all began in a small, crowded room at the Ambassador Hotel in Los Angeles on the weekend of the 1953 Pro Bowl. Gathered with me in the room were Kyle Rote of the Giants, Norm Van Brocklin of the Rams, Eddie

LeBaron of the Redskins, and about a dozen other NFL stars. There was good reason for our secrecy. In those days, we played under a rigidly paternalistic system. Had the owners known we were even *thinking* of forming a union, a lot of us might have been traded or cut. That's always the first reaction when labor tries to organize. You're going to tell us how to run our business? Why, you ungrateful pups!

Our initial meeting got off to an unforgettable start. Abe Gibron, the great offensive guard for the Bears, stood up, reached inside his jacket, pulled out a gun, and slammed it down on a dresser. Our jaws dropped. Then Abe said, "I know we all may get in trouble for being here. But, goddammit, we have to get a union. We have to be together, and, dammit, we *will* be together!"

Though none of us could tell whether the gun was real or just a toy (and I bet it was real), Abe had made his point. A players' union was worth fighting for, and he, for one, didn't give a shit what it cost him.

By the time the meeting ended, we'd all agreed to go back and quietly recruit our teammates. We asked them to start contributing annual dues; I think it was something like $125. There were two more years of meetings, always in the shadows, before the owners grudgingly agreed to recognize the Association—they wouldn't let us call it a union. Then we began negotiating our demands. By today's standards, those demands are laughable. In fact, during the 1987 players' strike, I mentioned them to Joe Klecko, the player representative for the Jets, and he looked at me as if I'd just crawled out of the Middle Ages.

The first thing we wanted was laundry money during training camp. Next we asked the owners to provide our football shoes. That was a big expense for us: The teams would issue players only one pair of shoes per season; you had to buy the two or three pairs you'd invariably need as replacements. (Today, of course, the shoe manufacturers practically beg players to wear their products free.) Finally, we demanded to be paid for pre-season games. Back then the owners maintained that exhibition games were played solely for our benefit, to get us in shape. Consequently, they didn't pay us a single dollar for a single down until the season opener.

The players changed all that, and, much later, their agents and lawyers changed everything else. But none of it would have happened without the Association, and the Association would never have existed without guys like Kyle Rote, one of its most tireless organizers. Not only was Kyle a very charismatic person—probably the only one the Giants' players would follow into something like this—but the Maras loved him so much they didn't resent it when he brought them our demands.

The irony is, Kyle actually didn't need a union. He was a big star making good money for those times. It was the Rosie Browns and the Jack Strouds and those who came later whom the union helped far more. Just like on the field, Kyle's performance taught me something: The people who really don't need the reforms are the only ones strong enough to force them to happen.

According to legend, an emergency order of sneakers helped account for the Giants' 47–7 annihilation of the Chicago Bears in the 1956 championship. Never put too much stock in legends.

True, we switched to sneakers that day because of the playing conditions. The temperature in Yankee Stadium hung in the low teens, and the wind howled at 30 mph. A few hours before the game began, I went out on the field wearing cleats. By that time of year, Yankee Stadium's grass invariably disappeared, and now the frozen dirt was as hard and slick as marble. I ran a simple pass pattern and could barely stay on my feet.

Typically, Wellington Mara had been testing the field all week. When he realized how frozen it was, he asked Andy Robustelli, who owned a sporting-goods store in Connecticut, to order us four dozen pairs of rubber-soled basketball sneakers. They arrived right before the kickoff, and from then on we had a lot less trouble with the traction. Yet here's what even the old-timers forget: The Bears also came out of the locker room shod in sneakers that afternoon. So, you see, we were all on equal footing.

But if the legend was wrong, the 1956 championship game marked something truly historic. The "Monsters of the Midway," as the Bears were nicknamed, were supposed to be the roughest team in football. As we quickly discovered, however, they had no idea what we were up to. Our offense and defense just kept outsmarting them, doing things they had never seen before and that are done all the time today.

The Bears were playing Bears football, which meant they were trying to mug us. But thanks to Vince Lombardi and Tom Landry, pro football had moved up to another plateau—and that game confirmed it.

As well as our coaches had prepared us, we weren't afraid to improvise on the field. We had decided that on third and long (a situation that occurred on our very first possession), we would work against J. C. Caroline, a good defensive back but a very aggressive one. We needed eight, and as I drove J.C. deep and broke it off to the sideline, he made his move back. On a good field, he might have gotten there. On a frozen Yankee Stadium field, he slipped, stumbled, and fell on his ass. The pass went for twenty-one yards, setting up our first touchdown—and the tone for the day.

Now cut to fourth quarter and the same pass play. By now we had the game locked up and were really having fun. This time a new cornerback read the play correctly and came up fast to stop it. So instead of breaking to the outside, I gave it a shake to the outside and raced straight downfield. Charlie laid the ball up for a twenty-nine-yard gain.

I had violated a cardinal rule: Never cross up your quarterback. But if Charlie had thrown to the spot called for in the huddle, the cornerback probably would have intercepted. I got away with breaking the rule because I knew my roommate. I knew he would read the same thing I read and anticipate my move. Charlie and I may not have conversed very much, but on a football field we could read each other's minds.

The other significant aspect of that game was the attendance: There were only fifty-seven thousand seats sold. That was more than five thousand short of capacity. For all New York's newfound love for the Giants, pro football still couldn't fill Yankee Stadium for a championship game. An NFL championship game not sold out! Still, there were enough paid admissions to give each Giant a victory share of $3,779.19. Uh-huh, that doesn't sound like much. But considering that I was making only fifteen thousand dollars in salary, it amounted to a 20 percent bonus. (The last time the Giants had won the championship, in 1938, each player had taken home a mere $504.45.)

That night we all headed to Toots Shor's for a major blowout. There were so many of us Toots had to set aside the entire back of his restaurant. God, we were on a high. Rosie Brown, who'd been awesome that day, lifted me clean off the floor, gave me a hug, and whooped out, "We're the champions!" Then everyone began chanting, "We're the champions! We're the champions!" It still took a long while to sink in.

The best part was watching Charlie's joy. He'd gone through so much incredible crap, the physical poundings every Sunday, the abuse from the fans and the writers. I was the official hero that year, but my roomie was the one who made it happen, who subordinated his ego, who did everything he could to make me look good.

Toward the end of the night, Charlie turned to me and raised his glass of scotch. He had that silly old Mississippi grin on his face. Then the man who never said anything said, "Giff, ah luv yew."

I didn't know whether to laugh or cry. All I knew was that I also loved that old goat—and was too damn happy to care about anything else.

CHAPTER 8

FOUR WHO CALLED THE SHOTS

Like the guys I called teammates, Vince Lombardi, Tom Landry, Pete Rozelle, and Roone Arledge couldn't be more dissimilar. Yet each, in his own way, showed me the most important single quality of an outstanding leader. I'm not talking about "genius." A lot of people possess genius, yet they can't get anything done with it. These four men made others want to excel for them. They inspired others to perform above their abilities. When you admire someone that much, you desperately want that person to respect what you're doing and to approve of how you're doing it. I suspect that's the secret of great leadership. It may even be a more accurate definition of genius.

VINCE

Writers have carved careers out of making Vince Lombardi into something he never really was. The man I knew wasn't anything like that myth. In fact, he was one of the most down-to-earth human beings I've ever met. Maybe that's why I never called him "Coach" or "Mr. Lombardi" or, even in jest, "God." To me, and to most of us who really knew him, he was simply "Vince."

When Vince arrived in 1954 to take over our offense, we didn't like him at all. He was loud and arrogant, a total pain in the ass. We had a lot of nicknames for him, most of them unprintable. Vince had been a good high school coach at Saint Cecilia's and an outstanding backfield coach at Army, but he didn't understand pro football. He didn't have a clue. He immediately tried to install Red Blaik's offense from West Point, the old option T. The quarterback, moving down the line of scrimmage, either pitches the ball to the halfback or runs it. Now, our quarterback was Charlie Conerly, whose days of running with the football were long gone—and he knew it. A lot of the things Vince wanted to do just wouldn't work in the pro game.

When Vince got up to the blackboard, he might have been teaching his fourth-grade math class at Saint Cecilia's. "This is the twenty-six power play," he'd announce. "The twenty-six power play, do you have that, Jack? The first step is for the right guard to pull back. He *must* pull back, *must* pull back, *must* pull back. He must pull back to avoid the center, who will be moving to the offside. So the first step is for the right guard to pull back. Got that, Jack? The *first* step is back."

We'd look at each other in disbelief. Here's a Charlie Conerly (whom Vince treated in the same way), having dodged bullets in the South Pacific and made All-America at Mississippi and lived through hell in the Polo Grounds, and he's hearing *this* guy tell him how to do it. You could see Vince was a terrific teacher, but these people had learned most of what he was teaching very early in their careers. They didn't require a lot of teaching. They required direction.

After our training-camp workouts, when many of the players gathered at a local beer joint, everybody began doing imitations of Lombardi. Some of them were quite hilarious. He just seemed a comical character to us, easy to parody. He had huge feet and big, long arms, and all those teeth. Someone once quipped that Vince had thirty-two teeth like the rest of us, but his were all on top. When we weren't laughing at him, our attitude was that we'd survive him.

Somehow, this guy would be exposed and gotten rid of. As far as we were concerned, it was just a matter of time.

Then Vince did something both humble and smart. He began dropping by our training-camp dorm after meetings to talk to us about different aspects of the game and to solicit our opinions of plays. At first that ticked us off. Charlie, Kyle, myself, and a few others were accustomed to coming back to our rooms at the 11:00 P.M. curfew, making the bed check and then sneaking out for a few beers. Now here was this bigmouthed rookie coach with a pasta name blocking our escape.

"How are things?" he'd ask, pulling out a chair from the desk.

"Uh, fine, Vince. Everything's fine."

"We're having trouble running the option play, aren't we, Charlie?"

Charlie, a man of few words if any, would pop his ankle and grunt something like "Yep." There was an awkward silence. Finally, I volunteered what we were all thinking:

"It's really not what Charlie likes to run. We really don't think it's going to be effective with Charlie."

"Well, what do you think about the fifty-four dive?" he replied. "How do you feel about the forty-nine sweep?"

Gradually, we felt comfortable enough to tell him. He'd just listen and nod. Then one night he suddenly said, "You know, if you don't mind, I could really use a little help from the older guys." Vince was a very intelligent man who sensed he was in trouble. So many coaches are so full of macho posturing that they'd have tried to tough it out. Vince knew better. What he was really telling us was "Come on, I *need* your help."

That changed the whole tone of our relationship. All of a sudden, we found ourselves wanting to help him. We discovered that he was a real guy, a warm, funny guy. He was very Italian in the sense that he loved to laugh, loved his pasta, and loved to have a few pops with his players. In later years, following practices, a bunch of us would drive over to his home in New Jersey, and his wife, Marie, would cook up a ton of spaghetti. We'd talk football and watch game films until Marie threw us out.

In terms of offensive strategy, Lombardi and the Giants learned from each other. Take the famous 49 sweep. When Vince installed it, he wanted the two guards who led the left halfback—yours truly—around the end to swing out several yards before they turned the corner. He wanted to be sure the penetration from our tight end blocking their linebacker didn't snarl everything up. Charlie and I disagreed. We felt the guards had to get to the corner as quickly as they could and turn it upfield. We knew that the defensive pursuit in pro football is too fast for that kind of maneuver. As big as Vince's ego was, he listened to us. We ended up running the 49 sweep half his way and half the way we thought it would work. The play turned out to be Lombardi's biggest ground gainer both in New York for me and in Green Bay for Paul Hornung.

As we became more familiar over the years with Vince and his system, we changed a lot of plays on the field. By the fourth quarter, we'd be kicking the other team's butt with an entirely different offense than what we started with. Unlike a lot of coaches, Vince was very flexible. And he truly believed in our ability to execute.

As much as Vince enjoyed winning, he became ecstatic over winning through deception. You could also see it when he played bridge. Playing an ace might win him the trick, but he got a bigger kick by trying to finesse the queen. He'd positively twitch with glee. It was the same with football. As much as he loved the fundamentals, trickery was his major turn-on.

We had a play called the 36 slant, in which Mel Triplett, our fullback, went off tackle as I hopefully blocked the linebacker. We'd do it maybe ten times that way, and then, suddenly, with the defense determined to stop that play, we'd fake the same action. Instead of blocking the linebacker, I'd slip around him and take a pass from Charlie, often for a big gain or a touchdown. When we'd look at films of the fake on Tuesday morning, Vince would practically have an orgasm.

Pretty soon teams began borrowing from Vince, which sent him ballistic. "Look at that, look at what they're doing with that!" he'd suddenly scream as we were reviewing game films of an upcoming opponent. "They got that from us! *They stole our play!*" Not that Vince wasn't above doing a little pilfering of his own. He'd say at practice, "We're going to put in this little dive play with a little counterfake to the left." And I'd say to myself, "Come on, we just saw the Steelers doing that last week.'' But Vince wasn't handing out any credit to the Steelers. When teams copied from him, it was a felony. When he copied from them, it was creative thinking.

Few coaches could motivate as masterfully. Henry Jordan of the Packers once said that Lombardi was the least prejudiced man he ever met: ''He treats us all alike—like dogs.'' That made great copy, but from what I saw, it just wasn't true. Vince treated all of us differently. He measured people so well that he knew exactly which buttons to push. He knew some guys needed goosing, some stroking, and some both. It drains enormous energy to coach like that. You start caring so deeply for certain players that you get involved with everything in their lives. That's how Bill Parcells coached the Giants, and he wound up with open-heart surgery. It finally got to Vince at Green Bay. I suspect he realized he couldn't keep doing it that way, yet he knew it was the best way to do it. So he retired at Green Bay after nine years (and five NFL championships plus two Super Bowls).

Vince was famous for his tirades, but many, I felt, were calculated. Especially the ones at our screenings of the previous Sunday's game films. That's when he'd really hammer someone's performance.

''Austin, look at that!'' he'd scream, running the offending frames back and forth on the projector. ''That's not the right technique! Drop that right leg! Drop that right leg! *Drop that right leg!*'' The poor victim would sink into his chair and cringe. Then we'd walk out to practice, and Vince would sidle over to a couple of us, flash his most malevolent grin, and whisper, ''I really got Austin, didn't I?'' He got us, all right, and while he seemed to enjoy it, his eruptions invariably had a positive effect on our play.

Only once did I witness Vince's theatrics backfire. We had a tough southern running back—I'll call him ''Jones''—who, rumor had it, carried a knife around with him. He also performed best when no one got under his thin skin. During one film session, Vince seized on some frames that showed the guy failing to block a linebacker. ''Look at yourself, Jones,'' he shouted, beginning his back-and-forth number with the projector. ''Hear me, Jones? Jones? Jones? Jones?'' After about a minute of this, from out of the darkness a very quiet, mean voice was heard: ''Run that one more time, Coach, and

I'll cut you." Vince gulped, swallowed deeply, and meekly hit the projector's forward button.

Put fifty men together for half a year, and you're going to see a lot of practical jokes. We loved playing them on Vince, just to watch him explode. Like the schoolteacher he once was, he liked to have his pieces of chalk laid out just so before he began a blackboard lesson. And like mischievous schoolboys, some of us would beat him to the meeting room to hide his chalk. Result: accusations followed by expletives followed, more than once, by the crash of a hurled blackboard.

During practices, Vince hated anyone crowding him. He liked to stand exactly four yards behind whatever eleven guys were working on offense. The rest of us, who were not in the lineup, were supposed to stand at least three yards behind him. Naturally, we took that as a challenge. We were continually inching up to him, which invariably freaked him out. One day he threw down an orange peel to mark the line of demarcation. "Everyone stays behind the orange peel," he ordered. "Get in front of it, and you do a lap around the field."

We took that as an even bigger challenge. Each time he turned to watch a play, we'd push the peel closer to his rear end and creep closer ourselves. Finally, we were right on top of him.

When Vince looked back, he went ballistic. *"I said, EVERYONE BEHIND THE BLEEPETY-BLEEP PEEL!"* he screeched, his face turning a familiar purple. Then he glanced down and saw where the peel lay. It cracked him up. Of course, as soon as he stopped laughing, he moved it exactly three yards back.

Eventually, Vince and I became very close. He once told the press that his two favorite players were Paul Hornung and myself. That's fitting, because Vince's impact on both of us was remarkably similar. Just as he turned my career around by making me "his halfback," he saved Paul's butt in Green Bay. Paul is the first to acknowledge that, until Vince came along, he'd been far from a smash in pro football. Ray Nitschke, the former Packer linebacker, said something interesting when he appeared at a roast of me a few years ago. He said that Vince Lombardi made Paul Hornung into his Frank Gifford, "only a little bit bigger, stronger, and faster" (I resented only the "faster"). Vince also developed the same affection for Paul, a kind of fatherly warmth we both returned.

One thing that really bothers me is that Vince will be largely remembered as a heartless dictator, the man who supposedly said, "Winning isn't everything. It's the only thing." He was talking, of course, about the *will* to win—as he tried to explain many times. As for compassion, he had loads of it. He'd be the first one there to help if you were in any kind of trouble. But all that strangers seemed to see was his incredibly dominating presence. It became the easy-to-pin-on label that the media chose to portray Vince.

After Vince retired, he made a ton of money giving motivational speeches to business executives. I attended one and got a huge charge from seeing all those big, powerful CEOs so in awe of him. Then Vince started his speech—and damned if it wasn't the old 26-power-play routine all over again. Repetition, repetition, repetition. They were mesmerized.

Our last conversation was almost as awkward as that first one in our dorm, only this time I was visiting his room. It was the summer of 1970, and Vince lay dying of cancer in a Washington hospital. Though he looked shockingly weak, he gathered himself together for me. I said something stupid, like "How you doing?" And he said something to change the subject, like "Not as poorly as we are," meaning the Redskins, the final team he coached. Then we talked about everything except the fact that this was probably our last time together. Finally, when I started out the door, Vince said something that really shattered me. As I awkwardly stood there, he looked at me and said slowly, "Frank, it hurts."

I'd rather remember him at his most alive. It's Tuesday morning, and we're watching films of the play-action fake off the 36 slant, the one that went for a TD on Sunday. "Look at that linebacker bite!" whoops Vince. "I told you, I told you! Oh, yes! *Ohhhhh yessssssssss!*" Though the room is almost dark, we can see his teeth glowing—all thirty-two of them on top. He's practically frothing. And we're laughing at him and laughing with him and, now that I look back on it, feeling something very close to love.

TOM

Tom Landry, I've long believed, was one of the first victims of a television paradox. TV can deliver brilliantly clear images, but too often those images distort the truth.

As the networks got into regular coverage of pro football, they began focusing a lot on the sidelines, especially on the coaches. It was often some no-talent director's way of exercising his ego by putting his stamp on the broadcast. He would cut from an occurrence on the field to a quick shot of the coach's reaction. It happens most frequently when a player gets hurt, and it was just one of the many things that led to Tom's cold, aloof image. They'd be carrying a Dallas Cowboy off, and here's Tom on the telephone, not even looking at him. So the perception grew that Tom was a heartless, unfeeling ice man. "There's Tom Landry with his customary hat on," some play-by-play guy would snicker. "We haven't seen a smile or a frown from Tom in fifteen years. The man is inhuman."

Bullshit. To understand Tom, who was probably the least-understood coach in football, you had to be down there with him. I don't care what Howard Cosell says, most people in the media don't have a clue about what's really happening on the field. Unless you've been part of it, you can't imagine how violent and brutal it is, how loud and confusing it is.

What few understood about Tom was that his genius lay in his total concentration. Unlike other head coaches, he called every offensive play for the Cowboys. No matter what was happening around him, he always had to be thinking about that next play. He had to program his mind like a computer. So while he might feel terrible about the guy who just tore his knee up, he realized that wasn't the time to grieve over him. He couldn't allow anything to interrupt his focus. Nor did he.

In my mind, what made Tom such a successful offensive coach was his brilliance as a *defensive* coach. He knew what plays and formations were easy or hard to stop because he'd already invented the game's most-copied defense, the famous 4–3. The key to this defense was absolute discipline. Everyone was supposed to do something very precise and *only* that something. He'd stand at the blackboard and say, "You do this, Robustelli, you do that, Grier, you do this, Modzelewski, you do that, Huff, you do this, Livingston, you do that, Gifford . . . and everything will be taken care of."

In the beginning, some of us would ask, "What if they don't do that?"

"They will," he'd calmly reply.

"But what if they do something else?"

"They won't."

"But what if—"

"There are no what-ifs," he'd finally interrupt. *"This is what's going to happen!"*

The remarkable thing is, he was rarely wrong. We'd be absolutely flabbergasted to see the other team make the exact moves that Landry predicted they would in a given situation from a given formation. Back then, the fans and the press didn't talk much about defense because they didn't know much about it. Nobody approached it as scientifically as Tom. He was the consummate perfectionist.

I know, because in the early days of my career I probably was his biggest screwup. Back then I was playing offense as well as defense, and therefore didn't have time to concentrate on the latter in practice as much as I should have. Though Tom never got angry, he always made his point. Once, in a game against Washington, I picked off a pass, returned it about forty yards, and then lateraled over to Tom, who went the rest of the way to score. When we reviewed the films on Tuesday, I couldn't wait to see the play unfold. Neither could Tom. He froze the play with the ball coming into my hands.

"Frank," he said, "you're in the wrong position."

"Well, I thought they were going to bring the left end all the way across," I explained. "I thought I could go for the ball and still maintain coverage."

"We don't think, Frank. What was the formation?"

"Brown right."

"And what do you do in a Brown right in this situation? You play off seven yards, outside the shoulder of the wide receiver. You have inside coverage with a circle back and outside coverage on a flair. You don't worry about the left end. He's not your man."

It was totally exasperating. Here I've helped him score a touchdown, and he won't roll the rest of the damned film! Needless to say, he was right about my position. The Skins had their back in a circle pattern, and I had inside responsibility. Had I played the correct defense, I wouldn't have made the interception. But I had to really leap for the ball. If I hadn't gotten to it, their wide receiver probably would have—and scored himself. Screwing up Tom's defense was a capital offense.

Tom Landry was an All-American running back at the University of Texas, flew thirty combat missions in World War II while still in his teens, was a Pro Bowler as a player-coach, made the NFL Hall of Fame the first year he became eligible, and led the Dallas Cowboys to five Super Bowls. Yet as remarkable as those achievements are, the media, I'm convinced, always resented Tom for not being "colorful." I've been with him off and on for many years. He's a kind, gentle person who deeply loves his wife, Alicia, his kids, and his religion. That also brought him resentment. He was characterized so often as a "born-again Christian" that it began to sound like a crime.

As for the knocks Tom's taken from some of his players, it helps to look back at the times. These guys were products of the sixties: pro-drugs and anti–everything that was in any way authoritarian. An intensely patriotic and disciplined leader like Tom Landry made a perfect target.

I think Tom was used by those players. Pete Gent portrayed him as a win-at-all-costs monster in *North Dallas Forty,* a coach who forced his players to take painkilling shots so they could play hurt. Hell, Pete Gent was at best the Cowboys' backup receiver. If he had actually played and suffered as much as he depicted himself in his book, I might take his complaints more seriously. But as I recall, Pete spent most of his career on the sidelines cheering for Bobby Hayes and Lance Alworth.

In another book, Duane Thomas nailed Tom with the label of "plastic man." The reality was, Tom not only made Duane a Super Bowl star, but he let him train by his own set of rules until his crazy behavior disrupted the team. As a matter of fact, Tom created coaches as well as players. Look at those who played defense for him with the Giants. Andy Robustelli, Dick Modzelewski, Jim Katcavage, Harland Svare, Dick Nolan, Em Tunnell, and Jimmy Patton all went

on to become assistant or head coaches. Not to mention head
coaches like Mike Ditka and Dan Reeves, both of whom were assistants under Tom in Dallas.

As close as I am to Don Meredith, we finally agreed never to
discuss Tom Landry in order to maintain our friendship. Don at
times would become maniacal on the subject of Tom. I think it all
went back to their attitudes toward football when Don was quarterbacking the Cowboys. Talk about oil and water. To Don, the game
should be played for fun. It was only a game! It also represented a
means to express his free spirit. He relished making things up as he
went along, and he was great at it. Tom, as I've already pointed out,
believed in a rigidly organized system.

Tom would send in a slant play designed to pick up three yards
and a first down. Don couldn't care less. He might have a weak
defensive back he knew he could work against. So he'd duck into the
huddle and, generating unbelievable excitement, say, "Okay, Bobby.
You beat that sucker, and I'll throw the son of a bitch as far as I can.
Okay, guys, I need some time. On three, break!"

The team would bust their asses for Don, but if it didn't work,
Tom would bust *his* ass.

Eventually, Don tried to subordinate his swashbuckling nature to
the good of the team. In his heart, I think, he realized that Tom's way
worked. At the same time, he was such an independent spirit that
he never stopped chafing at all that discipline. Don played brilliantly for Tom. He took the Cowboys to the 1967 NFL championship game and came within one frozen yard of upsetting the Packers,
not to mention becoming the first winning Super Bowl quarterback.
But it wasn't until Roger Staubach arrived, along with some big
offensive linemen and some outside speed, that the Cowboys finally
won it all. Staubach was the perfect quarterback for Landry because
he basically was an extension of Landry's systematic mind. I know
that Tom Landry loved Don Meredith and still does. And I think that
Don, in his own way, loves Tom. But having to do a Cowboy game
on *Monday Night Football* drove him nuts. He longed to say how he
felt about playing for Landry all those years. The problem was, I
don't think he really *knows* how he feels.

My primary feeling toward Tom is one of gratitude. I've learned
many things from him, especially the value of intense preparation.

So much of the way I prepare for challenges, whether it's a speech or a TV broadcast, I took from Tom. When the Cowboys' new management brutally fired him after twenty-nine seasons, I wrote him a note telling him how much he meant to me and to the game. While I'm sure he was hurt by it all—and I would've been devastated—you'd never have guessed. Shortly after Tom was fired, I ran into him at a Boys Club dinner in New York, and I brought up the subject. He quickly interrupted me, saying, "They have every right to do what they want with their football team. I've still got other things to accomplish. It's time to move on." It might be hard to believe for some, I'm sure, but I bet Tom was as happy for the return of the Cowboys and their Super Bowl XXVII victory as any other Dallas fan.

Tom Landry has always given off a sense of inner peace. Yes, he's a born-again Christian, and while I never saw him push his religion, he's a living advertisement for it.

PETE

On a balmy evening in 1970, I took Pete Rozelle to a Hollywood party. Our host was George Stevens, Jr., the TV documentary producer, and the occasion was the introduction of George McGovern to the town's Democratic elite. Pete and I were in Los Angeles for a league meeting, and when Stevens invited me to his party, I invited Pete to come along.

The room was jammed with TV's movers and shakers. I'd introduce them to Pete, they'd shake his hand, and then, as soon as they realized they'd never heard of him, hurry off. To them, he was just another nonentity lurking in a corner. What only he and I were aware of was that he'd just closed the largest deal in the history of television, a new NFL contract that cost the networks the then-astounding sum of $185 million. "If they only knew what you know," I said to Pete, and we both smiled. On that night, he was the biggest television guy in a room full of self-anointed biggies.

Pete Rozelle is a quiet man. In the thirty years I've known him, I've never heard him raise his voice. You'd come away from a three-hour lunch with Pete thinking, Wow, wasn't that a great conversation! Then, a few hours later, you'd realize that he'd said virtually nothing. Yet somehow he'd learned everything he wanted to know about what interested you. He's a world-class listener, the best one-on-one man I've ever met. Even the bitterest adversaries liked him and trusted him. Maybe that explains why he succeeded so brilliantly in the toughest job in sports.

Pete's stats are in the record books. When he became NFL commissioner in 1960, pro football's annual income from television was less than $2 million. When he finished negotiating his last network contract in 1987, the sport's take from TV had zoomed to $470 million a year—and there were twenty-eight teams in the league instead of twelve. More than any other individual, Pete made pro football what it is today: the true "America's game." He took a cottage industry and turned it into a billion-dollar operation.

But in so doing, Pete became something of a victim of his own success. As the size, popularity, and complexity of the NFL burgeoned, the pressures on its commissioner—the focal point of the game—increased proportionately.

In his relationships with the owners who elected him, Pete had to be a combination lion tamer, politician, and psychiatrist. On any given day, he'd have to tell some guy who'd voted for him that he was wrong. Now, almost by definition, a professional team owner is a tough, self-made millionaire who's convinced he's always right. They're guys who think they should be running the whole show, just as they run everything else in their lives. For want of a better analogy, they're like members of a small, exclusive church who want a high priest to handle their misdeeds. Just as long as he doesn't tell them what not to do.

So what did Pete do as one of his first official acts? He took on the biggest and toughest owner in the league. He fined George Halas, the legendary ruler of the Bears, for criticizing an official. He called up Halas to tell him himself. Typically, old George said something to the effect that he wasn't going to pay. And just as typically, Pete replied, "I want you in my office on Monday." He was making a statement to all of them: When you do something wrong, you'll be nailed, and I'm the man with the hammer.

Nor was Pete reluctant to punish a famous player. In 1963 he slapped one-year suspensions on Paul Hornung and Alex Karras, two of the league's biggest stars, for betting on NFL games. (To comprehend the impact of that, imagine Paul Tagliabue suspending Jim Kelly and Reggie White.) A year later, right before Pete's press conference announcing the players' reinstatement, he phoned me. He knew that reporters would want to interview Hornung, and he thought that I, being a good friend of Paul's, could help him pin down his current residence. After making a few inquiries, I tracked Paul to a club in Miami. The *Racquet* Club.

I quickly called Pete back. "Guess what?" I said. "The guy you're about to reinstate after a suspension for gambling is staying at a place called the Racquet Club. What's the press going to make of that— even presuming they can spell it right?"

"Oh, my God," he replied. "Get him out of there."

Now I called Paul. "Get your ass into another hotel, old pal," I told him.

The next day, Pete made his announcement, and Paul did a batch of phone interviews—from a Holiday Inn. That one I knew they could spell.

Pete took his heaviest heat following John F. Kennedy's assassination. After agonizing the rest of that terrible Friday and most of Saturday, he ruled that the NFL should play its normal Sunday schedule. For that, he was accused of everything from callousness to greed. It was a thoroughly bum rap. Though Pete kept it quiet at the time, he'd consulted by phone with Pierre Salinger, the president's press secretary and a fellow alumnus of the University of San Francisco. He reached him early Saturday morning in Honolulu. Salinger advised Pete to go ahead with the games, assuring him that canceling them was the last thing Jack Kennedy would've wanted.

In fact, Pete has always had a great relationship with the Kennedys. Ethel and he worked together on the board of NFL Charities. Ted, along with Senator Orrin Hatch, threw a big Washington reception for Pete after he announced his retirement, lauding and toasting him for all his accomplishments. The Kennedy family never disagreed with Pete's decision to play that game, and I know because I've discussed it with several of them over the years. If there's a single trait that binds that family, it's their awesome ability to put aside pain, pick up the pieces, and go forward.

Yet Pete's still getting hammered for that call. When the twenty-fifth anniversary of the Super Bowl arrived right in the middle of Desert Storm, there was a big controversy over whether the game should be played. So once again they dragged poor Pete out of the closet and kicked his ass. Columnists are always writing that he'll forever be haunted by that decision, that it's his one regret. He's not haunted in the least, and he sure as hell needn't regret it.

I watched Pete make the right moves over and over. Following the Giants' disastrous 1978 season, he played arbitrator in the bitter battle between Wellington Mara and his nephew Tim for control of the team. When the two could not decide who would run the football operation, Pete asked both of them to draw up a list of individuals they considered qualified to do it. If a name showed up on both lists, that man would become the team's new general manager. As it turned out, neither list contained the same name. So Pete picked the general manager himself. He tapped a little-known executive with the Miami Dolphins named George Young. It was the best thing ever to happen to the Giants. Bill Parcells also deserves credit for their turnaround, but the man who made the major difference was George Young.

Ironically, Pete's achievements in his job helped drive him away from it. Well Mara was the first person I know to see that coming. It was way back in 1964, after Well learned that Pete had negotiated a TV-rights package for the then-staggering sum of $14 million. He came up to me as I was dressing for practice and said something prophetic: "I almost hate to see that contract happen, because I know what it's going to do to our game. It's going to cause a lot of problems we don't have today."

Of course, not even Well, who genuinely loves the game, could have foreseen the agents and the lawyers and the labor disputes and all the afflictions that came with the big money.

Inevitably, it all got to Pete. Though he doesn't share his problems with anyone, I know he was truly hurt when money motivated Al Davis to move the Raiders from Oakland—a city that desperately needed something to feel good about—to Los Angeles, in total violation of the league's bylaws. The struggle between Al and Pete went on for years and was just one of the many problems that took the fun out of the job, the fun of building something tremendous.

During the last ten years of his tenure, Pete was constantly giving depositions or testifying in court or preparing to testify. There were legal wrangles on every side. It's not like running a corporation, where the chairman has a board and lots of committees to rely on. Only one man ran the National Football League, and it became too much. Every one of the twenty-eight teams at one time or another has been embroiled in some kind of hassle, and it all ended up on Pete's desk. He didn't have enough fingers to plug all the holes.

I saw what it did to him. He smoked more and exercised less. We used to play a lot of tennis (he'd cut a spin on the ball that drove me bonkers), and he just lost interest in it. When he and his wife, Carrie, dined at my house, the phone would summon him every five minutes. I'd say to him, "Good God, how long can you do this?" He'd shrug and make some wry joke. Then he began encountering serious health problems. Finally, one day in 1989, he called to say he was announcing his retirement the next morning. I felt three emotions almost simultaneously: flattered that I was one of the few he'd called, sad at the prospect of his moving back home to California, and relieved because I believed his decision had in all probability saved his life.

Shortly after Pete retired, ABC Sports president Dennis Swanson suggested we honor him and his wife at the network's affiliate meeting in Los Angeles. We put together a video of Pete's entire life, beginning with footage of him as a little kid. We also knew that Pete's favorite song was "Try to Remember" from *The Fantasticks*. So we asked Kathie Lee, one of his favorite people, to sing it at the affair. To open the festivities, I said some nice things about Pete from the dais, then the lights went down and the video began unwinding on a giant screen. Meanwhile, Kathie, who can milk an emotional moment like no one I know, started down an aisle from the back of the huge ballroom singing, "Deep in December, it's nice to remember . . ."

Schmaltzy? Sure. But by the time the song was over, our guest of honor—that unflappable, unemotional "Mister Smooth"—had given way to tears, as had most of the audience. It was wonderful.

I'm occasionally characterized as an "apologist" for the NFL. Defender? Yes. But apologist? No. For openers, there's been very little to apologize for. Look at what's happened to the league since I was part of it. Back in the fifties, I'd often see a championship game that wasn't sold out. Today pro football has become the toughest ticket in sports, a colossal entertainment machine that's enriched players as well as owners. And most of this has happened on Pete Rozelle's watch.

ROONE

Roone Pinckney Arledge, Jr.

Can you imagine a father passing on a name like that? I worked for the president of ABC Sports longer than I played for any of my coaches. Of the thousands of hours Roone and I spent together, his finest came during the 1972 Olympics in Munich.

When Arab terrorists invaded the Olympic Village to take Israeli team members hostage, Roone brought the story to the world as it unfolded. He moved into the ABC control room and didn't leave for nearly three days. I don't think he ever slept. I can vouch for that because the rest of us stayed up almost as long. The whole thing was happening just three hundred yards from where we sat. Once I walked outside the control room, turned a corner, and there was a terrorist with a sack over his head peeking out from the balcony of the building where the hostages were being held.

As I watched all of this unfold—in the studio and across those three hundred yards—I thought to myself, What a crazy world! It was my first encounter with the insanity of terrorism. Little did I suspect that, over the next two decades, that insanity would come to loom over our daily lives.

Roone conducted ABC's life-or-death marathon like some television Toscanini. As Jim McKay talked to the world, Roone talked into his ear. Conflicting rumors were pouring in on us, and Roone had to sort them out. "Jim," he'd say, "we got a report that somebody's dead, but I think it's bogus. We'll keep you posted. Now here's something we've picked up from the German police." Most TV sports presidents would've been sitting on their behinds watching some half-assed director or some little toy producer run the show. Roone was total hands-on. He fed Jim information, flew in Peter Jennings (who had been living in Beirut) for his Arab expertise, called most of the camera shots, even fought to keep us transmitting on the satellite when another network tried to snatch it away from us. He knew that he could do that story better than anyone in television.

Roone Arledge revolutionized sports coverage and, along the way, helped save ABC. Back when the network was literally a joke, the so-called "Almost Broadcasting Company," Roone's sports division was its only money winner. He created *Wide World of Sports,* gambled with Pete Rozelle on *Monday Night Football,* and turned the Olympics into dazzlingly produced home entertainment. He believed in a heretical philosophy: Instead of just bringing the game to the viewer, TV should bring the viewer to the game. He stuck cameras everywhere, on the sidelines, in the stands, in helmets and helicopters. He turned sports into drama, the only drama with slo-mo replay. For his cast, he reached beyond pretty talking heads. He hired people who could convey the emotion of the game and figure out what was happening behind the scenes.

You can't really understand an event, Roone liked to say, unless you understand the people who are creating it. *Wide World of Sports* is as much about people as it is about sports. Sports just happens to be the vehicle. Roone's so inquisitive about people that he wanted to know everything about the skier who takes that spectacular fall at the beginning of every show. He wanted to know where he came from, what he did, why he fell, what happened to him next. Roone would've made one hell of a reporter.

The many Olympic telecasts that Roone produced were basically expansions of the philosophy he brought to *Wide World of Sports.* I was quietly amused to see that same philosophy imbue NBC's excellent coverage of the 1992 summer Games in Barcelona. Amused because both Dick Ebersol, the president of NBC Sports, and Terry O'Neil, the executive producer of the telecast, were once protégés of Roone's at ABC.

Time and time again, I was at the receiving end of Roone's curiosity. On the air, he'd be the voice in my ear telling me where to take a telecast or what to ask someone next. In Munich, while Bill Russell and I were covering basketball, Roone would call and say, "Get Bill to be a little more personalized. Get his own experiences into the game more." When I covered the wrestling finals, and Dan Gable won a gold medal, an unprecedented achievement for the

United States, Roone was in my ear constantly. "Tell us more about Dan's background," he kept saying. Somehow, he knew that there was tragedy in Dan's family history that had made him focus totally on wrestling. As Roone did for everyone, he made me look good by making me perform better.

Roone loved using his sense of humor to turn a stress-filled moment into a piece of cake. As I prepared to open the telecast of the 1985 Super Bowl (ABC's first), he began counting me down through my earpiece to the second we'd hit the air. Roone, who is known for not being terribly accurate in his count, started at ten. As his count continued . . . "Nine, eight, seven, six" . . . he quietly said in my ear, "There are one hundred twenty-five million people watching. Be great. . . . two, one, *You're on!*"

The smile on my face when I came on the screen was not from my delight at being there. It was my appreciation of the boss's perverse humor.

Roone and I have shared virtually everything in our lives, our divorces, our children, our problems, and our joys. Basically, Roone is a kind, thoughtful, eccentric genius. He's also enormously good company, partly because he's so well-read. He's read just about everything and remembered almost all of it, a veritable human sop. As a result, he can intelligently discourse on virtually any subject.

It always amused me to observe Roone and Pete Rozelle conducting negotiations for ABC's *Monday Night Football* contract, which we had to renew every three years or so. Instead of making a formal bid, Roone would have lunch with Pete at Toots Shor's and then they'd amble over to the "21" Club for drinks. I'd leave them to do my sports report on WABC's early news, return to find them heading into dinner, leave again to do the late news, and come back to find them having more drinks after dinner. They'd usually go past midnight. And what did they talk about this entire time? Music, movies, art, books, politics, economics, the state of the world and of humanity. The next day, Roone would casually inform me, "We got it all worked out. It's a pretty good contract."

The big rap on Roone, of course, is his legendary reluctance to return phone calls. When he became president of ABC News as well as ABC Sports, everyone started telling the same joke: Now Roone has two offices you can't reach him at. Aside from the fact that he receives hundreds of calls a day, I think I've figured out the reason for Roone's elusiveness. His problem is that once you get to him, you've really *got* him.

Roone will leave his apartment in the morning, with maybe a dozen appointments lined up at his office, and the doorman will say, "Mr. Arledge, how are you doing?"

"Fine, Freddy. How are you today?"

"Not so well. I hurt my hip."

"You hurt your hip? I did that a few years ago. Listen, I want you to see this doctor. He's over at Lenox Hill. His name is Dr. So-and-so. Now tell me, where is the pain located?"

Half an hour later, Roone is still into Freddy's hip. He did the same thing with the late Cuban barber we shared, Gio Hernandez. If Gio had someone he wanted to get out of Cuba, Roone would sit there discussing it with him forever. Meanwhile, there were eighteen guys in his office waiting to decide whether to spend $100,000 for fifteen minutes of satellite time.

My theory is that Roone recognizes this about himself. Consequently, when he looks at a long list of callers, he knows there're only a few he can deal with in his unique way. Whoever he's talking to receives his totally channeled attention. He'll talk to the same person six times a day until the problem is resolved. Then he'll abruptly vanish, as he switches his focus to someone else. He may even disappear forever, especially if that person didn't give him his way. People at ABC have a droll phrase for that process. They call it "getting Rooned."

No one understands better than Roone the enormous politics that goes into television. I know of no other business—well, maybe the movie business—where you're required to deal with so many huge, yet fragile, egos. It's the dark side of the star system. But Roone believed in stars long before most network sports and news executives believed in them. Today they all do, because stars, many say, are the only things that differentiate the networks from cable anymore.

No star demanded more of Roone's time than Howard Cosell. And Roone gave it to him because, right from the first telecast of *Monday Night Football,* he recognized Howard's value. No sooner had we gone off the air than ABC's phone lines went crazy. Everybody wanted to complain about that bigmouthed guy with the New York accent. In fact, the Ford Motor Company, the show's biggest sponsor, called the chairman of ABC to demand that Howard be removed. Roone had to fight like hell to keep him on. He regarded Howard as a crucial ingredient in the show's formula, and, as usual, he was right.

Yet even after the show clicked and Howard became such an integral part of it, he'd get on Roone's case. He'd call him all the time or drop by his office. Since Roone kept an open office, Howard would either plow right in or stroll by and loudly clear his throat. He had opinions or complaints to register about everyone and anything. For Roone, it was exhausting; Howard tends to use up all the air. But Roone realized that Howard would sulk if he didn't brush and stroke him, maybe even pick up the phone and bitch to some reporter. So he'd hear him out and tell him how great he was doing. Roone always was one of Howard's most loyal supporters.

In return, Howard said some nasty things about Roone, as he did about everybody. Roone maintains a network of informants, so I know those comments got back to him. What he put up with from Howard constantly amazed me. After all, Roone was his boss. He could have simply told him, "That's it." Maybe the reason he didn't was that his perception of Howard was a lot like mine. Whatever had shaped Howard and made him that way could never be changed. What's the sense in flailing away at it? At the same time, Roone understood and accepted Howard's behavior because he basically created him. He gave this near-total unknown a national stage. Without Roone Arledge, Howard Cosell would never have become *HOW*-ard *CO*-sell.

In one sense, Roone's managerial style resembles that of another eccentric genius who fascinates me: Howard Hughes. Both mastered the art of the delayed decision. That irritated and frustrated a lot of people who worked for them. But in Roone's case, at least, he always wants to make his decisions at precisely the right moment, the moment when he's looking at the best options possible.

Take *Wide World of Sports.* Say you were the show's producer, putting together the ingredients for next week's episode. Since you couldn't find Roone to get the final word, you'd go ahead and prepare the show three different ways. Then Roone would arrive, take the best elements of all three, mix them together, and you'd have one hell of a show. Now suppose he had told you up front: "Go ahead on elements A, B, C, but forget about D, E, F." You'd have a show that worked fine on A, B, and C, when maybe, if you had labored on all of them, E would have emerged as the most terrific.

Roone brought the same style to the news division. On the afternoon of the premiere of ABC's *Prime Time Live,* one of the most touted magazine shows in TV history, Roone and I played golf. If he were anyone else, that would have amazed me. But Roone realized that, had he stayed at the office, everyone connected with the show would be leaning on him or performing for him. About an hour before airtime, he walked into the control room. Instantly, the level of intensity came up, and the level of performance soared. Everyone desperately wanted to please Roone. As far as I'm concerned, that's one mark of genius.

Another mark is to know when to come down hard, or at least seem to. Long before the Montreal Olympics, a very talented ABC producer named Dennis Lewin worked his tail off putting together a taped two-hour package to lead off our first night of Olympics coverage. He worked more than a year on that package, and it was excellent. About forty-eight hours before airtime, Roone screened Lewin's show and said, "I don't like it. We're going to drop it and go live with everything."

Talk about shock waves. Half the staff started running around yelling, "Roone doesn't like it! The tape package is out! The sky's gonna fall!" Meanwhile, Roone had quietly moved into the studio and was setting up his all-live premiere. "Frank, you're going to be doing wrestling and be stationed here. Chris, you're going to be doing gymnastics from over there. Keith, you're here. Bob, you're there. . . ."

The upshot was an electric show, pure, live television with an occasional tape package rolled in. It was what Olympics coverage should be all about. Roone, I know, didn't really dislike Denny Lewin's package. He simply wanted to take everyone to another level. He did, and they stayed that way for two weeks. Of course, Roone didn't mind squishing Denny to make it happen, either.

For as much as he plays, Roone is an excellent golfer. But at one time playing with him could often be maddening. Roone's Scottish, so he loves the game's rituals. The problem was, the whole round would seem like one long rite. "Okay, I'm a hundred fifty yards from the green," he'd mutter. "If I hit a seven iron, no, there's too much wind coming from the right. Maybe I'll hit a six iron, just punch the ball a little to keep it out of the wind. I have to bring it to the right anyway, so if I punch it, it's going to hook a little bit. No, that's not going to work. Maybe I'll . . ."

Finally, he would hit the damn ball. And on those occasions when he'd "skull" it, hit it right or left, his golfing partners would think, *What the hell was THAT all about?* Mercifully, that's all behind Roone, and he's playing better (and faster) than ever.

The happiest I've ever seen Roone was at his oceanfront house in the Hamptons on a freezing February night in 1977. He had just decided to accept the presidency of ABC News. With the pounding surf in the background, we listened to all the music from the Montreal Olympics, created by a brilliant young composer whom Roone had commissioned. Then we went for a walk along the beach. Though the temperature was so low the waves were leaving behind frozen puddles of foam, Roone was positively glowing. He'd done everything that could be done in sports, and now here was this huge new challenge.

Of course, at first the skeptics tore him apart. The big joke was that Roone was going to create a *Wide World of News* with Howard Cosell as its anchor. The irony is, that's pretty much what he did—and it's been great. What's *Nightline* about but bringing together the world's people so we can get to know them and understand the world's events? Who else could have gotten Mikhail Gorbachev and Boris Yeltsin to sit down for an international town meeting? I saw the same thing at the 1972 Munich Olympics when Peter Jennings interrogated Munich officials and politicians about the security at the Games.

While Roone was in the process of turning around the news division, he asked me to accept a Peabody Award for him. That's the most prestigious honor in broadcasting, and so the awards dinner was packed with journalistic heavies, many of whom knew very little about Roone Arledge. I suspect Roone didn't want to go himself because he was sick of all that ridicule.

Anyway, in my acceptance speech, I talked about how brilliantly

Roone had performed in Munich and what he would bring to TV news. "I know he'd want me to thank you for this award," I concluded. "But speaking for myself, I can assure you he'll be back for more."

As it turned out, Roone ended up with five Peabodys. This time he made us both look good.

CHAPTER 9

THE GLORY YEARS

*I*n my mind, at least, the most noteworthy sports event in all of 1957—hell, maybe in the entire decade—was the arrival of the greatest player in pro-football history.

I first saw Jim Brown carry the ball on television, back when he was starring for the University of Syracuse. Right off, I decided I didn't like the way he ran. He ran straight up and with virtually no body movement, almost as if he were wired so tightly that he could barely extend his legs. Jim's running style was anything but fluid, much less graceful. If this guy ever makes the pros, I chuckled to myself, he's going to get annihilated.

So much for first impressions. As the Cleveland Browns' first-round draft pick, Number 32 led the NFL in rushing in his rookie season. What's even more astonishing is that Jim accomplished that feat for eight of his nine years in the league. Jim carried the art of rushing to a new level. He did things no one has ever come close to doing. Jim Brown was the only opponent I would get up off the bench and go to the sideline just to watch—and I watched with awe.

It's how the Trojans must have felt when they saw Achilles take the field.

What most impressed me about Jim was his speed. For a 230-pound man, he had unbelievable quickness. Later, he was joined by another great Browns running back, Bobby Mitchell, who'd been a Big Ten sprint champion. Yet Bobby could not beat Jim in a forty-yard sprint. As a matter of fact, Jim would bet anyone in the league that he could beat him over forty yards. After a while, people stopped taking him on. Jim also had enormous strength. He would run up one side of a guy and down the other, and that's if he didn't just flat run over him. I can't ever recall one person stopping him. They might hit him; they might even grab him. But somehow or other, he'd kick right through them. Jim would have been great at virtually any position in football. What a linebacker, what a tight end, what a strong safety he would have made!

Jim's unique trademark was that once he went down, he was always the last man to get up from a pile. He'd pull himself off the ground as if every bone were broken and just make it back to the huddle before the next play was called. You'd think he was seconds from death. Then, *bang,* he'd beat your head off. Once we talked about all that. "Sometimes I'm really hurting, I'm really beat," he explained. "But if I get up slow every time, nobody's going to know whether I'm hurt or not."

For all Jim's prowess, the Giants occasionally managed to shut him down—a feat no other team could match. Most people think that was Sam Huff's doing: His one-on-one duels with Brown became the stuff of instant legend, or at least Sam's legend. But in truth, the Giant who stopped Jim Brown was Tom Landry.

What Landry did, and he was the only defensive coach doing it at the time, was to study "frequencies." From endlessly breaking down game films, he figured out how frequently an opposing team would run a certain play in a given situation from a given formation. After a while, Tom could predict almost exactly what Jim was going to do. In certain situations—first and ten, second and short, second and long, etc.—Tom would tell you he was going to carry the ball off right tackle, around end, or a quick trap. From another formation, Tom would tell us, "Expect a quick pitch to the left." In still another formation: "It should be a trap up the middle." At times it must have seemed as if we had their huddle tapped.

But even if Tom gave us advance warning, we still had to stop Jim before he got going. Otherwise, Newton's Law of Motion took over, and he was gone. That meant Modzelewski, Grier, Katcavage, and Robustelli had to wipe out Jim's blockers. If they did their job, Sam would be free to work from his middle-linebacker spot to nail Jim. Though the Browns had an awesome offensive line, those four guys were able to neutralize it enough to allow Sam to become famous as the Man Who Stopped Jim Brown. It had to piss them off when they'd read in the papers that "Huff made 20 stops of Brown." Sure he did, but only because Andy and Kat crushed their offensive tackle, Rosey and Mo their guards. Sam was a great player, but so were the guys in front of him. Against every other team, Jim averaged more than one hundred yards a game. Against Landry's defense, he averaged less than eighty yards and scored roughly half as many touchdowns.

Jim took some brutal beatings from the Giants, and none worse than our famous 1959 play-off game with the Browns. That day he was held to an incredible eight yards (partly, perhaps, because he suffered a concussion early in the game yet continued to play). Whenever Jim took the ball, it seemed like half the defensive team would stand him up and the other half hit him. By the end of the game, he looked like Joe Frazier after the Thrilla in Manila. Jim probably doesn't count that game because he likely doesn't remember it.

Jim wasn't an easy man to talk to, much less get to know. About the longest conversation we had was at the 1957 Pro Bowl when the two of us lockered next to each other. Though Jim hardly said a word all week, I sensed he wanted to talk to me about something. Finally, at our last practice, he got around to it.

"I'm just curious, man. What kind of dough are the Giants paying you?"

"Why?" I replied. "Have you got a contract coming up?"

He just shrugged. "Jimmy," I said, "I'll tell you exactly what I'm making. After I won the Most Valuable Player award last season, I signed a new contract for twenty-five thousand a year. And I'll tell you something else. If the Giants are paying me what I'm worth to them, you ought to make five times that much for what you're worth to the Browns. Because I'm not anywhere as valuable to the Giants as you are to the Browns.''

Jim flashed a very rare smile. Later, I heard that he was indeed in contract negotiations, and that he used what I told him in the way he deserved to use it. Hell, I hope he got ten times what I was making. You couldn't put a dollar figure on what Jim Brown did on a football field—not to mention the pain and abuse that come with being the target on twenty to thirty carries a game.

For the Giants, 1957 brought a temporary reversal. We finished second in the Eastern Conference, behind, yes, the Cleveland Browns, who were wrapping up one of the greatest runs in football annals: seven division titles in eight seasons. Yet the momentum had clearly swung our way. The Giants were about to launch their own run into the record books, winning five division titles over the next six years.

Though I made All-Pro again in 1958, the season started off with a real downer. In the fourth game, I injured my left knee—the good knee—and found myself contemplating life from my least favorite perspective: a hospital bed. On top of that, I had a bizarre experience. I guess everyone who has ever been hospitalized comes home with at least one weird story. Mine involves a surprise visitor.

Around sunrise one morning, I awoke to find a very large young man standing at the foot of my bed. It was still dark in the room, but I could tell he was trembling. Suddenly, he started shaking the bed. "I can't believe how shitty you Giants are playing!" he screamed. "What's the matter with you guys, Gifford?"

Since my leg was packed in ice and elevated, I could not rise to my defense, let alone that of the Giants. Now he started telling me how he could help the team. "I should be playing, not you assholes. I can play anything. I am the answer to your problems!"

As he ranted on, I stealthily reached for my water pitcher. If he made a move toward me, I intended to conk him with it and then scream for my backup support (which consisted of a 110-pound nurse sound asleep down the hall). Instead, he drifted over to the window and began rattling the venetian blinds. "I was in Korea," he said softly. "You're looking into the eyes of a dead man." Then he ran his fingers up and down the blinds, making what sounded like machine-gun noises. At that point, I knew I had to do something before he became totally unglued. I picked up the water pitcher. "Look, pal," I said. "If you really think you can help this team, get your ass down to Yankee Stadium. Otherwise, I'm going to clobber you with this."

Damn if that didn't do it. He stared at me for what seemed an eternity, then nodded, turned around, and quietly left. Not only that, he took my advice. As I learned later, he sneaked into our locker room at Yankee Stadium before practice and started haranguing everyone. Guys like Huff and Robustelli were so terrified they practically climbed into their lockers. When the police finally came to cart him off, he was drop-kicking footballs and anything else not nailed down all over the room.

At least, I figured, he was out of my life. Uh-uh. On another fall morning thirty-five years later, my secretary, Pat Connell, buzzed my extension. "There's a guy on the line who claims he visited you in the hospital in 1958," she said. "He says you should remember him because you almost hit him with a water pitcher."

I blanched. Suddenly, I had the weird feeling that I was trapped in a hospital bed. "Uh, talk to him, Pat," I pleaded. "Maybe he'll go away."

"Nope," she reported. "He's absolutely adamant about talking only to you."

I picked up the phone with a shaking hand. It was his voice, all right, and the first thing it said was, "I can't believe how shitty the Giants are playing!"

Only in New York.

THE DOCTOR AND THE CHAPLAIN

Thankfully, a lot of relatively sane people also came to see me during my various hospital stays. Among them were two Giants who never played the game, yet whom I remember as vividly as any of my teammates.

Dr. Francis J. Sweeny, our team physician, wasn't anything like

Marcus Welby. More like a miniature Wallace Beery, actually. Short and bandy-legged, profanely pugnacious, always bundled up in an overcoat, scarf, and galoshes and invariably toting a pint of scotch in his hip pocket. Doc Sweeny was one of football's true characters.

Doc's brother-in-law was Steve Owen, which may explain how he hooked up with the Giants. But right from his first game, this little guy became the team's biggest cheerleader. He quickly became notorious for cussin' out the officials. He'd run up and down the sidelines, his scarf flying, screaming across the field at them in his Bronx accent. His favorite oath wasn't the Hippocratic. It was "asshole," and when he wasn't using it on the refs, he'd hurl it at the team he hated most: the Chicago Bears.

George Halas, the Bears' owner and coach, had a habit of continually straying outside the two 40-yard lines, which NFL rules required a coach to stay between. That totally pissed off Doc. He'd be working on a player and suddenly see Halas running down to the 30-yard line as he followed a play. Doc would race over to our own sideline and start jumping up and down. "You asshole, get back!" he'd shout. "Get back where you belong, you old asshole!"

Doc liked to prescribe scotch almost as much as he loved drinking it. He thought scotch was far better than penicillin or any other treatment. After a tough road game, when we had dragged ourselves aboard a train to return to New York, he'd hunt down Charlie and me and hand us these little bottles of brown liquid. "Some cough medicine," he'd explain. "It's good for you, boys." Charlie and I could always count on Doc for a pleasant trip home.

The best thing about him was his wise attitude toward injuries. Except in extreme cases, he never recommended surgery. He understood that all many sport injuries need is rest. His usual recommendation was "Let's see if it will heal up." Even then his philosophy was in complete contrast to the attitudes of most coaches and owners, not to mention other team doctors. As I've said, the first thing many of them wanted to do—and still do—is cut. I've always wondered how many times unnecessary surgery is performed on players and how much damage it causes, even today's arthroscopic surgery. If I hurt my knee, Doc would pack it in ice and say, "It may be a little loose. Let's give it a rest." And that's what he did: no light work, no coach constantly asking me how I was doing. He just put me in the hospital to keep me away from all that pressure. In my view, Doc did a lot of good just by not doing anything.

Doc was lovable but far from flawless. During a pre-season game in 1962, I got sliced across the bridge of my nose by someone's cleat. I knew I was badly cut because blood started gushing down my face. I went to the sideline and, after a long search, finally located Doc. Typically, he was screaming and cussin' at somebody on the field. Once I got him to look at my gash, he said, "Oh, yeah, you're going to need a couple."

So we went down to the end of the bench, and Doc took out his needle. But even as he started sewing, he continued to glare out at the field. Someone was really pissing him off. Suddenly, the needle hit bone or something, because I felt as though I'd just been branded. "Doc!" I yelled. "What the hell are you doing?" Doc turned his head back to me, pulled out the needle, and discovered it had no thread. "Sorry, Frank," he said. Then he took out a spool of thread, weaved it into the needle, jabbed it back in, and, aaargh, hammered that bone even harder.

This time I didn't bother to protest. But I still have the scar—a very crooked-looking scar.

Doc's other sports passion was Manhattan College basketball, and he served as the team's doctor for more than forty years. Fittingly, he died of a heart attack right on the college's court. Everyone said, What a perfect way for old Doc to go. It sure was, and I bet he was running up and down the sideline chewing someone's ass when he went out.

Our team chaplain, the late Father Benedict Dudley, was more restrained yet no less lovable. We called him Father Ben, a quiet, floridly robust member of the Benedictine order who seemed as natural a part of the Giants family as the Maras.

All we knew about Father Ben's background was that he grew up on the same block in Philadelphia as Toots Shor. That figured, because he spent a lot of time at Toots's joint—and he had the whiskey veins on his nose to prove it. Father Ben would always have a Manhattan straight up. That was his drink, though as the night wore on, he might slide into a little brandy, which was Toots's drink. They often drank in the same circle, and it was hysterical watching thom. Toots would be throwing out a few "shits" here and a few "fucks" there, then he'd realize who else was sitting at the table. "Oh, excuse me, Father, excuse me, Father, excuse me, Father," Toots would stammer. Naturally, a few minutes later he was back telling whatever profane story he had started telling. Father Ben had a way of easing into the wall when the talk turned blue. It wasn't that he approved, mind you, just his way of not making things awkward.

Father Ben and I became very close. He'd show up early in training camp, and after practices I sought him out. And during the season, he'd come to my apartment in New York and play with my kids, who really loved him. Father Ben and I got into some long talks about some heavy subjects. As I mentioned, I've always been confused about my religious upbringing as a Holy Roller. When I went to Sunday school before the church services, I'd hear all about how Jesus loves us and was sent here by His Father to save us and all that. Then I'd go upstairs for the main service and hear that if you do this or do that, you're going to burn in hell for eternity. I just couldn't equate Jesus' love with all that hellfire and brimstone.

The fact that Father Ben was a Catholic also attracted me to him. Throughout my playing career, beginning at USC, I would often seek out a Catholic church on the morning before a game. It wasn't a good-luck kind of thing. It was just that I felt comfortable there. To me, this is what spirituality was and is—being in a quiet, holy place where one can communicate one's thoughts to God without somebody jumping up and down and hollerin' damnations.

Though Father Ben was not in the conversion business, we talked about everything from my religious confusion to the historicity of Jesus and the Bible. I found I could have fun with him, too, because we shared an irreverent sense of humor. Like every team in the league, the Giants would huddle up on our sideline before a game for a brief prayer. Father Ben never led the prayer, but he always was right in there with us. Once, just as we started forming the huddle, I tapped him on the shoulder and pointed across the field.

"Do you see that, Father? The other team is praying just like we are. I don't understand this."

"What don't you understand, Frank?" he asked.

"I don't understand how the Big Guy is going to deal with two teams asking Him for the same thing. Do you think it really helps to pray?"

Father Ben's voice became very slow and stentorian. "Yes, Frank," he intoned. "I've found that it does help to pray—particularly in the years that we have good personnel."

When I suffered the concussion that sidelined me for the 1961 season, Father Ben visited me in the hospital every evening. "Father," I said during one of those visits, "I don't think I've ever been this bored. I'd love a little touch of something. You know, Father, maybe just a little cocktail."

After hearing my complaints a few more times, Father Ben showed up at the door of my room one night while the nurse was giving me a pre-dinner checkup. As usual, he was wearing his Benedictine robe, which was very full and had big, floppy sleeves.

"Nurse," he said solemnly, "I need to be with Frank for a few moments. If you don't mind, we'd like not to be disturbed."

She shrugged, walked out, and closed the door behind her.

Father Ben moved awkwardly over to my bed—I could swear he was clanking—and swung my food-serving tray out in front of me. Then he reached inside his robe and brought out a bottle of gin. Next he pulled out some dry vermouth. That was followed by a bottle of rye and some sweet vermouth. Now his hand was up inside a sleeve. It reappeared with a plastic bag full of ice cubes and a tall, elegant shaker. Then came the glasses, the olives, and so on.

After I stopped laughing, I made myself myself an oh-so-dry martini, and he meticulously mixed his own Manhattan. Then Father Ben raised his glass and toasted the Lord's first miracle, the one in which He turned water into wine. A couple of rounds later, I raised a toast to Father Ben for his own miraculous powers.

It was the only happy night I've ever spent in a hospital—and I shared it with a truly lovable friend.

The 1958 season wound up with one of the game's most famous, and exhausting, stretch drives. After losing two of our first four and then hitting a winning streak, including a brutally hard-fought victory over Detroit, we found ourselves facing Cleveland at Yankee Stadium in the final Sunday on our schedule. The Browns needed only a tie to take the conference title. We had to win the game and, even if we did, we would have to beat Cleveland the next week in a play-off for the title.

Sure enough, the closing minutes of the fourth quarter found the Browns and Giants tied 10–10 and our season about to vanish. Cut to Pat Summerall's finest moment and one of the most dramatic in Giants history. Kicking with a sprained knee in vision-blurring snowflakes the size of half-dollars, Pat booted a forty-nine-yard field goal to keep us alive another week. Actually, no one knows how long Pat's kick traveled, because the snow had obliterated the yard markers.

Yankee Stadium was just as cold the following Sunday, and we were even more beat-up. But our defense completely shut out the Browns, and I played a part in the game's only touchdown.

It was a reverse to me from Alex Webster that began on the Cleveland 19-yard line. Lombardi had designed the play to take advantage of the Browns' strong pursuit, and it worked perfectly. As I reached the Browns' 8, I knew I could take it in. But out of the corner of my eye I saw my thirty-seven-year-old buddy, Charlie Conerly, wheezing along behind me. I just couldn't resist the temptation, so I flipped him a quick lateral. Charlie was totally stunned: There was a look of stark terror in his eyes. But he caught the ball and just made it into the end zone. On our way back to the bench, Charlie muttered to me between gasps, "Next time I give you the fucking ball, you keep it."

When the touchdown turned out to be the game winner, however, Charlie was only too happy to bask in the locker-room celebration. In fact, he and I told the press that my lateral was the way the play was supposed to work. "We practiced it all week," I informed them, as Charlie tried to look modest. And that's exactly how they wrote it.

Our play-off victory sent us into the NFL championship game against the new powerhouse in the Western Conference. It was a team that wore horseshoes on their helmets and fielded a quarterback who, just when you thought he was hopelessly roped and tied, proceeded to coolly kick the hell out of you.

JOHNNY U & COMPANY

It was our last pre-season game of 1956, and Charlie Conerly and I were itching for it to end. We were going against the Baltimore Colts in Boston's Fenway Park (in those days we played in some improbable places). The last flight to New York, where Charlie and I had planned a big night out, was 10:00 P.M. Since the kickoff was at seven, we figured that catching that plane would be close, but if all went right, we could make it.

Now there's three minutes left in the game, we're holding a fat 14-point lead, and takeoff is still more than a half hour away. Don Heinrich has replaced Charlie to mop things up. "Just run the damned football," we're both telling him. "Just keep that clock moving so we can get out of here."

Don does his best, but we fail to get a first down, and the Colts take over around their 30. Suddenly, Charlie turns to me on the sidelines and says, "Look at that goofy son of bitch."

He's referring to the Colts' new quarterback. The guy is gangly and stooped over and pigeon-toed, and he's obviously wearing someone else's jersey because he's got rubber bands holding up the sleeves. He looks like a six-foot gooney bird.

Charlie and I are still snickering, when *bang,* the guy hits one out in the flat. Then he hits another in the corner. Then he hits one over the middle. Suddenly, they're inside our 20, and Charlie and I are taking things very seriously. Now he rifles another one over the middle, this time for a TD. All of a sudden this gooney bird has infected his entire team, and we're forced to punt again. Back to work he goes, hitting sideline passes and using time-outs like a Bobby Layne. The goofy son of bitch is trying to win the game. And we're going to blow the flight!

"Who is that guy?" I ask Charlie. He goes off to find out, comes back and says, "U-na-tis."

"Sounds like a Greek drugstore chain."

Well, we eked out the win and just barely made our plane. But Charlie and I were so ticked off at "U-na-tis" that we really didn't enjoy our night in New York. We had no idea, of course, how ticked off we would be the next time we met him. That was that little sudden death affair in Yankee Stadium, the one they called "the greatest game ever played."

Johnny Unitas was a pure passer with a great touch. Most quarterbacks always put the same velocity on everything they throw, but Johnny could flick it, and he could smoke it. He made it amazingly easy for his receivers; he did everything but catch it for them. But what impressed me most was Johnny's toughness. He was a risk taker who continually put his body on the line. He'd hang in the pocket waiting for his receiver to get open when most other quarterbacks would've gotten rid of it. Consequently, he got hammered a lot after throwing the ball.

There was no way to count the times Johnny had the shit kicked out of him. But though he hurt his knees, ribs, and both shoulders, and lost most of his teeth, I never saw him come out of a game. He'd run the ball, too, and without any hook-sliding swoon. If he saw he needed an extra yard, he'd put his crew-cut, goofy-looking head down, and just do it.

As remarkably as Johnny performed, he was surrounded by equally remarkable talent. He had Ray Berry on one side and Lenny Moore on the other side—two Hall of Famers—plus a great fullback named Alan Ameche. Berry and Unitas developed unbelievable timing, and the hours of work they put into it at practices became an NFL legend. Say Ray ran a ten-yard down-and-out pattern. The average quarterback would wait until the receiver made his break to the outside before releasing the ball. Johnny would release it right on Ray's break, at the very instant he planted his outside foot to cut and a fraction of a second before the defender could recover. Some people claimed they could do it blindfolded. And, I'm told, they actually did on several occasions.

Berry was no speed demon. In fact, he was one of the few wide receivers even I could beat. But he compensated for a lack of physical talent with an incredible work ethic and total comprehension of the game. He became notorious for his intense study of game films. One day a newly married Berry was asked if his bride could cook. He hesitated, then replied, "I don't know, but she sure can run a movie projector."

Defensively, the Colts fielded the most awesome left tackle in the game. Big Daddy Lipscomb was six feet five and weighed around

290, which is big even by today's standards for linemen. Yet he was a racehorse with amazing quickness. If you didn't block him even away from the play, he'd run it down from the back side every time. He also had huge, gangly arms. I don't know how many of Charlie's passes he blocked just by "pushing the pile" and getting his arms up in the air. It was like trying to throw the ball over a condominium.

The most incredible play I saw Big Daddy make came in our 1959 championship game with the Colts. We tried a fake pitch to Alex Webster with our right guard pulling out as a decoy. Big Daddy bought the fake and, smelling blood, followed the guard outside just as we hoped he would. Meanwhile, I took a back handoff from Charlie and broke to the inside. My brain had already dismissed Big Daddy as a big hole opened and I started to kick into another gear. Somehow, some way, in midstep, Big Daddy hurled his body backward and thrust out a hand.

Whack! What felt like a bear trap clamped onto my ankle. I went down as if I'd been shot. He was so strong he damned near broke my ankle. God, it hurt. Later, when I looked at the films, I realized what an impossible physical feat he'd pulled off.

Lipscomb didn't enjoy a long run in life. He died shortly after leaving football, apparently of an injected drug overdose. That stunned us all, because he was infamous for being terrified of needles. You couldn't even give him a shot of Novocain. They say Sonny Liston died the same way, but, to me at least, not even Scowling Sonny was as scary as Baltimore's Big Daddy. I think of him once in a while—when I look at my ankle.

As disappointing as our sudden-death play-off loss to the Colts was for us, the game did wonders for the football business. In 1956 the city of New York fell in love with the Giants. In 1958 the rest of the nation fell in love with professional football—and it seemed to happen overnight.

The matchmaker, of course, was network television. Tens of millions of Americans watched Johnny U pull off his two brilliant stretch drives in their living rooms, and from then on, it seemed, pro football became the reigning entertainment spectacle. The fact that the game took place in New York was symbolically fitting. As the U.S. media capital, the city was full of writers, and when they started embracing the Giants, they began fueling the nation's love affair with the game.

Up until then, virtually all the New York sports pages dispensed during the football season were worshipful features about what a Mays or a Mantle was doing during his off-season. It used to really tick me off when we would slug our way to a big win over Cleveland or Detroit and the next day read headlines about Willie or Mickey or Whitey or Moose having a hangnail removed. One day, I suppose, some editor probably said to some sportswriter, "Did you know there were sixty-four thousand people at Yankee Stadium last Sunday?" No shit! Suddenly, we were not only being covered but glamorized. Journalistic heavyweights like Quentin Reynolds, Red Smith, Jimmy Cannon, Frankie Graham, Frank Conniff, and Jimmy Breslin began turning our grimy labors into prose poetry. God, there were great writers in those days!

Yet what writers need years to build television can create in an instant. I mean, it happens like *boom!* When I went back to Bakersfield after our 1958 championship defeat, my hometown friends no longer asked, "Where you been?" They said, "I watched the game. Sorry, Frank."

Certainly, I felt sorry for my two fumbles, which basically cost us the game. I was really torn up by it. But mercifully for me, sportswriting back then wasn't what it is today. If that Colts game had been the 1993 Super Bowl, there would have been fifteen thousand keyboard assassins in attendance, and every one of them would have drawn my blood. Sportswriters in the fifties were a lot less adversarial, not to mention less numerous.

In any event, I felt confident enough the following season to go for a major career change. I decided to try out for quarterback. This was no passing fancy. For openers, beginning in high school, a quarterback is always what I wanted to be. Yet every time I got a shot at doing it, something interfered, and I ended up somewhere else. I also knew I could handle the job. Probably, I was a couple of generations ahead of myself in that I could throw the ball as well as run it. Working the halfback option play, I'd already tossed twelve touchdown passes in only forty-one attempts, which was an NFL record. (The reason, I suppose, was that we were the only team that used the play.) To me, those two skills had the makings of a running quarterback, something that might also help diversify the Giants' attack. And as someone who'd been named the league's MVP, for the first time in my career I had the clout to say, "Look, Coach, quarterback is what I'm going to be."

Of course, knowing Jim Lee Howell, I put it a bit more diplomatically. During the off-season, I wrote him a letter that took me three days to compose. I laid out my case and assured him that, anytime he felt the experiment wasn't working, I would return to halfback. "I will not moan and groan," I wrote. "I will not give you a problem."

Next I set off on an even more delicate mission. Since my best friend was already installed as the Giants' quarterback, I wanted Charlie Conerly to hear about my proposal in person. So I flew down to Clarksdale, Mississippi, and, in the middle of a day of fishing, told my friend what I intended to do. Charlie was anything but distressed. "Fine with me," he said with a chuckle. "I'll help you all I can." I suspect Charlie was both bemused by my outlandish notion and secretly relieved. He hated practices, and now there'd be another quarterback to share the work.

The first problem I had to overcome was a major one. At the time I was the team's leading rusher and leading receiver. I'd have to make a hell of a splash to convince the Giants to give up both of those for a rookie quarterback. But Jim Lee agreed to let me try, in retrospect, I suppose, to humor me more than anything else. I started two exhibition games at quarterback, one against the Eagles and the other against the Lions. I did fairly well in the first but survived only half of the second. As I mentioned earlier, with the Lions game tied 7–7, I threw a "fly" to Alex Webster, who was wide open on the goal line, and damned if the ball didn't bounce right off his normally traplike hands.

I didn't get mad at him; God knows, I've dropped enough of them. But the Lions quickly went ahead, and in the locker room, between halves, Jim Lee came over to see me. He stared at his feet for a few moments, then finally said, "When we go back out, I'd like you to work a little bit at halfback. Uh, just to get the feel of it again."

He was even more diplomatic at the postgame press conference. "Gifford is a such a naturally graceful athlete," Jim Lee told the reporters, "that he could make it at quarterback if we were in dire need of him there and could concentrate on developing him.

But . . ." It was almost exactly how that big shot at Warner Bros. had summed up my acting abilities just a year earlier. And once again even I was able to translate the message: Thanks, Frank, but no thanks.

As it turned out, my failed experiment worked out great for both me and Charlie. In 1959 I made All-Pro again at halfback, and Charlie Conerly, the most underappreciated quarterback in the game, was named the NFL's Most Valuable Player. God, it delighted me to see that thirty-nine-year-old geezer finally get some recognition. The Maras even held a Charlie Conerly Day. More than sixty thousand fans packed Yankee Stadium to watch Charlie pick up $25,000 worth of gifts and a new Corvette. By then my once-reclusive roomie had really come out of his shell: Instead of having to beg him to go out, you had to beg him to stay in. His wife, Perian, meanwhile, had even written a book about her life called *Backseat Quarterback.* After those horrible early years, the two had emerged as the darlings of New York.

Indeed, for both Conerlys, that day erased a lot of bad memories. As he accepted the keys to his Corvette, Charlie looked up at those sixty thousand cheering fans, then gave me a wink and a grin. I knew he was thinking of all those idiots who'd ripped him up and down in our losing years at the Polo Grounds. Some of them were probably up in the stands at that moment, screaming his praises.

The following week, those same fans created quite a different scene, yet one I remember just as vividly. Before a wildly hyped crowd of 68,436, including about 5,000 standees, we clinched the conference title by walloping the Browns 48–7. Our victory, however, almost didn't make the record books.

By now Yankee Stadium on our home Sundays had turned into a three-hour cocktail party. After every game, to avoid the waiting drunks outside, I would leave our locker room with my kids and take a shortcut to my Concourse Plaza apartment by going out the dugout and across the field. I loved that time almost as much as the game. Jeff and Kyle would be racing around, and depending on the postgame condition of my body, I'd take a slow walk to the exit at center field—just savoring the pure joy and miracle of my being there. The maintenance guys would be starting to clean things up by then. You could hear the clank of the bottles being swept away. And even though the place smelled like a Third Avenue bar, there was a graceful presence about the House That Ruth Built that can never be duplicated.

On the Sunday we routed the Browns, our fans started celebrating the end of the game in the third quarter. With a couple of minutes still left on the clock, about a thousand of them poured onto the field. First they tore down the goalposts, then they surrounded both benches. I took one look at their eyes and was stunned at what I saw. I had never seen so many crazed expressions. So even though the game wasn't over, I grabbed Charlie and said, "Let's get the hell out of here."

Everyone else had the same idea. As both teams dashed for their locker rooms, I saw a little boy being buffeted in the crush. He was crying and all scuffed up—in real danger. I scooped him up as I ran and deposited him on top of the first-base dugout. "Don't go back on that field!" I screamed at him. And if I could have found his dad, I would have really whacked him.

Now we were in our locker room, starting to undress, when Timmy Mara came in and announced, "We gotta go back out. Paul Brown is going to demand a forfeit unless we finish the game."

"Bullshit," said Charlie. "No way am I going back there."

And he didn't. But the rest of us returned to the field and ran off a couple of plays while they kept the clock going. All the while we were encircled by fans, including some very elegant women in high heels. It was bizarre: They were so close we could hear them *breathing.*

On one play Mel Triplett took a handoff and kind of jogged through the Browns, who were standing around with very white faces, then vanished into the crowd. He must have kept running, because only the ball came back to us. At that point, I think we were all wondering how many of us would get out alive. It was the closest I've ever been—or want to be—to mob hysteria. The next day there was a big uproar over the failure of the police to give us more protection. Nothing much came of it. But years later, when the Maras finally built their own stadium for the Giants in New Jersey, they made sure there was a high wall between the field and the first row of stands. I bet I know exactly when the idea for that wall came to them.

We played the Colts again for the NFL championship and lost 31–16. No excuses this time either: They were still the better team. All I recall about that game is my brief conversation with the Colts' notorious Johnny Sample, who was both a great defensive back and a loudmouthed jerk. I was writing a football column for a news syndicate that year, and Johnny, then in his second season, must have seen it. Because the first time he tackled me, he said as we lay on the ground, "So you're the great Frank Gifford, the famous newspaper columnist. Why don't you put my name in the paper, mother-fucker?"

"I would, kid," I replied, "if I knew what it was." Sample became so furious he almost got thrown out of the game trying to realign my profile.

Little did I know that another tackle was in my future, this one a hell of a lot more violent. In fact, it would knock me out of the game—driving me into temporary retirement.

NO GIANT YET

The first Gifford huddle.
My brother, Waine, my sister, Winona.
I'm the one with the helmet on.

ALL IN THE FAMILY

The Gifford clan (*above*)
at one of our many
Depression-era homes
in the West.
From left: Waine; Winona;
my mom, Lola; me;
and my father, Weldon.
(*Right*) My sister, Winona,
made like Bonnie while my
brother (*on right*) and I later
fought over who was
the best Clyde.

GOLDEN MEMORIES

I gave Mom and Dad a fiftieth-
anniversary party in 1971.
Raising three kids in the
Depression was tough, but they
tried to never let us know how
tough. (*Left*) I was sixteen when
I proudly displayed a great
string of golden trout taken from
Wallace Lake in the
Sierra Nevadas.

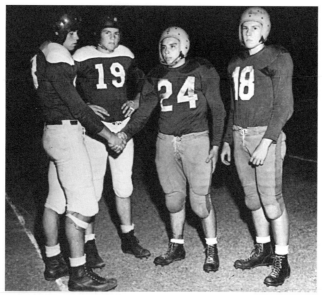

FOOTBALL HERO

As I proudly wear my Bakersfield High School Drillers number 19,
co-captain (and lifelong friend) Bob Karpe and I prepare to launch
our senior-year season against Covina High. Even then (as I turned
the corner) I was looking for cameras. A few years later, the 9 had
become a 6 at USC, where I did a little bit of everything, including
placekicking with another pal, Johnny Williams, holding.

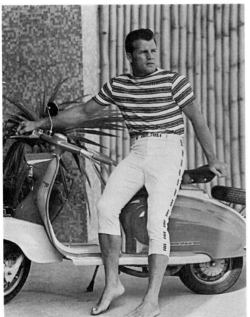

MODEL CITIZEN

By the late fifties, I was into acting, modeling, endorsements, and
taking a lot of my friends along for the ride—like Les Richter,
a former Rams great (*top*). All of these were for Jantzen's
International Sports Club.

ALWAYS IN FASHION

(*Above*) I like the one from *Esquire*. I don't wear a hat or gloves, but I thought, Wow, could I make an entrance at Bakersfield's Woolgrowers Restaurant in this outfit!
(*Right*) I could use a little more of this today—not the hair stuff, just the hair.

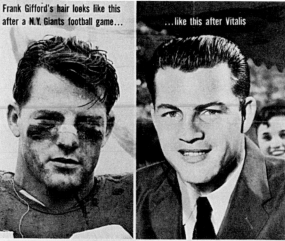

WISHING UPON A STAR

Warners had great plans for me,
according to their studio photographer.
Jack (as in the late Jack Warner),
however, thought my eyes were too little.
I did a lot of stunts and one-liners and
maybe the worst TV pilot ever made—
Public Enemy. I showed it to Cody and
even he walked out.

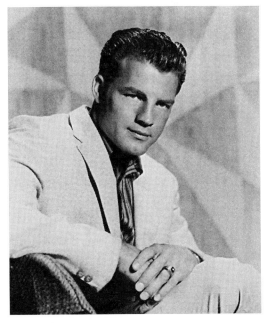

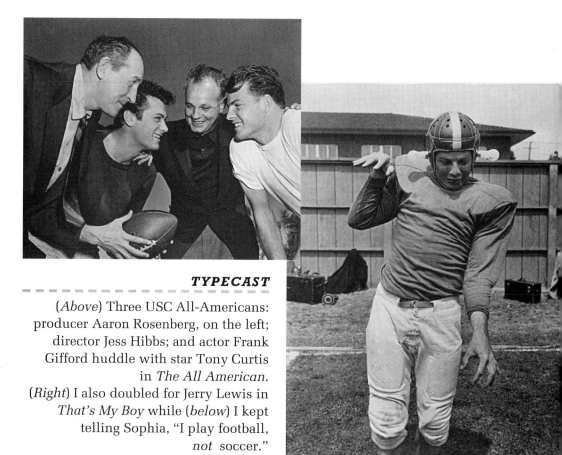

TYPECAST

(*Above*) Three USC All-Americans: producer Aaron Rosenberg, on the left; director Jess Hibbs; and actor Frank Gifford huddle with star Tony Curtis in *The All American*.
(*Right*) I also doubled for Jerry Lewis in *That's My Boy* while (*below*) I kept telling Sophia, "I play football, *not* soccer."

FAMILY MAN

My first wife, Maxine (*above*), was as bright as she was beautiful. A Phi Beta Kappa and homecoming queen, she taught me that books were for reading and classes were "to go to." (*Below*) My two guys, Kyle (on my right) and Jeff, came to all my home games at Yankee Stadium, and sometimes would sneak onto the bench.

BRIGHT LIGHTS

(*Above*) My first TV show was a Friday-night sports show in my hometown of Bakersfield during the off-season. I was a mess—but my buddy Ed Urner owned the station. Meanwhile, "on season" I was big on the New York dinner circuit (*below*). Here with Terence Cardinal Cooke, Toots Shor, and Arnold Palmer.

POLITICAL DOINGS

Richard Nixon was, and is, a great sports fan, and I often had him as my guest at Giants home games and our postgame parties.
(*Below*) In 1965 John Unitas and I were on the same team as we toured Vietnam, showing films and talking NFL to the troops.

GIANT STEPS

The year 1956 was a great one,
and my friend and roomie,
quarterback Charlie Conerly,
helped me celebrate being voted
the NFL'S MVP.
(*Below*) Vince Lombardi had
been the offensive coach for our
NFL champion Giants in 1956,
and later, in Super Bowl I,
I got an almost exclusive
pregame interview.

GLORY DAYS

Offensive linemen open the holes and make the heroes they have to read about; I had some great linemen. (*Below*) Some old Giants fans refer to this as "The Catch." It was one we needed to help beat the Steelers on the way to the 1962 Eastern Division title.

PARTING SHOTS

(*Right*) This was the end of the line for a couple of old warriors. It was the final game of Y. A. Tittle's career as well as mine. We lost to the Browns that day, but we both made it to Canton, Ohio, and the Hall of Fame. (*Below*) Wellington Mara, owner of the Giants, scouted me at USC, signed me on as a pro, and was my presenter at Hall of Fame Day in 1977.

MONDAY NIGHT FOOTBALL

What a trip! Over twenty-three seasons I've worked with, among others, Howard Cosell and Alex Karras (*left*), Don Meredith (*center*), and today's team of Al Michaels and Dan Dierdorf (*bottom*).

RENAISSANCE MAN

When you marry your best friend, it's hard to miss. Kathie Lee
and I share not only a wonderful love, but a wonderful little
guy, Cody, and as this goes to press, a little daughter, Cassidy.

CHAPTER 10

CONCUSSION AND COMEBACK

Around the time that I started going with Kathie, I gave her a word of warning: "I played professional football for twelve years. I made All-Pro at three different positions and Most Valuable Player once, and I'm in the Hall of Fame. But of all the things you're going to hear about me, the word you'll hear most often is 'Bednarik.' "

Kathie gave me a blank look. "Bednarik?" she said. "What's that—a pasta?"

She learned otherwise very quickly. In fact, I don't think a week has gone by in our marriage without someone bringing up Chuck Bednarik and the infamous tackle that sent me to the hospital. If all the people who've told us they were in Yankee Stadium that day actually were there, the Maras never would have had to sell another ticket. By now Kathie gets queasy whenever she hears the name "Bednarik." Too much pasta can make anyone sick.

It was November 20, 1960, and we were trailing the first-place Eagles 17–10 when, with a few minutes left in the game, I ran a crossing pattern over the middle. Just after I pulled in the ball,

Bednarik, the Eagles' great middle linebacker, caught me from the blind side and really nailed me. I must have glimpsed Chuck just before he unloaded as I tried a quick move that only made me more vulnerable. It was a great shot, and down and out I went.

I actually don't remember any of this, I don't think. My memory of that play—and most of that day and night—has been blurred by having seen the "hit" replayed on TV shows more times than the Hindenburg disaster.

In any event, as the ball bounced loose and was recovered by an Eagle, Bednarik leaped up and down over my stretched-out carcass, gleefully pumping his fist. (Tiny little Doc Sweeny, I later learned, not only gave poor Chuck a string of "assholes" but had to be restrained from attacking him.) Chuck later reassured me he was merely celebrating the fumble and not my demise. Though doctors diagnosed my injury as a deep brain concussion and kept me in the hospital for ten days, I felt fine the next morning (I think). In fact, I was chomping to get back in uniform.

That's all there was to it—and yet the whole affair took on a kind of mythical aura. It began with the writers, most of whom went bonkers. The late Fred Exley, in his classic *A Fan's Notes,* had me crumpled on the field "like a small, broken, blue-and-silver manni-kin." And the late Tex Maule of *Sports Illustrated* wrote, "Bednarik's violent, blindside tackle left Frank lying still and almost dead on the cold ground."

Hell, I wasn't anywhere near death. For me, the only scary part of the experience was finding myself stretched out in the locker room wondering how I got there and lying next to a stadium security guard who *was* dying. He'd been stricken with a heart attack, and people were banging on his chest and screaming. It was insanity, and particularly tough on my wife, who was waiting outside. Max-ine had been through a lot of my bumps and bruises, but she about lost it when someone—referring to the security guard—started mur-muring: "He's dead. It's so sad. He died."

My hospital stay seemed interminable, though I did get a lot of nice mail, most of which I saved. Here are a couple of my favorites. From the sisters at Our Lady of the Rosary Convent in Clinton, Massachusetts: "Dear Frank: We want you to know that the Giants

have a few enthusiastic fans here in our little convent home. We have had the privilege of watching the games on TV, and we have done our very best to pray the team to victory. Haven't you ever heard our cheers?"

And this from my old Texaco commercial director, George Cukor: "Dear Frank: Things might be worse. You could be working for Warner Brothers!"

I also heard from Chuck Bednarik, who sent me a telegram expressing his regrets, a get-well card, flowers, and a basket of fruit. I didn't bear him any resentment and never have. After all, his tackle had been perfectly legal. What was he supposed to do, ask me to turn around before he clobbered me? Nevertheless, I resorted to a bit of gamesmanship with Chuck. While I knew he was feeling bad, I put off returning his messages. Since, in a rare scheduling matchup, we were playing the Eagles again on the following Sunday, I wanted him to stay subdued. But after they beat us again, I thanked him for all his concern. Although Chuck was a great player, I think I made him immortal. Apparently, he's built a whole routine around our collision for the banquet circuit. It's like his new profession.

Hell, the way I see it, if I'd hit him a little harder, I'd have killed him.

On a February morning in 1961, I announced my retirement from pro football. Immediately, virtually everyone in the press concluded that the Bednarik incident had prompted me to quit. The truth, however, is a bit more complicated.

Granted, I didn't feel like leaping any tall buildings. A couple of weeks after I went home from the hospital, New York was struck by a huge snowstorm. To get the car out of the garage, I started shoveling. The next thing I remember, Maxine was helping me back to the house. I guess I passed out, because she said she found me just sitting in the snow. That scared both of us, though I attributed it to my inactivity as well as all the drugs I'd received in the hospital.

At the same time, my friends started hammering me to hang it up. Everybody I talked to said, "You've played enough. You don't need this anymore. Your health is more important than any game." People were looking at me as if I were some sort of zombie, some-

thing that had wandered back from the dead. Pretty soon I began looking at myself the same way. Maybe they're right, I thought. Maybe I'm going to topple over the very next minute.

Then, out of the blue, CBS offered me a long-term radio contract. I'd been doing a five-minute sports show for them for several years, and now, in addition to that, they wanted me to appear on a regular nightly basis on their New York station. Since the salary was nearly twice my pay as a Giant, I decided to make the break. Here I was a thirty-year-old running back with three kids. After nine seasons in the pros, I figured I had a couple more left in me at best. CBS spelled security—something, I guess, I'd been seeking ever since those cold nights in the back of a pickup truck.

Even so, I couldn't bear to cut all my ties to the Giants. After agreeing to terms with CBS, I asked the Maras to make me a team scout and was delighted when they consented. On game days during the next season, I would be in another city scouting the next week's opponent, watching for those "frequencies" that Tom Landry had so brilliantly exploited. Summing up my career as a scout, Arthur Daley, the *New York Times* sports columnist, wrote that I turned in "perceptive, illuminating and immensely valuable espionage information." I don't know where he got that—kind of makes me sound like a jock Mata Hari—but I definitely enjoyed my new role. It was a real kick to pick up an opponent's tendency to do something—say, blitz their weak-side linebacker from a certain formation in a given situation—pass it on to the Giants' coaches, and watch us take advantage of it the next Sunday.

Daley, a friend and a Pulitzer Prize winner, also got something wrong. He wrote that I stayed completely away from Yankee Stadium that year "like a reformed alcoholic who doesn't dare go near a saloon for fear of being tempted." In fact, I often worked out with my old teammates on Tuesday afternoons after handing in my scouting report, and sometimes on Wednesdays and Thursdays. At practices I ran pass patterns against our cornerbacks and discovered, to my immense delight, that I could still beat them. I also played a lot of handball, racquetball, and three-man basketball to stay in shape.

Even so, I never considered unretiring until the Giants traveled to freezing Green Bay to take on the Packers for the 1961 NFL championship. They annihilated us 37–0. Watching the game on TV

in my cozy New York living room, I suddenly said to myself, "God, what am I doing here? I should be out there. I can still play this game!"

During the next few months, I thought long and hard about attempting a comeback. I had missed playing football enormously. I had missed everything about it: the competition, the camaraderie, the recognition. I missed coming out of the dugout at Yankee Stadium with sixty thousand people on their feet, roaring their approval, the cheers getting louder and louder as Bob Sheppard intoned over the public-address system, "At halfback, Frank Gifford." You got the kind of adrenaline rush a bullfighter must get when he enters the arena. And I missed my ritual after the game was over: going out through the dugout with my kids and walking across the field to the exit the guard always kept open for me and then up to the Concourse Plaza to have a few pops with the guys. I honestly believe I got more excitement and joy in one day playing football than most people get in a lifetime.

I'll always remember the moment I made the final decision. It was a beautiful spring evening, and I was tooling home in my first convertible, a little blue Mustang. I had the top down and was feeling really happy. I was in as good shape as I've ever been, with a super job and a great family and a home in Scarsdale. It was a long way from the "oil patch," and I felt I had it all. Then it suddenly hit me. I'm thirty-one years old, and if I don't play football this year, then that's it, it's really over. In another year, I won't be able to play again. I can always go back to broadcasting, but now is the only time I can return to football.

I had to share my decision with someone, so I awakened Maxine and let her in on the scoop. "I'm going back and play," I told her.

"Play what?" she groggily mumbled. "What are you going to play?"

"I'm going to play football again."

By now Maxine was fully awake. "Honey," she said, leaning forward to catch a whiff of my breath, "who have you been out with? You been to Condon's?" (Eddie Condon's was my usual last stop before home.)

God bless Maxine. She was all for it, even though it meant selling the house, putting the kids through another change of schools, and making a cross-country trek. A move back to Bakersfield, I felt, was vital so I could just totally concentrate on getting myself into shape to make the comeback. After we got everything all packed up, I went to bounce my plan off Well Mara. He seemed pleased but quickly suggested I go to a neurologist for an electroencephalogram—just to make sure everything was still working right. Thankfully, it was. The day after the test, the Giants announced that I was rejoining them.

At the press conference, a reporter took me aback a bit with what seemed like a dumb question. "Suppose," he said, "you can't make it?"

"Don't worry," I replied with a cocky chuckle. "I'll make it." But for the first time I felt an uneasy feeling about my decision to return.

I made it, all right, but as it turned out, my comeback attempt was no cause for cockiness. You might say I was about to absorb a Giant lesson in humility.

While I was off in retirement, the Giants had acquired a new head coach: Allie Sherman, the only native of Brooklyn I had ever known who spoke with a southern drawl. Though Allie turned out to be a fine head coach, a lot of New York fans wondered why Vince Lombardi didn't get the job instead. How could the Giants let one of the greatest coaches in football history slip away? As best as I can reconstruct it, here's the story.

When the 1959 season ended, Jim Lee Howell lumbered into Well Mara's office and delivered a shocker. "Look," he said. "I just can't do this anymore. This game is really just too much. So I'm quitting coaching."

Jim Lee, you see, was basically a big old country guy who hated bright lights and fast ways. He lived in a place called Lonoke, Arkansas, and he couldn't wait for each season to end so he could hurry back to his farm there. I think he just decided, I've won everything there is to win. Who the hell needs all this anymore?

For the Maras, however, Jim Lee's timing couldn't have been worse. Before the season had started, Vince Lombardi had gone off to Green Bay to launch his dynasty there. Vince had finally become convinced that, with the Giants' success under Howell, he'd never get the head coaching job. Though he and Well were old Fordham classmates, and Jack Mara a dear friend, Vince knew that the Maras changed head coaches about as often as Halley's comet showed up. They'd even kept Steve Owen for nearly twenty-five years. They simply weren't the sort of people who fired coaches. (Of course, they hadn't met Ray Handley yet.)

Meanwhile, Tom Landry had already taken over the Dallas Cowboys when the expansion franchise opened for business in 1960. So suddenly Well and Jack were looking at a bitch of a situation: They'd lost their offensive genius, they'd lost their defensive genius, and now their head coach wanted to quit.

Appealing to Jim Lee's friendship and loyalty, the Maras asked him to coach one more year. That would give them time to find the right replacement.

Jim Lee was nothing if not loyal. He agreed, and the Giants went into the 1960 season with a lame-duck coach. When the word reached Green Bay that Howell was leaving, Lombardi went ballistic. I know personally how stunned he was, because we had continued to stay in touch. Vince, I'm certain, would never have gone to Green Bay had he known that Jim Lee was going to retire. Nor would the Maras have allowed him to go.

So the intrigue began. The New York sports press decided that there were only two possible candidates for Howell's job: Lombardi, whom the Maras wanted and who presumably could get out of his multiyear contract with the Packers, and Allie Sherman, who had returned to the Giants from a coaching stint in Canada to replace Lombardi as offensive coordinator. The writers liked the second option but came down hard on the first. All of sudden, a barrage of articles appeared demanding that new NFL commissioner Pete Rozelle hold Lombardi to his Packers contract. They put on a lot of pressure, and they all made the same point. If the NFL players couldn't jump from team to team, why should a coach be allowed? Who the hell do the coaches think they are?

In the midst of all this, I got a call from Vince. He was coming to New York to learn his fate from Rozelle. Would I like to have lunch after the meeting? So we lunched, and I'd never seen him so down. Basically, he'd been told by Rozelle to honor his contract. But what bugged Vince even more was his conviction that Allie Sherman had lobbied the press to the point of manipulating it. I have no idea as to the truth of that. But I do know that losing out as coach of the Giants was the most painful defeat of Vince Lombardi's life.

After he retired from the Packers, I visited him in Green Bay as part of an assignment for NFL Films. We looked back on his incredible record with the Packers, and then I said, "Too bad you couldn't have done this in New York." Suddenly, Vince looked very sad. "Frank, I'll always be convinced I could have accomplished exactly the same things with the Giants. My greatest regret is that I didn't get the chance."

At least Vince got a shot at revenge. Remember that 37–0 whipping the Packers gave the Giants in the 1961 NFL championship? Lombardi was prowling one sideline that day and Sherman the other.

Allie Sherman's stewardship of the Giants was very much an up-and-down affair. During his first three seasons as head coach, he won three conference titles, then saw the team suffer its own version of the Great Depression. The Giants dropped out of contention for more than a decade, and Sherman, before getting fired in 1969, became a punching bag for what seemed like the entire city.

In my mind, Allie was a terrific offensive coach but not a great head coach. A left-handed quarterback at Brooklyn College, he was picked up by the Philadelphia Eagles and learned the game from Greasy Neale, the famous Eagles coach who was considered a brilliant offensive innovator. Allie had a good sense of the passing game, and he loved to employ it. But when it came to dealing with real players rather than with blackboard *X*'s and *O*'s, Allie's style hurt him a great deal.

Whereas Lombardi knew how to step on his players' toes, how to praise them when they performed and rip their asses when they screwed up, Allie wanted to be one of the guys. Instead of saying, "This is the way it's going to be," he tried to cajole his players. He tried to deal with each one of us psychologically. Then he'd play these little mind games with us that not only were debilitating for him but weren't very effective. That doesn't make Allie Sherman a bad guy. In all honesty, I think Allie just wanted to be loved. That's an okay approach if you're an assistant. But it's the first step on the way out if you're a head coach.

Allie's timing also worked against him. He inherited a bunch of players right at the very peak of their game, guys who studied the game and thought like coaches on the field. They could see what would work and why it would work, and they improvised on both sides of the line of scrimmage. Allie was smart enough to recognize that, and at first he subordinated his ego to their talent and experience.

There always comes a point, however, when a head coach wants to mold a team in his own image, to "make it my team." I wince whenever I hear a coach say that. I winced when I heard Ray Handley say it in his second year after he took over the Giants. It usually means out with the old before there's enough of the new to compensate. That, in my view, happened with Allie Sherman, who housecleaned with a broad sweep. Stars like Sam Huff, Dick Modzelewski, and Rosey Grier were traded. Others started looking over their shoulders and, for the first time, thought about retirement. Unfortunately, Allie didn't have other stars to replace them. It doesn't take much to disturb the balance of a great football team. In 1963 we led the NFL in scoring on our way to another conference championship. In 1964 we plummeted to last place, and the stunned, frustrated fans at Yankee Stadium began singing "Goodbye, Allie." They sang that song to death.

I know a little bit about what Allie endured because my kids were attending Scarsdale schools with his kids. I mean, it was brutal. I'd go to football games to watch my son play on the same team with Allie's son, Randy. As soon as they took the field, you'd hear "Goodbye, Allie" from the parents in the stands. You'd hear it in restaurants and on the streets. I don't know how Allie or his wife, Joan, or his kids survived all that abuse.

He got one nice thing out of living in Scarsdale, though. One of his neighbors turned out to be the late Steve Ross, the legendary founder of the Warners conglomerate and a fervent Giants fan. After Allie was fired, Steve hired him to work on all sorts of projects for Warners, and he proved a great success. More recently, Allie's done ESPN's Monday-night pre-game show, critiquing the two opposing teams each week. Fortunately for me, he doesn't turn his sharp bite on the weaknesses of the announcers.

Some may knock Allie Sherman as a coach, yet everyone I know respects his intelligence, not to mention his resilience. There's no question in my mind that Allie could have continued coaching somewhere—but not in his beloved New York.

My first training camp after returning to the Giants was the toughest of my career. Things went wrong right from the start. In the first week of camp, in a blitz-pickup scrimmage, I mistimed a block on a good friend, Tom Scott, and felt a sharp twinge in my back. I almost fainted. The next morning I couldn't get out of bed. It was two weeks before I could work out again, and then I pulled a hamstring. Suddenly, I began wondering if God wanted me to stay at CBS. I began questioning whether my comeback was a mistake. The sportswriters were asking the same question, and, I knew, so were my friends and family.

By now Allie Sherman had decided to switch me from halfback to flanker. That was because Kyle Rote had exchanged his uniform for the sweatsuit of an assistant coach, which left the flanker position open. Allie also wanted to go with his big running backs, Alex Webster and Phil King. The position wasn't all that new to me since, during my years at running back, I'd also worked as a wide receiver. I also knew that a wide receiver in the pass-heavy offense Allie was developing with Y. A. Tittle would be a major player.

Well, it turned into a nightmare. My biggest problem was getting in sync with Y.A., who had joined the team the season I was away. Some quarterbacks throw soft balls and some throw hard balls. Charlie Conerly threw passes so soft that, in practices, I used to fool around by catching them one-handed. It was that easy. Y.A., on the other hand, had a howitzer for an arm. He also had a sidearm delivery that gave his passes a unique trajectory, a ball that often came to you as a blur out of the line of scrimmage. In addition, I had to adjust to Y.A.'s timing. Charlie would toss the ball just as I made my break to the inside or outside. Y.A. would hold on to the ball a split second longer and then bang it to me after I made my break. Same accuracy, but fractions of a second later and with a hell of a lot more velocity.

Though I dropped almost everything Y.A. threw me at first, I felt reasonably sure we'd eventually jell. But in the final exhibition game against Philadelphia, with my back killing me and my hamstring tight as a drum, I dropped three passes that were right in my hands. It was the perfect cap to my whole pre-season. I felt mortified.

On opening day, against the Browns in Cleveland, I found myself on the bench. Allie Sherman had picked up a player from San Francisco named Aaron Thomas to start at flanker. I told him I understood. Allie, I knew, was taking the team apart, and maybe I was one of the parts he didn't want around. I didn't really resent him for it. If I'd been the coach, I probably wouldn't have played me, either.

Deep inside, though, I was shattered. It really hurt. Suddenly, I'd gone from All-Pro running back to second-string wide receiver with a bad back—me, a guy who'd been a star most of his career. Though I laughed about it with friends, I'd never felt so down in my life. So I started spending a lot of time with Toots Shor. It was cheaper than a shrink and a hell of a lot more fun. I'd stop off at his huge Park Avenue apartment in the early evenings before he went to the restaurant and pour out my troubles while he poured himself brandies.

After one game in which I didn't play a single second, I went straight to Toots's place from the airport. He quickly set me down at the circular bar in his living room. "I saw the game," he said. "You're feeling rotten, aren't you?"

"Toots, I think I'm going to quit."

"You can't do that, pal," he said gruffly. "You just can't."

"Toots, I didn't even get into the game. And we *won.* It really hurts, Toots. Not that I didn't play, but that they didn't even need me."

We went through about half a bottle of brandy. Then inspiration suddenly seized Toots. "I'm going to take you to a doctor friend of mine," he said. "This guy is just what you need."

"What's his specialty?"

"Curing celebrities. [Which I'm sure to Toots was a better credential than a degree from Johns Hopkins.] He's got a list of patients that reads like a Who's Who. You know, Fonda, Ameche, Gleason, even George Patton. They all go see him. This guy's a medical genius."

Naturally, I was intrigued. So Toots made a call, and a few minutes later we were sitting in the doctor's office just a few blocks up Park Avenue. The next thing I know, the guy's jammed two damp cotton swabs up my nostrils. Whooeeee! Suddenly, I felt twenty feet tall. Quit football? I walked out of that office ready to take on the Cleveland Browns single-handed.

Thirty years later, I noticed a picture of that doctor in the New York *Daily News*. The headline on the story said, COCAINE DOC DIES. And here's the second paragraph: "The colorful doctor was best known for treating his patients' aches and pains with cocaine. His clientele included a mix of personalities from the worlds of art, show business and even the military."

Right—and at least one dumb jock.

In any case, I decided to take Toots's advice and stick it out. The next week we flew to St. Louis to play the Cardinals. Since Aaron Thomas had hurt his knee the previous Sunday, I knew I might get a chance to play. I couldn't sleep at all the night before that game. When the sun finally came up, I took a long walk and found myself standing outside a Catholic church. I went in, knelt down, and thanked God for everything I'd been given in my life. And I didn't ask for anything more. When I left that church, I felt almost as good as when I left Toots's doctor.

Sure enough, Allie started me at flanker. I was still thinking about that church visit—could this be the Big Guy's doing?—when early in the game Y.A. looked at me in the huddle and asked, "Can you beat Fischer?"

He was referring to Pat Fischer, a tough little Cardinals cornerback who later became an All-Pro with the Redskins. "Yeah," I replied, trying to sound very confident. "I can beat him deep."

"Beat him on the fly?" said Y.A., arching his eyebrows.

I just nodded. So Y.A. called the play: "Strong right, split left, B circle. I'll need some time, guys. On three . . . break!"

At the snap, I took it straight up the field and gave Fischer a little move to the inside, as if I were going to take it over the middle. He bought it, and I blew by him. But I was shocked how quickly he recovered, and he was right with me when Y.A. had to let it go. Seeing me covered, he just let it rip. Basically, Y.A. was throwing it away. I don't know how the hell I got there. I sure wasn't that fast. And when I left my feet, the ball was still way beyond me. As I dove for it, I literally caught the end of the ball. Somehow I pulled it into me before turning sideways and crashing into the end zone. It was the luckiest catch I ever made. And I would have loved to have been with Toots at that moment. Suddenly, I knew everything was going to be okay from then on.

Boy, was it ever. Not only did I start the rest of the season, averaging twenty yards a catch, but I went to the Pro Bowl in a third position—something no one had, or has, ever done. UPI named me NFL Comeback Player of the Year. It wasn't the MVP award, yet considering how my comeback started, that honor struck me as near miraculous.

Y.A. and I had developed a great rhythm, and I owe him much of my success that season. He wanted his pass patterns run precisely the way they should be run: so many steps upfield, the fake, the cut, the drive inside or out. We worked and worked on each pattern until we had it as choreographed as a ballet performance. Y.A. would take the snap and sprint back, never backpedal, always the same number of steps, always the same number of yards, then plant that rear foot and fire the ball. It always arrived in the right place at the precise instant I came open. Y.A.'s passing routine was so exactly calibrated that, after about a half hour of practice, he'd have literally dug a hole with the right foot that he planted before the throw. We'd have to move to a new spot on the field.

Our favorite pattern was the zig-out, and it became our bread-and-butter play against man-to-man coverage. My job was to drive to the cornerback and give it a hard move to the inside, looking back at Y.A. He would time his pump-fake to my inside move and the cornerback had to commit. At that very instant, I'd plant my inside foot and break hard to the outside. I loved that play, and so did Y.A. We shortened a few careers with it over the three years we were together.

Y.A. was a real superstitious character who insisted that we adhere to a culinary pre-game routine. It started the Saturday night before the sixth game of the '62 season. We were staying at the Roosevelt Hotel near Grand Central Station, and late in the evening a bunch of us on the offense set out for a bite to eat. We walked and walked, but found no restaurant open. Finally, we landed in this ratty old Italian joint, literally a hole-in-the-wall. After checking the menu on the stained wall, Y.A. suggested that we all try the spaghetti and meatballs. Amazingly enough, they turned out to be marginally edible. The following day we launched an ulcer-risking, nine-game winning streak.

For the next three years, on the night before every home game, Y.A. dragged us to that dump for spaghetti and meatballs. To this day, the mere thought of those reddish-brown mounds makes me queasy. But Y.A. loved to slop that stuff down almost as much as he believed it was helping us win. Nor, unfortunately, did he mind sacrificing our gastrointestinal systems to the cause.

Once again, we won the Eastern Conference crown and played Green Bay for the NFL championship. Everyone wanted revenge for the clobbering they'd handed us the year before, but this time the Pack had the weather on their side as well as Lombardi. The winds at Yankee Stadium averaged close to 40 mph. You can throw in rain and you can throw in snow, but you can't throw in a gale. Y.A. threw balls that day that landed behind me and in front of me, and at times passes I thought were meant for someone else. It was impossible. We were a passing team, the Packers were a running team. We lost 16–7.

That night my late lawyer, Howard Epstein, hosted a party for both teams at his Sutton Place apartment. I invited a lot of Giants and also asked my friend Paul Hornung to bring some of the Pack. That was a big mistake, because they were all over the place, dancing, toasting each other, continually crowing: "NFL champions! NFL champions!"

At last it came time to adjourn to Toots Shor's. Since I knew it was going to be freezing, I'd arranged for a limousine for myself and Maxine. So out the door we walked, my wife in her full-length mink with my limo waiting at the curb, when guess who we see. Max McGee, Jim Taylor, and Paul Hornung with wives and girlfriends— all trying to hail a cab. They were having absolutely no luck (hey, this was Sunday night in New York) and were freezing their butts off.

Seeing that was my only enjoyable moment of the day. Even so, I couldn't allow them to turn to ice. As my driver started pulling away, I told him to hold it up. "Hey, Paul," I called out. "You and the guys need a ride?"

I've rarely seen men that big move so fast, not to mention their shivering ladies. As they all piled inside my limo, I couldn't resist taking a shot. "Maybe you guys kicked our asses," I said. "But you've still got to go back to Green Bay."

While it wasn't six points, it felt almost as good.

THE GOLDEN BOY

Of all the guys I played against, Paul Hornung may be the unlikeliest to become a close friend. We started hanging out together around the time that Vince Lombardi transformed Paul into a bigger version of myself. A Heisman Trophy winner at Notre Dame—when he began losing his blond hair, they dubbed him "the Golden Dome"—Paul came to the Packers as their number-one draft pick and floundered around as a part-time quarterback until Lombardi arrived. Vince figured out very early that Paul wasn't going to be his quarterback. Like me, Paul wasn't a great passer; he was a good passer. Like me, he wasn't a great runner; he was a good runner. Like me, he wasn't a great receiver; he was a good receiver. And he could also kick. So recognizing his versatility as well as his limitations, Vince made Paul his halfback and built his offense around him. Paul *became* me.

Whenever I hear the phrase "a creature of excess," I instantly think of Paul. He maxed out on everything: sex, food, booze, fun, laughter, friendship, and life. You might call him a sophisticated Bobby Layne. While Bobby liked the honky-tonks, Paul was strictly uptown and upscale. He loved to visit New York. When the Packers came in, or when he'd visit with me in the off-season, I'd take him to Toots Shor's, "21," Eddie Condon's, P. J. Clarke's, all my spots. But Chicago was his town. He knew Chicago infinitely better than I knew New York, and everybody in Chicago knew him. I couldn't stay up with Paul on those nights when we bounced around Chicago. He'd bury me before he even warmed up.

Nobody loved Paul more than his teammates. In fact, I used to look at him and wish I had the same sort of rapport with my guys. What made Paul's popularity with players so unusual is that he wasn't what you'd expect a jock to be. He wasn't ugly, he didn't swear a lot, and he never broke his nose. Paul was as much a glamour boy as Joe Namath and a hell of a lot better-looking. You'd expect guys to resent him for it. Yet he had close friends on both sides of the line of scrimmage, the little guys as well as the big guys, and they're still his friends today. I never met anyone who didn't like Paul Hornung.

As great a player as Paul was, he became an even more legendary socializer. He loved to hang out with his guys, but he really came to life partying with big shots and entertainers. He truly relished the glamour and the glitz. Most of the action he created himself. One of the Packers said it best: "Paul could turn a trip to the drugstore into an event." Most likely, he'd never get to the drugstore—but he'd leave a lot of well-tipped bartenders and happy females along the way.

I received a firsthand view of Paul's effect on women when I helped get him a job with the Jantzen company. He, I, and a bunch of other famous jocks traveled the world shooting ads for Jantzen sportswear. It was the early days of endorsements for pro-football players. We were underpaid, but we had some great times.

One trip took us to Hawaii, where Paul was going with a beautiful heiress. She lived in a spectacular penthouse on the island of Oahu. One night we all met for dinner at the Colony Surf, a classy Oahu restaurant on the ground floor of the condo building in which the heiress lived. There were myself and Maxine, Bob Cousy and his wife, Ken Venturi and his wife, and a few others.

When Paul showed up with his date, it became instantly evident that the poor woman was as zonked as she was gorgeous. I mean, she was just paralyzed with fatigue. Paul probably had been partying with her for forty-eight straight hours, because while there was love in her crossed eyes, her voice had a bad case of the mumbles.

Paul, on the other hand, just bounced into the room. He was ready to rip and looking to make a move on anything there. And what happened to be there was an even more gorgeous singer working the piano bar. Half an hour later, Paul had joined her for a few duets. One hour later, he was putting the heiress on the elevator. Two hours later, he was leaving with the singer. Knowing Paul, he probably stopped off at the heiress's apartment after he left wherever the singer lived.

On another occasion, in 1962, Paul's social connections came close to getting yours truly in trouble. The Giants were playing the Cowboys in Dallas. The evening before the game, the phone rang in the room in which Alex Webster and I were staying. It was Paul calling from Green Bay.

"What are you guys doing tonight?" he asked.

"We're going to bed," I replied. "Paul, we're playing tomorrow."

"Oh, come on, guys. You've got to give my friend a call. He's having a party, and you've got to go. He throws the world's most unbelievable parties. I mean, *unbelievable.*"

How could we turn down a request like that? Paul, was right, of course. The party was beyond anything we'd ever encountered, or should have. Naturally, I hung around just to make sure Alex got home all right. About sunrise, I dropped him off at our hotel and went to put the car we had borrowed in the garage. Meanwhile, Alex staggered into the lobby—and straight into Wellington Mara, who was on his way to mass.

"Good morning, Alex," said Well.

"Uh, good morning, Mr. Mara," mumbled poor Alex, trying to unscramble his eyes. "Looks like a great day."

"Yes," came the reply. "A great day for a *game.*"

I'm sure Well never blabbed to anyone, yet somehow Y. A. Tittle, a very straight dude, found out about our little escapade. It was about 105 degrees in the Cotton Bowl that afternoon, and Y.A. must have run poor Alex twenty times in a row. Pretty soon he was heaving and wheezing in the huddle; we thought he was going to die. As for me, Y.A. sent me on long fly patterns every chance he got. The amazing thing was, we wound up blowing the Cowboys out of there. Alex stumbled and bumbled for a hundred or so yards, and I think I scored three touchdowns. For some reason, the details are a little fuzzy.

Though I didn't learn of it until later, Paul's phone line was being tapped when he made that call. The next season, Paul and Alex Karras were slapped with one-year suspensions by Pete Rozelle for betting on pro-football games. While Karras got angry and attacked the NFL, Paul characteristically took it in stride. He told Pete, "Yes, that's what I did; it was stupid, and I deserve what I got." I know Pete respected Paul for that. Unfortunately, a lot of fans still believe that Paul bet on his own team. In fact, it came out in the investigation that he did not, as was explained time and time again by Pete. It was and is a bum rap that should be forever laid to rest.

While Paul really didn't sweat his suspension—it was almost as if he'd gotten a ticket for speeding—his friends worried about what a year off would do to him physically. After all, he was never in great shape to begin with. I don't think he had a single visible muscle. He was also the only guy I knew who was capable of gaining ten pounds overnight. So we all feared that he'd party his body out of the game. Instead, Paul came back after his reinstatement and had a fine season. Maybe he'd been getting some exercise we weren't aware of.

Today Paul is married to a wonderful lady named Angela. They live near Louisville, Kentucky, where he hosts a popular syndicated TV show. I love watching it, because it's classic Hornung. The set is sort of a saloon, and Paul picks the winners of upcoming basketball and football games before a studio audience, who behave exactly like saloon patrons.

"No way is LSU going to lose to Georgia by six points," he'll announce with that familiar cocky grin. "Maybe two points, but never six." Then the Georgia fans will begin booing, and Paul will start shouting "No way! No way!" and everyone will end up laughing and cheering and having a terrific time. I guess it's ironic that an athlete who was suspended for gambling now hosts a gambling show on television. But to Paul it's just all great fun—in other words, exactly like his life. Wherever his hairline ultimately ends up, Paul Hornung will always be pro football's Golden Boy.

Add another *t* to the word "title," and you basically have why the Giants won their third straight in 1963.

Right from the opener, when Y. A. Tittle threw for three touchdowns and bootlegged for another against the Colts, that thirty-seven-year-old buzzard pranced through the season like some high school phenom. Thanks largely to Y.A., the Giants finished the year as one of the three highest-scoring teams in the history of the league. After we scored the first seven times we had the ball against Cleveland, Paul Brown hailed Y.A. as "the best passer in football." After we beat the Cardinals, St. Louis coach Wally Lemm said, "We're probably seeing the best year any quarterback has ever had."

It was the Cardinals, however, who subsequently handed us our only upset of the season. That game was played at Yankee Stadium on November 24, two days after the assassination of President Kennedy, and I've never played under more eerie circumstances.

Though we figured no one would show up, the stadium was filled to overflowing with long lines outside. I suspect a lot of people showed up without tickets, expecting they'd get in when everyone else stayed home. As for the players, there was no groundswell to cancel the game. Like everyone else in America, we were in shock. But also like most everyone else, we had a job—and our job was to play football. Even so, you could just feel the impact of that terrible tragedy on everyone there. The players played as though they were sleepwalking, and the fans seemed disoriented: They cheered at the wrong moments and were quiet during the right ones.

The most bizarre moment, however, came before the game started. Somebody had a TV going in the locker room, and all of a sudden we heard a commotion. "Holy shit!" one of the attendants shouted. "Someone just shot Oswald!"

For all our new offensive prowess, we didn't clinch the conference title until the final game of the season against Pittsburgh. That's the game in which everyone says I made the greatest catch of my career. A photo of it even showed up in *Time* magazine above the caption *He had it all along.* Hell, I barely had it for a nanosecond. Yet the play did display how precisely Y.A. and I had honed our rhythm. By halftime we had a 16–3 lead over the Steelers, who needed a win or a tie to take the title themselves. Y.A., as usual, was all over the locker room digging for information.

"What do you think you can do with that guy?" he asked me, referring to Glenn Glass, a Steeler cornerback who'd been covering me like Saran Wrap.

"When we're in that strong-right formation," I told him. "He's looking for the zig-out, and he's really playing me tight."

Y.A. filed that little tidbit away for emergency use. The emergency came early in the third quarter, when our lead had shrunk to six points, and we faced third and long on our own 23. We needed that first down to keep our drive alive and take some of the momentum out of a tenacious team that had been pulling games out all season.

In the huddle, Y.A. looked at me and just nodded. He called a strong-right zig-in, which meant I'd go straight at Glass, give him a hint of an inside move, drive hard outside, and then break it back across the middle. It worked to perfection. I ended up with a couple of steps on Glass, but Y.A., under heavy pressure, drilled a line drive about six inches off the ground and beyond my normal reach.

There was no way I was going to get the first down by diving for it. That was totally impossible. So I simply extended my right hand as far as I could, sort of like a shortstop stretching for a hot liner in the hole. All I was hoping to do was flip the ball up in the air. But—plop!—somehow the damn thing stuck in my palm. It was the weirdest thing that ever happened to me on a football field. Yankee Stadium erupted with one huge roar as we picked up the first down and regained the momentum.

After we went on to win by sixteen points, Buddy Parker, the Steelers' coach, called that completion "the turning point. It would have been a different game if Gifford hadn't caught that ball. He shouldn't have got it, but he did. I still don't know how he did it."

Believe me, Buddy, neither do I. Next to my getting conked by Bednarik, it's the play that old-time Giant fans bring up more often than any other.

In our championship game against the Chicago Bears that season, Y.A. tore up his knee in the first half. We had dominated the Bears on our very first drive, which ended with Y.A. hitting me for six in the corner of the end zone. We thought it was going to be a runaway. But when Y.A. went down, so did our offense. Our defense played great, but they couldn't do it all. Though Y.A. came back for the second half, playing on guts and Novocain, it just didn't work. George Allen, the Bears' defensive coach that day, knew Y.A. couldn't maneuver and came at us with everyone but the ushers. Poor Y.A. ended up throwing five interceptions in our 14–10 loss. But he also tossed an astonishing thirty-six touchdown passes over that fourteen-game season, which helps explain why he finished it as the NFL's Most Valuable Player and locked up a spot in Canton, Ohio.

It was to be his—and my—last great trip.

A BEAR, A LION, AND AN EAGLE

One of my most vivid memories of the 1963 championship game has nothing to do with the game itself. A few days before we played it, I gathered with the rest of our offense in a training room to study films of the Bears' defense, while in an adjoining room our defense watched films of the Bears' offense. Suddenly, we heard a eruption of laughter—followed by much oohing and aahing—through the wall. A moment later, Sam Huff stuck his head in. "You guys gotta come see this," he said with a grin.

We all trooped next door, and they reran the film of a play from a Bears-Lions game. Apparently, the outside linebacker for the Lions had been giving the Bears' tight end fits whenever he tried to get off the line of scrimmage. Of course, it's customary for linebackers to do that. But this tight end decided he'd had enough with custom. On the play we watched, he started off the line, stopped, then stepped back and whomped the linebacker right on the button. He just knocked him flat-ass cold. We were astounded. I mean, offensive players just don't do that to defensive players. They get to know them—you know, ask about their wives and kids. Defensive players have too many chances to get even.

No one seemed more impressed than Sam. "Can you believe that?" he said when the lights went on. "Who the hell is this guy?"

He was, of course, Mike Ditka.

Ditka may have been the toughest tight end ever to play the game. The only one I ever saw who rivaled him was Mark Bavaro of the Giants. But while both of them could carry three tacklers on their backs, Mike would be smacking them and kicking them as he dragged them along. You just didn't want to get near him on a football field. If Dan Jenkins wrote a book about Mike Ditka, he'd probably call it *Semi-Crazed*.

After playing a dozen great seasons with the Bears, Eagles, and Cowboys, Mike brought the same competitive fire to coaching. He learned that profession as an assistant to Tom Landry in Dallas, and his system of *X*'s and *O*'s in Chicago was basically the one Tom taught him. That system gave the Bears six division titles and a Super Bowl championship.

I'm not into the psychoanalysis of Mike that became a cottage industry in Chicago before he was fired. I do think, however, that some of his media critics were perhaps as mentally unbalanced as they accused him of being. All I know for sure is that, as a coach, Mike loved players like himself. He was never fast or extraordinarily big, but he was unbelievably committed. So he'd keep a player with less talent than another player just because he liked his determination, his ability to overachieve. Later, Mike's heart attack forced him to control his temper, and severe arthritis slowed him down. It was kind of sad to watch him on the sidelines. All Bears coaches have always run up and down the sidelines (it must be a genetic trait), but Mike just couldn't do it anymore.

Mike's mind, though, remains in frighteningly good shape, especially when it comes to the media. I know, because he played a mind game with the *Monday Night Football* team every season.

On the Sunday before Monday-night games, Al Michaels, Dan Dierdorf, and myself—along with our producer, Ken Wolfe, and our director, Craig Janoff—often meet with the head coaches for a background question-and-answer session. Most coaches are gracious, open, and outgoing. Not Mike. To gain an edge, I suppose, he invariably invited us up to his hotel suite—*his* turf. From then on, we always knew what to expect.

When we entered the room, Mike would be sitting before the TV deeply immersed in a Sunday football game. He never got up. In fact, he barely looked up. As we took chairs, one of us would try to break the ice. "So who are you starting at quarterback tomorrow?" maybe I'd ask.

Mike continued to stare at the TV screen.

"Is Harbaugh going to start?"

Mike glanced up, regarding us as if we had just gotten off a UFO. "Of course Harbaugh is going to start," he growled. "He's my kind of guy, don't you know that?" Suddenly, he turned his head to yell at his wife, who was somewhere off in the bedroom. "Diane, did that call come through yet? No?" He shrugged, shook his head, and returned to the TV.

It was all a charade, of course, because Mike was actually very happy to see us. He loves the limelight, but he's also an absolute genius at using the media to send messages to his players, his owners, and his fans. Once he would give us his full attention, he might compliment a Bears receiver: "That kid may be slow and small, but he gets it done." Or he might knock one of his linemen: "If that guy doesn't shape up, he's gone." Mike figured we'd incorporate that stuff into our game commentary, and he wanted those two players to hear about it. Mike's great television, and he got more close-ups than Liz Taylor. But he also played us like a fiddle.

Every time we left a sit-down with Mike Ditka, closed the door behind us, and stepped into the hallway, we always did the same thing. We'd look at each other and collectively exclaim, "What bullshit!" Yet we always enjoyed and admired the performance, just as I had when Mike was a player.

Along with its other challenges, switching to flanker brought me into close proximity with the football world's most vocally belligerent species: the cornerback.

What is it about these guys? Why are they such incorrigible trashmouths? When some cornerback babbled trash at me, I used to think, What a waste of energy! How self-defeating! But having played the position myself, I understand that it's the nature of the job. Cornerback is a very lonely position; you're really naked out there. When you get beat man for man for a touchdown, you look like a clown in front of millions of people. Consequently, good cornerbacks develop a genuine dislike for the guys they cover, who have all the advantages to begin with.

First of all, you're usually talking about a $100,000 guy covering a million-dollar guy. Who should win that war? If a Jerry Rice doesn't win it most of the time, he's not going to make a million bucks. And not one defensive back I've ever known can cover a really good receiver like Rice without help from another back or help from a pass rush. They're not supposed to. No matter what baloney you hear from the broadcast booth, it just can't be done. So if you're that poor little cornerback, why not give them "You cocksucker, you motherfucker" a few times? They probably figure it enhances their already slim chances of doing the job.

Despite all their disadvantages, the good cornerbacks stick around for a surprisingly long time. The best I ever played against was Dick "Night Train" Lane, who seemed to stick around forever.

When I came up in '52, Night Train was with the Rams, and when I retired in '64, he was with the Lions, and in between he starred for the Cardinals.

Night Train had a spidery body, and spidery guys usually can't run fast. He was an exception, and his speed, plus his amazing reach, made it almost impossible to get around him. Night Train had arms about a yard longer than most arms. He knew exactly when to time a little nudge with the elbows, a little brush with a forearm, a bump here, a trip there. He had all the tricks and a great talent. He was the most disruptive cornerback I ever played against, and nothing can screw up a passing game more. In his rookie season, Night Train set an NFL record with fourteen interceptions—and that's when a season meant only twelve games. He caused me so much grief that, before playing against him, I'd lie awake at night trying to visualize myself beating him. Then I'd fall asleep and have bad dreams about him. Night Train ruined my Saturday nights as well as my Sundays.

I did become good friends with another great cornerback: Tom Brookshier of the Eagles. Sort of like myself, Brookie was an overachiever. He came out of a tiny military college in New Mexico, a little raw but very aggressive. Actually, aggressive is an understatement. Hell, he'd mug you if he could. I couldn't stand Brookie at first. He'd jaw all the time, complete with allusions to my ancestry, which made me love to beat him.

Once, when I went man for man against Brookie on a crossing pattern, he tore half my jersey off. I'm not exaggerating. To catch the ball, I had to rip it out of his hands. Meanwhile, he desperately clawed at anything he could grab. I ended up with a long completion, and he ended up with a large handful of red, white, and blue jersey.

As time went on, Brookie became tougher and tougher to beat. He really improved with age, as did our relationship. We kind of graduated into broadcasting together. He worked local TV in Philadelphia while I worked local TV in New York. Then we ended up covering pro football together for the CBS network, and we had many, many laughs. I must confess that we did most of our research bending elbows late at night. During his prime, Brookie spilled more booze than most people ever consume. But like a lot of us, he discovered that life is better when we can remember it.

Brookie never quit jawing, though. During the past few years, he's hosted a call-in sports show on the radio station he owned in Philadelphia. I love to get on the air and rib him. It's almost as though we're still going one-on-one on the football field. In fact, one of those duels inspired the line I lay on him most often. "Come clean, Brookie," I'll say. "The only trophy you have in your trophy room is a handful of my jersey."

The beginning and end of my pro career had a sad symmetry. In 1964 the Giants came full circle, winning only two games and reverting, for the next couple of decades, to the mediocrity in which I had joined them.

I can't say whether Allie Sherman's housekeeping before that season began was too sweeping. Sam Huff certainly thought so when Allie swept him to Washington, and he's been bitter about it ever since. What I do know is that the Yankee Stadium roof fell in on Y. A. Tittle. His vision suddenly unraveling, his rib cartilage so damaged he literally couldn't stand up after getting knocked down, the man who'd taken the Giants to three consecutive division titles saw the fans turn against him.

Before the last game of the season, and the final game of both our careers, I found myself standing next to Y.A. on the steps of the Yankee Stadium dugout. He looked up at the December sky and said, "Frank, this is what I loved more than anything else. This one moment just before you go out on that field. No one could ever understand what this dadgummed stadium has meant to me."

As rotten as the team had played that season, Y.A. still felt the joy and the accomplishment of the previous three. Unfortunately, the crowd did not. He was introduced—and the boos rolled across the field like thunder.

Though I felt the same way as Y.A., I really wasn't sorry to see it end for me. I'd played twelve seasons, done just about everything I wanted to do, and now I was looking at thirty-five years old. It seemed time to move on. Fortunately, CBS was handing me the perfect job to move into: working the local news on the network's

New York station and serving as TV analyst for all the Giants games. Unlike a lot of pro athletes who find themselves at loose ends after retiring, I'd known for some time that broadcasting was waiting for me. It was as if my life were beginning all over again. I felt both excited and relieved. After all, the mike doesn't hit back.

At the end of that final game, I again found myself next to Y.A., this time on the sideline. Aaron Thomas was playing in my spot; a rookie named Gary Wood had replaced Y.A. Someone took a great picture of the two of us side by side, looking very tired and very sad. Today it hangs in my home, and whenever I gaze at it, everything about that moment floods back.

The Browns were kicking the crap out of the Giants—wasn't this where I came in?—and a rain of jeers poured down from the stands. They were good fans, and they had every right to expect better than we gave them. The problem was, we simply couldn't give it anymore. We'd been part of a dynasty, but football dynasties can never be built to last. They can topple in a blink: All it takes is losing a couple of guys and an attitude. Now we were the wrong team at the wrong time in the wrong place.

I turned to Y.A. to tell him how I felt about it all ending. But I couldn't find the words, and besides, he seemed in shock. So we watched our football careers run out in silence. There was nothing more to do and nothing more to say.

CHAPTER 11

IT'S A HELLUVA TOWN

Time: An autumn Sunday night, circa late 1950s
Place: Toots Shor's restaurant in the core of the Big Apple

On one side of the packed dining room sits Earl Warren, the distinguished Chief Justice of the Supreme Court. On the opposite side sits Frank Costello, the notorious boss of the New York mob. Scattered at tables in between are Ava Gardner, Mickey Mantle, John O'Hara, Ed Sullivan, Rocky Graziano, Chet Huntley, Eddie Arcaro, Red Skelton, and Red Smith. I'm ensconced at the table directly to the right of the entrance from the bar, the best table in the house. My dining companion is Jackie Gleason. Yes, the Great One himself.

The stage has been set; the players are in place. All that's missing is the master of ceremonies. At around 9:00 P.M., a huge fat man with bloodshot slits for eyes appears at the entrance and surveys the room the way a painter might contemplate a blank canvas. Toots Shor is deciding how he'll paint the night.

Toots nods to several people but deliberately ignores Gleason. It's a major part of his routine. Finally, he strolls by our table, stops abruptly, and looks back at Jackie with obviously feigned surprise. "Beast!" he growls. "What are you doing in my joint?"

Jackie, who is in Toots's joint virtually every night, lowers his glass of scotch long enough to snarl, "G'wan, ya fat Jew dirtbag."

"G'wan yourself, ya fat mick lush," responds Toots.

"Clamhead!"

"Crumbum!"

After a few more rounds of this, Toots settles himself into a chair and orders a brandy. I know that these two are bosom pals as well as I know that their razzing has just begun.

"The food here is the worst food in America," observes Jackie when his steak arrives.

"You sure suck it up," replies Toots.

"Just look at this steak. This ain't food. This is garbage."

By now Toots is getting visibly miffed. "Beast, either eat it or get out."

Jackie's eyes take on a mischievous gleam. "Clamhead, even the hamburger you buy is already rotten. I'll bet you five hundred dollars that if you took a pound of hamburger out of your refrigerator, it would turn green in a half hour."

As all of us knew, Toots never spent a great deal of time in his kitchen. Nevertheless, he couldn't resist a wager any more than he could ignore an insult. "Harry," he says to his maître d'. "Get me a pound of hamburger."

Minutes later the three of us are staring at a large mound of extremely tired-looking red meat plopped in the center of our table. Other diners gather around us, side bets are offered and taken, rounds ordered and reordered. By now Toots and Jackie, with eyes glued to the hamburger, are absolutely destroying each other with loud insults. The entire room is in hysterics.

Finally, the hamburger does what any hamburger will do if left out long enough, especially Toots's hamburger. It starts turning greenish brown. Toots looks astonished. "I'm going to kick my chef's ass," he vows as he pays off Jackie, who is now chatting with Rocky Graziano. Toots gives him a disgusted look. Then he notices a burly man with a grizzled beard who has just sat down at a banquette.

"C'mon, kid," he says to me, grabbing my arm. "I want you to meet Papa Hemingway."

As Toots leads me across the room, past Ava and Ed and Earl, a voice inside my bedazzled brain is echoing Ralph Kramden: "Homina, homina, homina . . ."

Obviously, I'd come a long way from Jack's Deli. But that's pretty much what it was like to be a New York Giant back when the Giants owned New York. Someone wrote that we were treated like "princes of the city." Winning tends to do that, I guess, especially in a town that worships winners. All I know is that I felt I knew everyone in New York.

The best nights were Sunday nights in the autumns of the late fifties and early sixties. After every home game, Charlie Conerly and I would host cocktail parties in our apartments at the Concourse Plaza, across from Yankee Stadium. About thirty or forty people would show up. At some point in the party, I'd always seek out Charlie, who'd usually be off in a corner sipping a drink and popping his ankle. Then we'd both look around the room. We'd see a movie star or two, a hot singer, some TV personalities, a couple of Pulitzers, maybe even the former vice president of the United States. (I hate to president-drop, but that's what Richard Nixon became.)

"Do you believe this?" I'd invariably say to Charlie. "Two guys from Clarksdale, Mississippi, and Bakersfield, California. Not bad, huh?"

Around seven o'clock, when we were all flying pretty good, a group of us would scoop up our wives, head for the subway stop at 167th Street and the Grand Concourse, and all pile on the D train. There'd be Charlie and me, Kyle Rote, Alex Webster, Harland Svare, Rosie Brown, Don Heinrich, Pat Summerall, and occasionally a few others. First we'd have dinner at Toots's, then maybe catch some jazz at Eddie Condon's or the floor show at the Copacabana or see what was doing at Manuche's or P. J. Clarke's. We loved to end the night with a bowl of P.J.'s famous chili. Even after I discovered it came out of a can, it still tasted better than caviar.

But the person who really introduced me to New York, not to mention most of the celebrities at my parties, was the inimitable Toots. He showed me a glittering new world, and then he helped me fit into it. You might call him my Henry Higgins, except that he became a dear friend as well as my social mentor.

Toots grew up in a tough neighborhood in Philadelphia. When he was fifteen, his mother was killed in a car accident; five years later, his father committed suicide. After he hit New York, Toots parlayed his size—he was about six-three and weighed around 270—into a job as the bouncer at the Five O'Clock Club, one of the town's speakeasies.

If Toots had written his own epitaph, it would say this: "I was the last of the real New York saloonkeepers." No matter how fancy his decor or famous his customers, he always called himself a saloonkeeper. In those days, saloonkeepers drank, and no one drank like Toots. He might do two bottles of brandy a day. His restaurant became almost a shrine to booze. "Show me a man that don't drink," he used to say, "and I'll show you somebody I don't want to be with."

I know that sounds like self-destructive macho bullshit, but back then drinking carried more of a cachet than an onus. Before the drug culture took over, New York was a booze town. If you were in advertising or publishing or broadcasting, you got your work done in the morning and started knocking them down at lunch. By the time the happy hour came along, you were into double martinis. Booze got to several of the guys I played with, and it probably should have bitten me, too. But because I had to perform on the air a lot, especially in the evenings, I never became a major drinker. Besides, by the time I arrived at Toots's from the studio after the late news, everyone was often so bombed there wasn't enough left of the night to catch up.

Even though I leaned more toward Cokes than brandy, Toots liked me right off. He was a passionate Giants fan who knew everything we were doing and when to dispense the commiseration when I wasn't doing well. Maxine and I would sit with him and listen to his stories all night, always at the head table. Of course, you never got his undivided attention. Either he'd be popping up to insult someone or he'd be taking calls at the table. He'd have Mickey Mantle on one line and Frank Sinatra on another and some congressman on a third. He knew everybody from every walk of life. To some people, Toots was just a loudmouthed, name-dropping drunk. And I guess he was all of that. Yet those who really knew him truly loved him. We loved him for his humor and wisdom and loyalty and generosity. In those days, in that society, Tootsie was a god.

One of the more famous Toots Shor stories involves Jackie Gleason, which is fitting, because he was Toots's favorite "bum." One night, while I was sitting at the bar, Toots bet Jackie that he couldn't beat him in a race around the block. They were supposed to start together from the door and run in opposite directions around a block between West Fifty-first and Fifty-second streets. Toots chugged off, with Jackie heading the other way. As soon as Toots got out of sight, Jackie hailed a cab and rode the rest of the race.

He was lolling at the bar when Toots came panting in. Toots paid the bet and staggered to the men's room to dry off. Suddenly, he burst back into the bar. "Wait a minute, crumbum!" he screamed at Gleason. "How come you never passed me?" We all roared.

Toots was also responsible for the longest weekend—make that *lost* weekend—of my life. A few days before we had to report to our 1959 training camp in Vermont (the camp at which I planned to try out for quarterback), I got a call from Toots. "Why don't you and Charlie come down to my summer house on the Jersey shore," he said. "Sinat's opening in Atlantic City, and we can all go catch him."

I called Charlie. "Fine with me," he said. I called back Toots. "Fine with us," I told him. "But no heavy partying, okay? Camp opens on Monday, we gotta be ready, and we don't need any press." Right. So here's how the weekend went:

Friday, 11:00 A.M.: Toots's limousine driver picks up Charlie and me at our hotel. "How's Toots?" I ask him. The guy chuckles. "Wait till you see him," he says.

Friday, 1:00 P.M.: We learn what the driver meant when we arrive at Toots's house in New Jersey. He's waiting for us at the door. All in golf clothes—and half in the bag. We adjourn to Toots's club and tee it up. I've never seen a man test a golf cart like Toots does. It's not just his bulk; it's his impatience. He can't wait to finish the front nine so he can hit the clubhouse bar on the way to the back nine. It was a great way to play the game if you didn't care about remembering it.

Saturday, 6:00 P.M.: Charlie and I get into the limo for the drive to Atlantic City. Toots, who's been drinking all day, falls into the limo. Actually, he kind of rolls in one door and out the opposite door. After we help him up, he announces that he's forgotten something. He reenters his house and emerges with his beloved wife, Baby. He's carrying a bottle of vodka. She's carrying a bucket of ice, three glasses, some tonic water, and some limes.

"Bye-bye, Baby," calls Toots as we finally drive off.

Saturday, 8:00 P.M.: With our vodka supply nearly depleted, we arrive at the 500 Club in Atlantic City. It's the town's premier nightspot and, although I'm not supposed to know it, allegedly owned by the mob. The entrance to the 500 Club is packed with people waiting for the big stars who always show up for a Sinatra opening. It's the first time I've ever seen paparazzi. *Lots* of paparazzi.

"Well, look at that," chuckles Toots as we drive up. "They're all waiting for us!" Charlie and I take one glance at those cameras and scrunch deep into our seats. I mean, our boss is Wellington Mara, who expects his players to live the way he does—like a saint. "Oh, no, man," I say to the driver. "Please keep going."

Too late. Toots throws open the door—and out rolls an empty vodka bottle. At the sound of it breaking, everyone runs over to the limousine. "Who's that?" they're shouting. "Who's that?"

"It's Tootsie!" proclaims our host. "The world's prettiest Jew!" Then he opens the door wider and points to us. "And here," he proudly announces, "are *the* two biggest stars of the New York Giants!"

Saturday, 8:15 P.M.: Toots insists on going backstage to greet "Sinat," as he calls him. Toots worships Sinat. So off we go to Frank's dressing room, where we find him having dinner with Natalie Wood and Robert Wagner. Though Toots is clearly shitfaced, Frank treats him very graciously. I feel embarrassed. As a player, I don't like the jerks who barge into our locker room before a game. Now, just to be polite to Toots, I'm one of the jerks.

Saturday, 9:00 P.M.: Toots escorts us to a ringside table, then kind of nods off. He just plops his head on Charlie's shoulder and begins snoring. His snores sound like a water buffalo's. Meanwhile, Sinatra is putting on a hell of a show. But just as he starts to wind it up, Toots comes out of it.

"Sinat!" he shouts. "Sing 'Melancholy Baby'!" (Baby, of course, being Toots's wife.)

Frank ignores Toots and continues with his act.

"C'mon, you wop bum. Sing 'Melancholy Baby.' "

Suddenly, Frank doesn't look quite so gracious. People around us are clearing their throats.

Now Toots reaches into his pocket, pulls out a wad of hundred-dollar bills, and tosses one at Frank's feet. " 'Melancholy Baby,' " he burps.

Frank coolly scoops up the bill, slips it into his own pocket, and keeps right on singing.

Toots throws up another hundred dollars. " 'Melancholy Baby.' "

Frank puts this one in his pocket, too. Toots starts to throw yet another bill when suddenly a massive hand clamps down on his wrist. "That's enough," growls the guy attached to the hand. Toots looks into his face, gulps, and puts the wad back in his pocket. He looks very pale and very sober.

Later, as we're leaving the club, I ask the maître d' if he knows who just shut up Toots.

"Fischetti," he replies. "Big man from Miami. He and Sinatra are like brothers. Your friend is lucky he ain't dead." Charlie and I really need this.

Sunday, 3:00 A.M.: We're back at Toots's house. He's sobered up, had his hangover, and started drinking all over again. Us, too. For some reason, we decide to play football in his living room. Charlie is the center, and I'm showing Toots how well I can play quarterback. But the game is abruptly called when Toots falls down the entire flight of stairs that leads to his bathroom. He's out cold.

Remember the old saying, there's no way you can hurt a drunk? It's not true, of course, but in this case it applies. When our limousine departs a short while later, Toots is upright enough to cheerfully wave us off.

What a weekend! We were on our way to training camp, we hadn't been shot, nothing was broken, and we'd had a hell of a time.

Monday, 9:00 A.M.: Burlington airport, Burlington, Vermont. Charlie and I, still holding our heads after a few hours of sleep, are searching for a cab to take us to training camp. "Need a ride?" asks a familiar voice. It's Well Mara, who's been waiting for us. As we drive off, Well turns from the wheel and says, "So how was Sinatra's show?" Then, with a huge grin, he tosses us a Vermont newspaper.

Our arrival in Atlantic City had made the wire services—complete with pictures. One of the captions went something like this: "New York restaurateur Toots Shor (front) and Giants stars Frank Gifford and Charlie Conerly (rear) alight from their limousine at the 500 Club last Saturday. Preceding them is a bottle of vodka (lower left)."

Great way to begin a season . . .

Even four decades ago, a pro athlete's life in the nation's media capital came with an almost guaranteed perk: the product endorsement. For whatever reasons, the ad agencies offered me more than my share. They did not meet with rejection. Hell, I endorsed anything that was legal.

Between TV, radio, and magazine spots, I sold Vitalis hair tonic, Mennen after-shave, Dry Sack sherry, Wilson sports equipment, Rapid Shave cream, Lucky Strikes, Planters nuts, and Willard batteries. No wonder my teammates started calling me "the male Betty Furness." And they had it right, because later I would replace Betty doing Westinghouse commercials.

The funniest fiasco was my TV commercial for Rapid Shave. It showed me shaving my foam-covered mug as a voice-over described my beard as "tough as sandpaper." Cut to a hand holding another razor smoothly shaving a strip of sandpaper smeared with Rapid Shave. That was the pitch: This cream can even barber sandpaper. What no one knew, including myself, was that the "sandpaper" actually was a piece of Plexiglas smeared with jelly and sprinkled with sand. When the Federal Trade Commission found out about it, it blasted the ad off the air. The press loved that story. *Newsweek* even ran a shot of me shaving—I looked in deep pain—above a caption that said, "Red-dogged by the FTC." Ouch.

My happiest endorsement gig was for the Jantzen International

Sports Club of Champions. That's a fancy name for a group of famous jocks, many of whom I recruited to promote Jantzen's line of sportswear. What a deal! All-expense-paid location trips to places like Hawaii, Rio, and Majorca, plus all the free sweaters, shorts, and shirts you could carry home.

My involvement began with a call from a guy named Homer Groening, who was Jantzen's ad director. Homer was also the father of Matt Groening, the cartoonist who later created *The Simpsons.* That's how Homer Simpson got his name: Matt named his cartoon father after his real father. Anyway, Homer wanted me and Bob Cousy to do an ad for Jantzen bathing suits. We were delighted to oblige. After the ads appeared, I quickly started getting calls from some real superstars: "Hey, man, how do I get one of those Jantzen deals?" I just gave them Homer's number. Didn't even ask for a commission.

We ended up with Paul Hornung, Jerry West, Bobby Hull, Dave Marr, Don Meredith, and a few others, and all of us became close friends. Considering our salaries at the time, those trips were price-less blessings, especially for our wives and kids.

The most memorable was to Majorca. I don't think we made too many friends for Jantzen among the Majorcans. First, we beat a team of locals in a basketball game arranged by Homer. I suspect none of them knew who Jerry West was, but they sure remembered him after that day. Then, when we got some free time, Don Meredith and I went to a bullfight. Big mistake.

It was the first bullfight for both of us, and being typical Ameri-cans, we chose to do our part to support the local grape industry—and then root for the underdog. We were sitting right in the middle of the crowd wearing big straw hats and trying to act like natives when the first picador stuck his first lance into the first bull.

Don, who'd had too many grapes and too much sun, let out a loud "Booooo." Naturally, I chimed in. I could hear some people around us muttering in Spanish.

By the time the picadors began really working on the bull, Don and I were on our feet. "Run, you sumbitch!" screamed Don, the consummate color man.

"Yeah," I echoed, and, as if preconditioned, I started with the play-by-play. "Head for the gate!" I screamed. Though our neighbors couldn't understand our words, they definitely caught our drift. Their muttering grew louder and a whole lot meaner.

When the bullfighter finally appeared, we totally disgraced ourselves. Apparently, he was a very famous bullfighter, but in our condition, he just looked like a fancy-dressed fop with a padded crotch who was picking on this poor, scraggly-assed animal. It seemed unfair, and we let everyone know it. Suddenly, Don and I found ourselves surrounded by a group of tall, glowering men. They didn't say a word, but the look they gave us was a universal one. Man, they were scary.

"Señor Gifford," said Don. "Isn't it time to mosey back to the hacienda?"

"Splendid idea, Señor Meredith," I replied.

And we made tracks out of there mucho pronto.

As happened with my football career, my broadcasting career blossomed in New York. Yet both careers sprang from the lowly roots of Bakersfield, and my attitude toward each was forever shaped by my tough, poor, plainspoken California town.

I owe my start in television to the newspaper business. In 1957 a good friend named Walt Little, who was the sports editor of one of my hometown papers, asked me to write a twice-weekly column about my life in New York. If I had lunch with Mickey Mantle or Rocky Graziano, for instance, I'd tell the folks back home what Mickey and Rocky had to say. I enjoyed writing that column immensely—writing is something I've always regretted not pursuing—and apparently so did the readers. Because one day Walt suggested I do some moonlighting for Bakersfield's TV station, which was owned by a friend of ours, Ed Urner.

That's how I came to host a Friday-night sports show on KERO-TV in 1957. Consisting of score wrap-ups and interviews, the show followed the Friday-night boxing bouts and ran as long or as short as the number of knockouts. One night my guest was a reclusive resident of the Mojave Desert who had just been voted into the Baseball Hall of Fame, Wahoo Sam Crawford. We had a major national scoop, because nobody knew where this guy was: We had found him living way out in the desert. Needless to say, on this, my first outing as a TV host, I came prepared with a list of questions that could have run to eternity. Unfortunately, this is how the interview unwound:

ME: It must have been a great thrill to hear you were elected to the Hall of Fame after all these years.
WAHOO: Yup.
ME: Uh, have you heard from any of your former teammates?
WAHOO: Nope.

As I worked down my pad to my final few questions, I mentally calculated, with a glance at the studio clock, that I'd be out of questions with about twenty minutes of air time remaining. With a feeling akin to stark terror, I chucked the pad, looked my guest in the eye, and said: "Wahoo, you must have known some great guys in your career, guys you played with, guys you played against, managers . . ." Well, his eyes lit up like a pinball machine, and suddenly he was off. We could have done forty minutes easily.

I had survived my first major television test, and also learned a vital lesson. I should never have had that pad of questions. And I should have known my guest and my subject much better than I did. If I had, we would have gotten straight into a great chat without wasting all that time before I hit the right button—the *panic* button.

Now fast-forward to another interview four years later. By now I'm a bit more experienced. I've filled in for Phil Rizzuto on his CBS Radio show, but those were only five-minute spots during the baseball season. I've co-hosted the pre-game show before CBS's NFL telecasts, but there I had help from partner Chris Schenkel. Now I'm about to launch a career as a WCBS sports reporter, appearing every night as part of the New York station's half-hour radio newscast. Like any entertainer, I wanted my debut to go really well. And nothing, I knew, would impress my bosses more than leading off with a dynamite guest.

A few days earlier, I'd seen Joe DiMaggio lunching at an Italian restaurant on Park Avenue. I'd said hello to him, and he'd said hello to me. Back then he was even more reclusive than he is now, but I found out the hotel where he was staying and took a very long shot. The hotel operator put my call straight through to his room. My heart was doing somersaults as I waited for him to answer.

"Joe?" I began when he picked up the phone. "This is Frank Gifford and I have a request for you and I'll understand perfectly if you can't do it but I'm retired from football now and I'm starting a radio show and I'd like to have you as my first interview but like I said I'd understand if you're too busy to . . ."

"I'd love to, Frank."

". . . do it because I realize how . . . Huh? You would?"

"Absolutely. Do I come over there, or do you want to come over here?"

"Uh, what would be easier for you?"

"Whatever is easier for you. If you'd like to come over here, we can do it right now."

Unbelievable! Ten minutes later I'm standing in Joe DiMaggio's hotel room with my tape recorder clasped in my sweaty hands. The first thing that struck me was that he wasn't nearly as tall as I thought. Not that he looked little, but to me he'd always seemed like the tallest man on television. Anyway, he couldn't have been warmer or more gracious. We talked for so long that we were able to cut the interview into segments and run it nightly over my first five shows.

Though I can't remember what we talked about, I still think about that afternoon. Joe DiMaggio went from hero to legend to myth, and I caught him in the legend period. But what I'll never forget is how lonely he seemed. He didn't care whether I came to his room or he came to the studio, because apparently he had nothing else to do that day. I've been lonely, too, so I know it when I see it. Joe DiMaggio was one of the loneliest men I've ever met.

The other thing I remember is suggesting that he take up golf. I had just started playing golf myself and found it wonderful for both a competitive personality and a loner—a game you can play with a foursome, threesome, twosome, or by yourself.

"Golf would be very difficult," Joe replied.

While he didn't explain that, I knew what he meant. He meant that it would be hard for him to go to a golf course and look bad before a lot of strange people. Joe is a perfectionist. He could never settle for looking less than perfect at anything.

Nevertheless, I pressed him. "You really ought to try it, Joe," I said. "Golf has all kinds of benefits."

"I just might do that sometime," he finally said.

Today I run into Joe on golf courses all the time. We've played in the same charity tournaments, and I've watched him in many more. What I love to see is how beautifully he relates to other people on the course. He'll stop to sign autographs endlessly or chat with anyone who wants to chat. Since he'd gone out in public so rarely, I suspect he never knew how much people love him.

I don't know whether Joe took up golf because of me, nor would I ever ask him. But if he did, I'd be as proud of that as I am grateful for his kindness to a rookie radio reporter more than thirty years ago.

The newspaper business was also responsible for my big break in television. In early 1962, around the time I decided to try a football comeback, New York was hit by a newspaper strike. To Norm Walt, the general manager of WCBS-TV, that looked like a window of opportunity. He called me into his office.

"We've decided to expand our local evening news from ten to fifteen minutes to take advantage of the strike," Walt informed me. "We thought we'd add some weather and some sports. Since you're already doing sports on the radio side, you're the natural choice."

"That's great, Norm," I told him. "But I've got training camp coming up in July."

"July? Hell, this strike is going to last for a week at most. You'll love doing a TV newscast."

Norm was right about that. I appeared on both the six o'clock and eleven o'clock reports and enjoyed every second of it. Suddenly, I was reaching a whole new demographic: Even little old blue-haired ladies started stopping me on the street. But Norm was way off on the duration of the strike. It dragged on for months. So when training camp arrived, I confronted an uncomfortable task: getting Allie Sherman's permission to continue doing the newscasts while playing football. No one, I'd been told, had ever tried to work both those jobs simultaneously.

Though Allie had a big thing about outside interests distracting a player's focus, he agreed to a compromise. During the season, I could do the early news but not the late news. That, in his view, would be like breaking curfew every night. After the season, I was free to do both.

It worked out so well that I did those two newscasts for the next nine years. Followed on the early news by Walter Cronkite, starring terrific talents like Robert Trout, Morton Dean, Jim Jensen, and Carol Reed (the first of the folksy weatherpersons), our show owned the New York market for a long, long time. We killed everybody. Best of all, that show really taught me television. I went out with the camera crews, worked with the guys who edited the film (later the video-tape), and wrote all my own scripts. Television was so new then that viewers were quick to forgive goof-ups, especially if the goofer-upper happened to be a New York Giant. They just figured you were too busy to learn this stuff.

I have some truly fond memories of my years in local news. One night, right in the middle of one of my reports, the TelePrompTer started going crazy. Instead of the paper rolling up in front of my eyes, it began rolling down. Which meant I had to scrunch lower and lower in my chair to follow the descending words. By the end of my report, my chin was resting on the edge of my desk. Everyone was in hysterics.

Between the early and late shows, I'd usually dine at Toots Shor's. One night, as I was passing by the bar on my way back to WCBS, a thoroughly sloshed Jackie Gleason called me over.

"Where ya goin', football player?"

"Back to do the eleven o'clock news, Jackie."

"No kiddin'? Hey, how 'bout me coming with you? I'll do the weather."

"Uh, gee, Jackie, I don't think that's a great idea. Besides, Carol Reed might not like it."

"Not like *me*?" And with that he threw his arm around my shoulders and dragged me out the door.

A few minutes later, we arrived at my tiny office in the Vander-bilt Building near Grand Central Station. As I sat down to finish my script, Jackie wandered off to inform my colleagues of his plans for the weather report. I could hear him coming on to Carol Reed: "Hey, pretty lady. You and I are gonna be great tonight. Va-va-voom!"

I kept waiting for our director to say something, but how could he? This was CBS's biggest star.

Now it was time for all of us to walk to the studio, which required a long elevator ride down, a stroll across the waiting room of Grand

Central Station, and a climb up some stairs. Jackie was with us every step, or in his case every stumble. I'll never forget that scene at Grand Central. Here, trooping through the crowd of late commuters, came the guy who carried our TelePrompTer followed by Bob Trout followed by Carol Reed followed by me. And bringing up the rear was the Great One, waving to all with a huge, glassy-eyed grin. When Jackie reached the top of the stairs, he turned, looked out over the waiting room, and roared, "And awaaaaaay we go!"

Now we were inside the studio, facing the moment of truth. Jackie was still insisting on doing the weather, and everyone was still terrified of telling him otherwise. Since he was a complete mess, I could see a monumental disaster looming. At the last moment, however, Jackie was enough of a pro to realize he had two choices: Go on the air and make an ass of himself or go back to Toots's for another pop. Never have I seen anyone that large disappear that fast.

After the show, I returned to the restaurant out of curiosity. Sure enough, there was Jackie—holding court once again in a corner of the bar.

"What's with this guy?" I asked Toots. "What's his problem?"

Toots motioned me to a table, sat down, and for the first time since I'd known him, spoke in a quiet, thoughtful way.

"The Beast is a binger, Frank," he said. "He binges on booze and he binges on food and he binges on life. That's why I call him Beast, and there's no man I love more. While I'm sure no shrink, I think he binges out of guilt. His old man deserted the family when Jackie was just a kid. Now it kills Jackie the way he treats his own family, vanishing on them for days. I guess it all adds up to a lot of guilt and a lot of binges to forget the guilt. All I know is I love the bum."

Toots stared into space for a long while. His eyes were moist. Then he snapped out of it, rose, and went off to greet another of his "crumbum" friends.

Just a few months later, Jackie asked me to play in a golf tournament he was organizing. It was at the late Fred Waring's resort on the Delaware River in Pennsylvania. So the day before the tournament began, I drove down, dropped off my clubs, and checked in. "I'm Mr. Gleason's guest," I told the desk clerk.

"Yes, he said to expect you," he replied. "Mr. Gleason would like you to join him for dinner around eight."

I noddod, wont up to my room, showered, and changed my clothes. At precisely eight o'clock, I headed for the dining room. "Mr. Gleason's table," I said to the maître d'.

"Right this way, sir. He should be down shortly."

An hour or so later, I was still sitting alone at that table. I felt like a total idiot. People kept coming over to say hello, and I kept having to explain I was waiting for Jackie Gleason. "Oh, sure," they'd say with an incredulous look. "You're waiting for Jackie Gleason."

Finally, I left the dining room, returned to the desk clerk, and got the number of Jackie's suite. It was at the end of a long hall. As I approached it, I saw several huge trays sitting by the door. They were covered with food, most of it half eaten, and some bottles of booze, all of them empty. As the saying goes, I didn't bother to knock. I just went to bed.

Oh yes: Jackie didn't show up for his own golf tournament, either. A great talent but a tragic man.

Moving from local television to network television, as I did when I traded my Giants jersey for a CBS Sports blazer in 1965, was a bit like jumping from college ball to the pros. The game stayed the same, but the crowds got bigger. Though I still made some fluffs—I pronounced Pittsburgh as "Pissburgh," which did not enchant Steeler fans—I felt surprisingly comfortable in front of the camera. Maybe all those years as a talking stuntman weren't such a waste.

CBS handed me a full plate: pro football, some college basketball, a bit of golf, and host duty on a batch of *Sports Spectaculars,* CBS's attempt to imitate ABC's *Wide World of Sports.* My easiest gig was covering the Masters golf tournament. The Masters at the time was controlled with an iron fist by Masters co-founder Cliff Roberts. If you wanted to televise the tournament, you did it his way or not at all. Roberts had become comfortable with me from watching the local news while living in New York. He flat-out told our producer, Frank Chirkinian, and the head of CBS Sports, Bill MacPhail, what he wanted me to do.

Talk about boondoggles! All I had to handle was what we laughingly called the "invocation" and the "benediction." I'd come on the air, standing in front of a bunch of azaleas with lots of little birds chirping, and announce, "Hi, I'm Frank Gifford, talking to you from

Augusta National Golf Club in Augusta, Georgia, where in keeping with the tradition of the Masters golf tournament we will not be interrupting important play with commercials. We want you to enjoy the Masters as it's meant to be enjoyed. And so now, let's go to the action."

At the end of the broadcast several hours later, I'd come back to say, "This is Frank Gifford. I hope you've enjoyed the play here today at the Augusta National Golf Club. We also hope that you appreciated the fact that we did not interrupt important play with commercials."

That was it—my entire day's work. The rest of the time I'd follow my friends from the tour like Dave Marr and Ben Crenshaw and just have a lot of fun. I did the Masters for about five years. Nice assignment.

In my early years covering pro football, I found it difficult to be harshly critical of guys whom I'd played with and against, and had come to know as friends. Nor was I prodded to do so, as is the practice today with the annual influx of ex-athletes and coaches. It was a laid-back atmosphere and, for the most part, a lot of fun. As for my missing being on the field, no way. That was totally out of my system.

For NFL games, CBS gave me the color-analyst role and teamed me with terrific people: Jack Whitaker, Chris Schenkel, Jack Buck, Ray Scott, and Tom Brookshier, my old Eagle adversary-turned-friend who handled pre-game and postgame interviews. Technically, that was a highly primitive era for live sports coverage. You had to be ready for anything. For instance, it's not every day that a sportscaster finds himself with forty minutes of dead airtime to fill. That happened to Tommy and me when a Giants pre-season game ended forty minutes early and our local station carrying it had no programming ready for such a void. Consequently, we had to ad-lib the entire rest of the broadcast. It was a totally forgettable forty minutes, highlighted by our camera capturing the stadium lights going out, the players' bus departing, and the maintenance men cleaning up the stands—beer cans and all.

To me, the most memorable game we covered was the Packers-Cowboys NFL championship on New Year's Eve in 1967. Not so much because of the game itself, though that one was a classic, but because of the insights it gave me into Don Meredith, who was then playing quarterback for the Cowboys.

The story actually begins the previous season. By that time, Don and I had become really good friends, always getting together when the Cowboys visited New York. That season they'd wrapped up the Eastern Division title well before their final game, a meaningless one with the Giants. But the game should have meant something to Don. He had such a lock on the NFL passing title that all he had to do was complete a couple against the Giants to officially win it. On the Saturday night before the Sunday game, which I was working, Don called me. He had a little joke about contacting me by phone. "Give me three quarters," he'd say, "and I can always find Frank. He's either going to be at home, at work, or at Toots Shor's. He's that predictable."

This time Don found me at work. It was around 10:00 P.M. "Hey, buddy," he said with an extra glow in his voice. "A bunch of us are going to check out the Big Apple tonight. How about joining us?"

"Hey, Don," I said. "I'd like to, but it's a little late. And you'd better get some sleep. You've got a passing title on the line tomorrow."

"Forget it. Piece of cake. Besides, we're having a lot of laughs. Come on and join us. You're a member of Le Club. I'm your guest." (Le Club, a fancy private disco, was the hot spot in the Big Apple— and charged accordingly.)

A few hours later, I got a call at home from my friend who managed Le Club, Patrick Shields. Don, he reported, had just been walking on top of his bar, buying drinks for the house (on my account, of course) and in general raising hell.

Later, I got another call from Don himself. "Gotcha!" he screamed. "I *told* you I could always find you!"

"Well, where else would I be at three in the morning? And where the hell are you?"

"I have no idea, ol' buddy." His voice dropped to a whisper. "Maybe," he said, "maybe you better trace this call."

For some reason, Don had the worst game of his life the next day. I think his completion stats were 0 for 18, or something just as horrendous. And needless to say, he lost the passing title. Yet it didn't mean a damn thing to him.

But when something affected his team and his pals, Don bled deep inside. As was the case a year later when the Cowboys lost that NFL championship on a frozen field at Green Bay. Don battled as heroically as I've ever seen a quarterback battle under such miserable playing conditions. The temperature in Green Bay was 13 below zero. With only seconds left, and the Cowboys clinging to a three-point lead, Bart Starr followed Jerry Kramer's block over the goal line to give the Packers the victory.

As Tom Brookshier interviewed the ecstatic Packers in their locker room, I dropped by the Cowboys'. I found Don slumped bare-chested on his stool, his head practically between his knees. He looked like the survivor of a gang mugging: There was blood all over him and a huge bruise under his eye. Meanwhile, I could see the Packers celebrating on a TV set in a corner. Jerry Kramer, an All-Pro player who made a great career more memorable with that one block, went on and on and on about how brilliant the play was and how wonderful his team was. You couldn't get him off.

As I listened to all this, an idea hit me. I called our producer, Bill Creasy. "Why don't we get a camera in here and interview some of the losers, too?" I suggested. "Hell, they only lost by a quarterback sneak. And we've got plenty of time to fill."

The answer came back in my headset. "Frank, they won't do that. You can't get any of those guys to come on, and we can't ask them. It just isn't done, man."

"So let's be the first. Besides, I think I can get Meredith to talk with me."

There was a pause, and then: "If you feel that strongly, go ahead and take a shot."

So I did. "Don," I said to him, "why don't you come on and say what you feel about today? It's not like you guys got killed. You got beat on a frozen home field by a lousy quarterback sneak."

"You really think I should?" he said, lifting his head.

"Yeah, I really do."

"Okay."

As Don put on his bloody T-shirt, a camera was wheeled in from the Packers' locker room and a couple of lights were set up. When our producer threw it to me, I plunged right in.

"Don, you came so close. How does it feel to lose this one?"

"The way I look at it," he replied softly, "we didn't really lose it. Dadgummit, we didn't lose anything." Then Don proceeded to do something highly un-Don-like. He poured his heart out in public. With his voice choking on his emotions, he talked about how proud he was of the guys he played with, how hard they had played that day, how awful he felt for them, how he blamed himself for the loss, but how losing like that was really like winning even though it almost felt like dying. It was a passionate, spontaneous, no-bullshit television moment. It was wonderful.

The next morning, I called Don to thank him. "By God, ol' buddy," he said with a huge laugh. "You won't believe what's been goin' on! I'm getting calls from all these people in your business. They want me to go on talk shows, they want me to go on quiz shows, they even want me for a TV movie!"

I sensed instantly what had happened to Don. The people who create celebrities in America had caught a glimpse of the deeply feeling man behind the devil-may-care image—and they loved what they saw. Televisionwise, you might say, those few minutes of air-time put Don Meredith in play.

That weekend brought a second surprise, and this one I would have gladly done without. To get home for the rest of that New Year's Eve, my broadcast buddies—Jack Buck and Tom Brookshier—and I chartered a small private plane. It was supposed to take us from Green Bay to Chicago, where we could transfer to other flights.

By the time we arrived at the airport, night was descending along with the mercury. It must have been 15 or 20 below. The plane was a single-engine job with only four seats. Jack and Brookie climbed in the back; I sat alongside the pilot. Just as we took off, the door by my right arm popped open a bit. "What do I do about this?" I yelled to the pilot. He glanced over and shrugged. "Just give it a little yank," he said, then returned to the controls.

I yanked and yanked some more. But so much wind was pouring in as the plane climbed that the door wouldn't close. I looked at the backseat and saw that Jack and Brookie were huddled inside their jackets. What really shook me, though, was the sight of frost forming on their eyebrows. My God, I thought, these guys are starting to freeze!

As I held on to the door handle with one hand, I punched the pilot's shoulder with the other. "We got a problem," I shouted, pointing over my shoulder.

He glanced again at me, then back at Jack and Brookie. This time he seemed impressed. His exact words were: "Oh, shit!"

Finally, our pilot came up with a plan. "I'm going to nose it up a bit and reduce speed," he said. "That should cut the wind resistance enough for you to get it closed." So he did, and when we'd slowed down, I opened the door as far as I could and then tried to slam it. *Boing!* The handle broke off in my hand.

Now the door was open at least four or five inches. Howling, icy wind filled the entire cockpit. Jack and Brookie were practically on the floor, their jackets pulled over their heads.

Frantically, I ripped at the fabric that covered the inside of the door. Enough of it came away to expose a metal strut, which I grasped with all my strength.

"I'm taking it back to Green Bay," the pilot shouted. But as he started to make his turn, the plane began bucking. "Jesus, it's so cold the controls are sticking," he informed us. "We better put it down around here."

"Like where?" I squeaked.

He peered ahead. "I know a crop duster's strip up there. Not very long, but we don't have any choice."

As I desperately clung to the door strut to reduce the wind flow, the pilot fought the freezing controls all the way down. He even had to brace his knees against the instrument panel in order to haul the balky stick back. After we hit that Humpty-Dumpty little strip, we bounced about ten feet. Then we skidded for what seemed like a mile. When we finally emerged from the plane, everything was pitch black. Since there were no lights on what passed for a landing field, another hour—hell, another fifteen minutes—and our landing probably would've been impossible.

Whenever Jack, Brookie, and I get together, we relive that experience. And when we do, I always tell Brookie the same thing: "Remember all the trashmouthing you gave me as a cornerback? If it hadn't been for Jack Buck, I'd have pushed that door all the way open."

· · ·

CBS also assigned me to the first Super Bowl, and as with Don Meredith, my friendships with the guys on the field brought me an exclusive interview. Well, sort of exclusive. Though the Super Bowl wasn't as huge an extravaganza back then, the stakes in pride and prestige never loomed larger. That 1967 game matched Vince Lombardi's Packers against the Kansas City Chiefs, but the real clash was between two leagues. For the first time, the old-guard NFL was taking on the upstart AFL. We're talking serious bragging rights.

As for the TV coverage, CBS and NBC co-telecast this initial championship and decided to share the same pictures. Thus, about all that would differentiate the two telecasts were our pre-game shows. That's where I came in. Throughout the preceding week, I'd been spending time with my old coach, Vince Lombardi, and had talked him into giving me a live, on-the-field interview right before the game started. When I informed my bosses, they flipped. It was unheard-of for a pro coach to do that, especially a legend-in-the-making like Lombardi. CBS advertised that interview as if we'd landed God—and to some, I guess, we had.

Now it's ten minutes to kickoff and I'm standing in the middle of the Los Angeles Coliseum watching Lombardi lead his team out of the tunnel. As he runs past me, he catches my eye and vigorously shakes his head. No interview! Stunned, I drop my mike and run after him. When he sees that, he picks up speed. So do I. I can't believe I'm chasing Vince Lombardi in front of one hundred thousand people.

"You gotta do this interview, Vince," I shout.

"Oh, no, I can't," he shouts back.

"But you gotta. We've been promoting the hell out of it!"

At that, Vince stops. "Okay, okay," he growls. "But make it quick. Really quick."

I grab him by the back of the neck and literally lead him to where my mike is lying. As the cameraman sets up, I suddenly notice something about Vince that helps explain his strange behavior. That macho bulldog whom an earthquake couldn't rattle is clearly a nervous wreck. He's actually trembling. When I asked him why later, he told me he'd been getting calls all week from NFL owners. *The Bears' George Halas:* "Vince, you gotta whip their butt." *The*

Colts' Carroll Rosenbloom: "Vince, you gotta kick their ass." *The Steelers' Art Rooney:* "Vince, you gotta . . ."

No wonder the poor guy is a basket case. Vince isn't just playing the Kansas City Chiefs: He's leading a crusade against the forces of darkness.

Meanwhile, I've got my own problem. Just as Vince begins answering my first question, I notice a figure sprinting across the field toward us, coattail flying and microphone in hand. It's Paul Christman, my counterpart at NBC, who's obviously determined to horn in. In desperation, I start tossing Vince my second question before he's finished fielding my first. It doesn't matter. Christman bursts into the camera shot, thrusts his mike between us, and says, "Vince (gasp), let me ask you (gasp) this . . ."

What the hell: Everything came out okay. Lombardi and the NFL got their victory—by 25 points. And I got my exclusive interview (if only a question-and-a-half's worth).

In the winter of 1966, some people in Washington made me an offer I couldn't refuse. To help boost the morale of the troops fighting the Vietnam War, a war I had yet to question, the USO decided to send them films of NFL games. Then someone took that idea another step: Why not send some NFL players along to personally show the films? That's how I came to board a flight to Saigon one morning to meet up with three aging but still active NFL stars: Sam Huff of the Redskins, Johnny Unitas of the Colts, and Willie Davis of the Packers.

We ended up visiting bases throughout Vietnam over an unbelievably exhausting twenty-two days, lugging around a movie projector and the film highlights of the 1965 season. Though we had a military escort—a lieutenant so young we called him our "babysitter"—we'd basically hang around airports until some helicopter pilot agreed to give us a lift somewhere into the boonies. I never have, or ever will, experience anything like that trip. It went from the weird to the bizarre to the almost surreal. At times I felt as though we were trapped inside a jock *Dr. Strangelove.* A few excerpts from the diary I kept:

Saigon: After I land, our baby-sitter guides me through the military rigamarole for new arrivals. They do everything but tattoo me. Then he drops me off at a Vietnamese hotel with two pieces of advice. 1) "Don't walk the streets at night. It's not healthy." 2) "When you return to your room, always look under the bed."

Willie Davis arrives. We're rooming together. The first thing Willie says is, "Did they tell you something about looking under the bed?"

"They did."

"What are we looking for?"

"Willie, I think we're supposed to look for strange packages. You know, things that can blow our asses off."

Willie rolls his eyes. "I had to come all this way for that?"

We keep up a running gag about that for days. But I'm also thinking a very serious thought. I'm remembering all that hokey stunt work I did in all those phony war movies. Well, this war is real—and so are the stunts.

The next morning we sit in on a headquarters briefing by General William Westmoreland. He talks about the huge labyrinths of underground caves near Saigon that the Vietcong hole up in. Every now and then, he reports, we capture some of the cave dwellers and discover that their skin pigmentation has changed. They've lived underground for so long that their skin has actually turned white. I think, What incredible dedication! What a will to fight! And our guys don't want to get drafted, let alone go to Vietnam. For the first time, I question whether we can win this damn war.

The South China Sea: We're jammed into a tiny, twin-engine plane en route to one of the navy's biggest aircraft carriers, the *Kitty Hawk.* Before heading out to sea, we fly over an area the B-52s have just bombed. Unbelievable devastation—it looks like a moonscape. I'm still absorbing this when the pilot shows me how to work the radio. I fiddle with the dial and hear a sexy female voice. It's none other than "Hanoi Hannah," North Vietnam's version of Tokyo Rose.

Hannah says all the clichés: You American boys shouldn't be here, you should be home with your families, you'll just die here, and so on. Then she puts on a recording. My God, it's Barbra Streisand singing "People." Here are my eyes looking down on totally obliterated countryside while my ears are hearing the moving lyrics.

Dinner aboard the carrier with some navy brass. One is so hawk-ish he makes George Patton sound like Jane Fonda. After we all have a few drinks, he starts telling us how he could "end this fucking war in a half hour. We could do it with the ordnance on just this ship. But they won't let us. Those asshole peaceniks don't understand what this world's coming to. We've got to stop dicking around with these gooks and *take 'em out!*" Willie, Johnny, Sam, and I exchange looks. Then we stare at our plates. No one says anything.

I can't sleep that night, can't get over the whole crazy scene. Around four in the morning, I wander topside. I end up in the flight room, sipping some coffee with a bunch of pilots. Naturally, all they want to talk about is "pasta" (aka Chuck Bednarik). Suddenly, a guy walks up and says, "Hi, Frank, I'm Dick Anderson. Bobby's brother."

Bob Anderson, a former New York Giant and All-American run-ning back at Army, is a good friend of mine. So I'm delighted to meet his brother, who bears a marked resemblance to Bob. We talk for about a half hour. Then Dick says, "Are you going to be here for a while?"

"Sure," I reply. "I'm just hanging out."

"Good. I'll be back in a little bit."

I figure he's going to the head. After what must have been less than an hour, Dick returns, and we pick up our conversation where we'd left off. When we finally say good-bye, he apologizes for keep-ing me waiting so long.

"That's all right." I shrug. "Where were you, by the way?"

"Oh, I took a little run up north."

Only then does it hit me. While I was finishing my coffee in that cozy flight room, Dick Anderson had jumped into his fighter-bomber, flown a few hundred miles, dumped a load of something on the enemy—God knows how many MiGs and SAMs he'd had to dodge—and flown back. He was so casual about it you'd think he'd gone out for a pack of cigarettes. I think there's a phrase for that kind of thing: the right stuff.

Near Quang Tri: It's getting weirder. A well-connected South Viet-namese colonel, we're informed, is insisting on meeting Unitas.

Apparently, he once lived in Baltimore, became a huge Colts fan, and regards Johnny as his idol. The problem is, the village his battalion is holding lies so deep inside Cong territory that Johnny can't find a copter pilot willing to take him there. Even the guy who finally agrees has a big condition.

"He's only willing to touch down for about five seconds," Johnny tells me. "We've got to hit the ground running. Then he'll come back for us in a couple of hours. Hopefully."

"Wait a minute, pal," I say. "What's this 'we' and 'us' shit? The guy wants to meet *you*, Johnny."

I wind up going with him, anyway. The pilot does exactly as he warned. He touches down just long enough to dump us in the middle of this big stockade surrounded by trenches: I feel like John Wayne. And sure enough, as we leap off the copter, there's a South Vietnamese colonel waiting for us—his chest covered with medals and his face with a broad grin.

"Johnny U!" he exclaims as he pumps Unitas's hand. "Greatest football game ever played!" I can't believe it: even here in the jungle.

To make a bizarre story short, the pilot does indeed return for us. But not before the colonel treats us to a huge feast inside his thatched-roof headquarters. A bunch of his aides join us, along with his American counterpart, a colonel in the U.S. Army who's acting as an observer.

"This meat is great," I tell the American colonel as I lick my fingers. "What is it?"

"Don't ask," he mutters. "Just eat."

"C'mon. What is it?"

"Dog. It's roast dog."

"Oh."

Near the Laotian border: Now it's Sam's turn to get us in a fix. For reasons I have absolutely no recollection of, we find ourselves in the mountains visiting some Montagnard tribesmen. There's no one more feared, by both sides, than these incredibly ferocious fighters, who still wear loincloths and use crossbows and seemingly couldn't care less about dying.

Our baby-sitter gives us only one piece of advice: Don't take photographs. The Montagnards, it seems, are very superstitious about having their pictures taken. So naturally, the first thing Sam does upon entering their compound is aim his frigging Polaroid and click one off.

That sends the chief into a frenzy. He's screaming at us in Montagnard. He's jumping up and down. He's telling our baby-sitter he wants Sam to hand over the photo. Sam, of course, doesn't want to surrender it.

"For God's sake, Sam, give him the damn picture," I plead. "This guy is *really* tough. And something tells me he's about to whip our asses and then cut them off."

Sam shakes his head.

"I have a better idea," says Willie Davis. "Let's give the guy Sam instead."

At that, Sam reluctantly hands over the photo. Now the chief starts pointing at Sam's camera. Uh-huh, he wants that, too. Behind him, all the other Montagnards begin crowding closer. Some of them are fingering their grenade belts, which also carry a variety of truly ugly-looking knives.

"Look, I know Sam," I whisper to our baby-sitter. "There's no way he's gonna give up a camera he paid for with his own money. Better get us out of here any way you can."

He does—by having us do an about-face and start walking very, very fast.

It's Majorca all over again.

Near Saigon: Our trip ends with a downer. A copter drops us off at a little town occupied by a battalion of American troops. We show them our film highlights, and then, since this is a special event, they break out the beer. Lots of beer. The Vietnamese variety, I've already noticed, is stronger than hell. Now I notice that a lot of these young kids seem really out of it; God knows what else they've been drinking or smoking.

All this is happening on the fifth floor of a walk-up. In Vietnam, they build them around interior courtyards with the stairways in the center. All of a sudden, we hear a horrible scream. We race out the door, look down at the courtyard, and see one of the kids writhing on the ground. He's fallen all five stories, and he's busted up bad. Now the problem is how to get him to Saigon for medical help.

Everyone is running around trying to find a helicopter pilot or a jeep driver willing to brave the Vietcong, who are everywhere after dark. Everyone is cursing and arguing. No one seems in charge. Meanwhile, this poor kid is unconscious and twitching.

I feel awful. Is it our fault this has happened? Are we really doing any good by being there? That triggers larger questions. Should American troops be over here in the first place? Is any of it worth one kid's broken body? I started this USO tour as an unapologetic hawk. I'm ending it, I guess, as a bird of another feather.

Upon returning home, I went to see Fred Friendly, the legendary president of CBS News. I'd been chafing for some time about being confined solely to sportscasting. Believe it or not, I envisioned myself getting into network news as well—and my visit to Vietnam had stoked that desire. Friendly was kind enough to look at my diary and discuss my impressions of the trip. Later, he wrote me a letter strongly encouraging my interest in broadcast journalism. But as chance would have it, Fred was confronting his own career crisis. Just a few days after my visit, he quit CBS in a bitter dispute over its commitment to Vietnam coverage.

Meanwhile, I was experiencing disillusionment of a different sort with CBS. It went beyond being typecast as a house jock: I simply didn't feel at home in that house. In those days, CBS's sports division was a cliquish, hard-drinking, good-ole-boy operation, and I never became one of the boys. Maybe I didn't like to party enough. Wherever the blame lay, I felt increasingly alienated from CBS Sports.

Enter Roone Arledge. Golf first brought the president of ABC Sports and me together: We both belonged to Winged Foot, a world-famous club near my home in Westchester County. Roone and I quickly became friends. Besides our love of golf, we were both going through unhappy marital situations, and we shared those problems with each other. I liked him enormously. Not just for his warmth and charm, which were hard to resist, but for his remarkable innovations at ABC. He'd already revolutionized Olympics coverage and invented *Wide World of Sports.* The surest sign of Roone's impact was the darts my bosses at CBS started tossing at him. Pure envy, I suspected.

On an early spring day in 1970, Roone asked me what I thought about pro football on Monday nights.

"Sounds like a great idea," I said.

"How would you like to be part of it?"

Hell, there was nothing I'd rather do than work for Roone Arledge. Unfortunately, his timing was premature. "You know I've got a year left on my CBS contract, Roone," I replied. "I just couldn't do it."

"I figured you'd say that. What would you think about Howard Cosell doing the show?"

I'd been around Howard just long enough to form an opinion. "Not much," I said.

"I figured you'd say that, too. Got any ideas?"

My mind flashed back to that locker room in Green Bay. "Why don't you talk to the Cowboy? You know, Don Meredith. I can't imagine anyone who'd be more perfect."

"Don Meredith?" Roone said. "Interesting. I'll think about that."

As it turned out, of course, Roone took only half my advice, because he must have sensed I was only half right. He hired Don, but he also took Howard—and their chemistry proved to be dynamite. As for me, I watched that first season of *Monday Night Football* with more than a little interest. Though some of Howard's shtick still left me cold, the show seemed different and exciting. It had a unique beat.

So while I played out my CBS option, my lawyer and dear friend Ron Konecky hammered out a deal. ABC wanted me for the play-by-play role, which made me nervous. I'd never done play-by-play before. Nor did I want to hurt Keith Jackson, whom I would be replacing. Keith is an elegant, gracious man who went on to do remarkable work covering college football.

But the package ABC offered me contained some irresistible assignments: the Olympics, *Wide World,* even the evening newscast on ABC's New York station. It seems they were unhappy with the guy handling their sports wrap-up. He considered himself above giving viewers the day's scores, which was, after all, his most important function. Instead, he'd come on and proclaim things like, "Bowie Kuhn, the brilliant commissioner of baseball, has told me personally that the national pastime may expand to Milwaukee and furthermore that . . ."

Uh-huh, it was Howard. For the rest of our long relationship, I never mentioned my replacing him on that newscast. And thankfully, neither did he, although I'm sure that was just one of the many things that irritated him about the new "jock" in the booth.

My happiness during the next few years was marred by the misfortunes of someone I loved. As I embarked on a new job and a new life, the man who opened New York to me was in the process of losing both. Poor Toots! I'd long known that he was a terrible businessman. He let people steal him blind. And I knew what a soft touch he was for anyone down on his luck. How many times had I seen him tap one of his well-heeled patrons for a hundred-dollar bill and slip that same bill to some guy slumped at his bar?

Even so, the news of Toots's downfall really shook me. When I heard, I helped arrange a big benefit dinner for him at the New York Hilton. Everyone came—Gleason, Bob Hope, you name it—and we raised $200,000. Then the IRS got wind of it and said Toots couldn't have the money. He owed too much to the tax man, it seemed. He owed a lot of people. God, I felt bad about it.

By then Toots had been reduced to working as a figurehead at someone else's joint. A lot of guys who once would have given anything for a slap on the back from him—not to mention an insult—avoided going there. That place finally closed, too. I'd see him hanging out at other bars, looking like some old derelict elephant. The herd wouldn't let him run with them anymore. He had no job, no place to go, and nobody to pal with. I think that killed him as much as the cancer that finally got him. Toots died at seventy-three, about the same age at which my dad died. There weren't enough celebrities at his funeral to fill a single table at his old joint.

I think of him almost every day. I'd love to raise another glass with him. I'd like to say, Here's to you, ya bighearted bum. And thanks.

CHAPTER 12

LIVE WITH FRANK & KATHIE LEE

O ccasionally, when Regis Philbin is on vacation or ill, I'm asked to sit in for him on *Live with Regis & Kathie Lee.* I know I'm not anywhere near Reege's league, especially when ad-libbing those opening fifteen minutes of "host chat" that give the show its unique zing. On the other hand, I've had a lot of fun and a moment or two myself. Here's a transcript of one of them.

KATHIE: Hi, everybody! Regis is off, but Frank Gifford is here with me today.

FRANK: And last night. *(Chuckles from audience)*

KATHIE: May I say you're looking extremely sexy?

FRANK: Thank you, but I'm a little nervous.

KATHIE: He always gets nervous before he has to come here. Why is that?

FRANK: Well, what you do here is so dramatically different from what we do on *Monday Night Football.* Hmmmm. I wonder what it would be like if we did that show the way you and Regis do this show.... *(Voice rising)* ... Welcome to Giants Stadium! Tonight the

Washington Redskins versus the New York Giants, a big game in the National Football Conference. Hello again, everyone. I'm Frank Gifford along with Al Michaels and Dan Dierdorf. We're about ready for the kickoff, but first . . . Al, what did you do last night? *(Laughter)* And, Dan, I hear you've got a little commercial engagement at the Bergen Mall tomorrow. *(More laughter)* Uh, there's Rodney Hampton returning the kickoff. We'll get to that in a moment. So, Al, how are the kids? And, oh, I didn't want to mention it, but I'm gonna be at Macy's. I have a NEW CLOTHING LINE! *(Loud guffaws as Kathie cringes in mock chagrin)*

Okay, so it's not Tracy and Hepburn. Yet that little scene illustrates a very big reason why our marriage works. Offstage as well as onstage, Kathie and I have an unbelievable amount of fun. It's really a key to our relationship: It's never too early in the day for a laugh, and it's never too late for laugh—and we laugh a *lot*.

But let me back up a bit. I take most of the blame for the breakup of my marriage to Maxine. She is and always has been a very shy person, which was one of the things that made me love her. I loved her a great deal. She was a wonderfully tender, sensitive, beautiful, shy woman—all the things a man dreams of. Yet later on, when Maxine had to deal with my celebrity, that shyness really hurt her. I was shy, too. But after a while, after you do it over and over, you learn to stand up in front of a few hundred people and give a motivational speech or schmooze your way around a business convention or a sports conference. Maxine couldn't do that. She hated crowds; she was accustomed to living a very private life. So as the spotlight on me became more intense, my wife just withdrew from it. We started growing in totally different directions.

Only later did I realize how tough our life together was for Maxine. Here she was raising our three kids while I was off doing all the things I'd never, ever dreamed about doing—radio and television and movies and commercial endorsements and whatnot. Almost from the moment I was elected the NFL's Most Valuable Player, I was hardly ever home. Work became my narcotic of choice, my entire focus. And it destroyed my marriage. I should have been mature enough to recognize what was happening. I should have seen that what I thought was benefiting the both of us was actually damaging Maxine. If anyone should feel any guilt for our breakup, it's me.

My second wife, Astrid Lindley, was a half-English, half-Norwegian former aerobics instructor whom I met in the mid-seventies. Besides speaking five languages, Astrid could ski and play tennis and do a whole lot of athletic things, all the things Maxine wouldn't or couldn't do. In other words, we could share my love of physicality. That's not necessarily a good reason to marry someone, but it was definitely the main reason for our first becoming involved.

It wasn't very long into our marriage before I realized it was a mistake. We saw things in different ways. I was on the road all the time, much more than I am now, either for *Monday Night Football* or for my commercial commitments. Astrid was totally caught up in teaching aerobics and exercise in general. She was almost addicted to it. All of a sudden, I realized that the heart of our relationship—doing things together—we weren't doing at all. We didn't do anything together. Pretty soon we began constantly complaining about each other's life, and that's when I knew it would never work. Today I have absolutely no animosity toward Astrid, and she tells me the feeling is mutual. It was simply a six-year mistake for both of us.

I first met Kathie Lee Johnson in 1982. I was filling in for David Hartman on *Good Morning America,* and Kathie was in early that morning to do an entertainment segment. As she has recalled, I was bending over my dressing-room table, putting in my contacts and attired only in my jeans. She claims she liked what she saw (frequently referring to it as her first insight into what a "tight end" was all about). But all I can remember of our first encounter was how ungodly perky she was for that ungodly hour (5:00 A.M.).

Shortly after that, as I watched Kathie one morning—again on *GMA*—I was stunned by what I saw. For some reason, she was doing her "on camera" from six-foot-five-inch David Hartman's chair. She was craning her neck to read the TelePrompTer and looking for all the world like a turkey—albeit a very pretty one.

I immediately called the studio and, following her segment, got her on the phone. "You look like something eating fruit out of the top of a tree," I told her. She laughed, I laughed, and then I advised her never to sit in David Hartman's chair again. Later we discovered we had the same birthday. That triggered a lot of kidding, and thus began a four-year friendship that, amazing as it may seem (at least for me), remained platonic for the entire four years.

In my mind, at least, I was the least likely candidate for another marriage. By the time Astrid and I separated in 1984, I was in fervent agreement with that great old country-and-western line: "I can't afford to half my half one more time again." Besides, I was enjoying spending a great deal of my off-time in Jupiter, Florida, with my pal Tim Mara. I love to fish, and we had bought a boat together, along with another former Giant and Jupiter resident, Tucker Frederickson. I also spent a lot of time with Don and Susan Meredith in Santa Fe, New Mexico. The Cowboy and I even had a running joke: If I ever even contemplated saying "I do" again, he was authorized to cut off what "I do" it with.

Meanwhile, Kathie was still reeling from the breakup of her first marriage and involved in a series of destructive relationships. I mean, we're talking about a thoroughly confused woman. Here was a little, vulnerable born-again Christian, the product of a family as close as the Cleavers, who was a virgin on her wedding day. And all of a sudden the marriage collapses, and she's plunged into the two roughest worlds imaginable, the worlds of New York and network television. She was learning, but having to learn on the run can be awfully tough. Sometimes she'd get teary-eyed when we discussed it. Kathie, I sensed, was looking for security—but, as the song says, in all the wrong places.

Feeling protective toward her—kind of older-brotherish, I guess—I even tried fixing Kathie up with a couple of my buddies. Sometimes we'd do a foursome at lunch, but for some reason, Kathie and I would end up talking to each other the whole time. That didn't do much for her blind dates. Then came *The Odd Couple,* the benefit performance Don Meredith and I put on for his wife's Santa Fe theater group in 1985. *Good Morning America* flew Kathie to Santa Fe to cover our opening, and she did backstage interviews with both of us.

After the show, which went over better than anyone had expected (particularly me), Don and I invited Kathie back to his and Susan's home for a "victory" party. It was a great night. Never had either one of us worked so hard, and we were savoring the triumphs and laughing at the near misses. Kathie also seemed to have a great time, but about all I can recall is seeing how often and openly she laughed—both with us and at us. Later we drove Kathie back to her hotel, and I told Don to keep the engine running. I walked her to her room, kind of cupped her face, and gently kissed her. "Have a good flight," I said, and that was it. Years later, Kathie told me that was the first time she felt anything at all about me sexually. "It scared the hell out of me," she confided. As for Don, when I got back in the car, he was all ready. "You're just *leaving* her there?" he zinged.

By now I was living the absolutely perfect bachelor life—and feeling perfectly bored. I was just drifting, wondering if I wanted to stay with *Monday Night Football,* join CBS's morning show as a co-host, or just pack it in and buy a ranch in Santa Fe. I couldn't decide what I wanted to do—or whether I wanted to do anything. The word, I guess, is malaise. Or maybe it's funk.

In any case, on a spring day in 1986 Kathie and I had another of our friendly lunches, this one at a Mexican restaurant on West Sixty-ninth Street. Fittingly, it was named Santa Fe. My divorce from Astrid was just weeks from being final. As for Kathie, she'd broken up again with her latest boyfriend, with whom she'd been having a long, turbulent relationship. She sounded awfully blue and looked even worse. I'd never seen her face so drawn. Finally, after a couple of margaritas, my concern for her just burst out.

"That's it," I said firmly. "You've got to give yourself a break and get off this. You're being hurt too much. So from now on, you're hanging out with *me.*"

After lunch I walked her over to Columbus Avenue, gave her a little peck on the cheek, and headed south toward ABC. Kathie was going the opposite way; she lived in a little town house on Seventieth Street. All of a sudden, I stopped, turned, and just watched her walking up the avenue. *God,* I thought, *she really is adorable.* At that very instant, Kathie glanced over her shoulder. Just like in the movies, her eyes found mine. And then we both smiled.

The rest of this tale played out in Long Island's Hamptons, where Kathie had bought a small summer place. I started driving her out there, spending the nights at the nearby home of my lawyer, Ron Konecky. When it came to fixing up her place, Kathie was like a little waif. Every time she picked up a hammer, she'd break a nail. Then everything would stop for the next twenty-four hours while she dealt with *that* nail, rather than the one she'd started to hammer. So, being good with my hands, I wound up helping her with everything, from salvaging the plumbing and the wiring to planting trees. (Fifty-one trees, to be exact.) And I found myself enjoying it immensely. Just being around Kathie, I discovered, was enormous fun. She radiated energy and joy.

In late June I introduced Kathie to my circle. The occasion was a big dinner party at the Hamptons home of two dear friends, David Mahoney, a former CEO of Norton Simon, and his wife, Hillie, during the weekend of the U.S. Open. At one point in the evening, Kathie and I wandered out on the deck. There was a spectacular full moon coming up, and so, putting my arm around her, I said something like, "God, what a beautiful moon." Then I turned around to see some of my buddies grinning at us. *Evil* grins.

From then on, they just loved to tell that story—or at least a highly embellished version of it. In this version, which took on almost mythical proportions, I allegedly said, "Oh, Kathie, there's the moon." To which Kathie, gazing adoringly at my face, breathlessly replied, "Oh, really, Frank?" The story has followed me everywhere. Just last fall, at a coaches' meeting preceding a Jets-Bears game on *Monday Night Football,* Jets head coach Bruce Coslet strolled up to our entire *MNF* crew and said, "Hi, guys, how you doing?" Then he raised his eyes skyward and exclaimed, "Look, Frank, the *moon!*"

It was at a party the following weekend, however, that everything Kathie and I felt for each other suddenly popped into focus. This was at the home of another of my favorite couples: Marianne and Tony Ittelson, a former top executive of the CIT Group. The Ittelsons owned a Singing Machine, a device that allows you to record your own vocals over the doctored tapes of your favorite artists. Everyone was too timid to try it—except, of course, Kathie. She put on the Barbra Streisand–Neil Diamond version of "You Don't Bring Me Flowers" and began singing Barbra's part. Fueled by a bit too much vodka, I jumped in as Neil. I sang so horribly (it would be charitable to call me tone-deaf) that Kathie cracked up. Then we did it again, and we both got hysterical. By our third attempt, virtually every guest at the party was rolling on the floor. Recently, Kathie told me that was the moment she really knew we were Right. All I knew was that I had never met anyone like her. I had never felt quite what I was feeling. I wanted to help her, I wanted to laugh with her, I wanted to *be* with her.

Over the July 4 weekend, I finally met Kathie's family. It seemed as if I'd been hearing about the Epsteins forever, and now they were coming up from Maryland to meet the man their daughter had been talking about. I felt, to say the least, uneasy. After all, there was a twenty-three-year age gap between Kathie and me. In fact, she was a year younger than my oldest son. What were her parents going to think? Here's some old goat trying to get into their daughter's britches?

Shortly after they arrived at Kathie's house, I showed up bearing gifts and essentials such as bagels, croissants, muffins, fish, chicken, corn, you name it. Fortunately, I was given a running start, because they all turned out to be big football fans. I liked them instantly: Joanie, Kathie's mom; Aaron, her dad; sister Michie, brother-in-law Craig, and niece Shannie. I had heard such glowing praise for all of them that I was waiting for what I expected to be the disappointing reality. How wrong I was. They turned out to be all that Kathie had told me they were and more. Kind, gentle, thoughtful, unbelievably family oriented, and above all, a lot of fun.

Even so, things were a bit awkward that day until loud music started blaring from the house across the way. Apparently, a bunch of teenagers had rented it for the weekend. Since we could hardly hear ourselves talking, I said, "Why don't I go over there and try to quiet them down a little?"

To which Mr. Epstein, a former career navy man who'd been very reserved so far, replied, "I've got a better idea. Let me get my bazooka, and I'll blow them away."

That joke blew *us* away—and broke the ice. I ended up having a great weekend with them. As I've said, they're wonderfully warm, open people, very proud of Kathie and very protective of her and one another. Having grown up as I grew up, it was kind of a revelation, a look at the family unit as it should be. In fact, I began telling Kathie about my own family—which could charitably be described as nonnuclear—so that she could also appreciate the contrast.

The story that made the deepest impression on her concerned my maternal grandfather, Joseph Hawkins. Grandpa Joe was a big

man in every sense of the term: tall and hefty, with huge bushy
eyebrows and a great mane of shocking white hair. He never really
held a job, but he did very well at the pool hall and the card table.
I guess you could call him a professional gambler. Joe was also very
handsome, and everyone seemed to love him. His wife, Ora, however, was anything but lovable. She loomed almost as large as Joe,
and whenever one of her grandchildren acted up, he or she was
certain to receive a hell of a whack. The other thing I remember
about Ora was her "whiskers": She must have had to shave at least
weekly.

It was common knowledge in our family that Ora was very tough
on Joe. There were even some who wondered how he endured it for
so long. Or at least they wondered about that before a legendary
dinner at the Hawkins home. As it was later related to me, Joe looked
up from his meal one night and inquired, "Is there any bread?"

Man, Ora just exploded. "We'd have some bread," she shouted,
"if you weren't such a . . ." What followed was a long litany of Joe's
failures as a man, husband, and provider.

When Ora finally ran out of wind, Joe arose, quietly donned his
vest, his gold watch and chain, and his coat, and announced, "I'll go
get us some bread." Then he walked out the door—and totally
vanished. I mean, he just dropped off the planet. For the next few
years, sightings of my grandfather would be reported in various
spots around California. But every time Ora and my parents went off
to check them out, they proved erroneous. No one's ever discovered
what happened to Joe Hawkins.

Anyway, shortly after I told all this to Kathie, we were having
dinner at her house in the Hamptons. I'd been kind of mean and
grouchy that night. I forget what triggered it, but somewhere into the
steak I realized I'd forgotten to do something important. I jumped up
and announced, "I've got to go."

Kathie's eyes welled with tears. And then, with a blend of concern and mischief only a born actress could manage, she said,
"You're not going for bread, are you?"

But back to our courtship. A few weeks after the Epsteins' July
4 visit, Kathie and I went to London, where I was covering an
exhibition game between two American pro-football teams. Before
the game, I did an interview at a local radio station while Kathie

waited in the anteroom. My voice drifted out to her, and what she heard was this:

INTERVIEWER: Are you enjoying London?
ME: Yes, I'm here with my fiancée.

"What?" she exploded when I walked out. "Why did you call me your fiancée?"

"Well, er, because, um, you are," I stammered. "Besides, I didn't want them to think you're some bimbo I'm traveling the country with."

The conversation—and her understandable confusion—continued over dinner that night at Annabel's, a chic private club. We'd arrived just as it opened at eight-thirty, which, unbeknownst to us, was a good two hours before even remotely fashionable Londoners made the scene. Consequently, the dining room at Annabel's was totally deserted. The waiter who seated us was still wiping his mouth from his own meal.

All went absolutely beautifully until, after a couple of glasses of wine, Kathie started crying. "Why did you call me your fiancée?" she again asked.

"Because you are," I again replied, feeling like a dumb teenager.
"You mean we're going to get married?"
"Uh-huh."
"Well, why don't you *ask* me?"
Somehow it just wouldn't come out. "Ask me," she repeated. "Go ahead, just ask me."

All of a sudden, it seemed so simple, so right. I stopped squirming, took a deep swig of wine, leaned forward, and whispered, "Kathie, will you marry me?"

"Wellllll . . . yes," she said. Then she paused, demurely batted her eyelashes, and added, "As long as you insist."

Once it was out in the open, marrying Kathie seemed the most obvious move of my life. As the saying goes, I simply didn't want to live without her. So when we got back to the States, I bought an emerald-cut diamond ring and gave it to her during one of her singing engagements in Atlantic City. Kathie was in her suite between rehearsals, and I just laid it on a table in front of her. I was only half joking when I told her the ring was as much for her mom

and dad as it was for her. I wanted them to know I was in this for
real, and not just taking a whirl around the floor.

Later on I took Kathie to Florida to meet my two sons, Jeff and
Kyle, and she was an instant hit. We all went waterskiing along the
Inland Waterway. My boys are pretty good athletes, but Kathie,
who'd never been on water skis before, proved their equal in guts if
not in skill. They just fell in love with her.

The wedding was on October 18 at my friend and attorney Ron
Konecky's beachfront home. It was a beautiful Indian summer afternoon with cool Hamptons breezes and a warm "Bakersfield" sun.
All my close pals and their wives were there, as were Kathie's. It was
also the last time I would see my mom up and around, happy and
healthy. She passed away rather suddenly just a month later. I'm
glad she got to know Kathie in person, because they shared a common spiritual bond. They had spoken often on the phone prior to
our wedding, and when I overheard them sharing biblical thoughts
and passages, I sensed that all was well between them.

Kathie and my mom actually met on Friday night before the
wedding at the Regency Hotel dining room. I had sent my car to pick
up Mom and her friend George Byers at the airport, and when Kathie
and I learned the plane was late, we decided we'd have a glass of
wine and wait dinner. However, it wasn't long before they arrived,
and after the formalities of introduction were over, I asked Mom
what she would like to drink.

Sternly observing our wineglasses, she curtly replied, "Water
will be fine. Just *fine.*"

I had already told Kathie that Mom thought alcohol in any shape
or form was a sure ticket to a fiery eternity. But to make a tense
moment even tenser, when I nodded to Kathie for her order, she
announced, "I'll have a martini."

Now Kathie had never had, and never has, a martini. Yet somehow (perhaps in defense of her female territory) it just came out. It
was breath-catching time. And then my mom began to smile, I
started to laugh, and we all broke up.

It turned out to be a great weekend: a big party on Friday night
at the Salty Dog in Sag Harbor, with singing, dancing, family and
kids all over the place (mostly my grandchildren), followed the next

day by the simplest of wedding ceremonies at Ron and Isobel's. My friend Ross Johnson, who would later make James Garner famous in the TV adaptation of *Barbarians at the Gate,* was my best man, just as I had been his seven years earlier when he married his wife, Laurie.

Kathie and I had both worked out the vows we wanted to exchange, and I can assure you there was nothing about obeying, only about loving and sharing. Two things we had both discussed at length were a prenuptial agreement and children, not mine but the possibility of "ours." I've nothing against prenuptial agreements (they're right for a lot of people), but the thought of one for us seemed totally contradictory to what we both felt and wanted: a lifetime together. As for children, I jokingly told Kathie, "What more could you want? I'm making you an instant grandmother!" And indeed, my daughter, Vicki, already had Michael and her daughter Kyle, and a year later there would be daughter Rory. Meanwhile, my older son, Jeff, and his wife, Caryn, had little Jessica with Christiana soon to arrive.

I could joke about that, but I was not joking when I told Kathie that, while I didn't want any more children, I would never deny her the right to make her own decision. As far as I was concerned, to deny her that pleasure—one I had already known and shared with another—would have been the ultimate in selfishness. I should admit, however, that the joy I've found in our little Cody and anticipate from his new sister, Cassidy, come not from my willingness to sacrifice but from Kathie's wisdom about what would complete our life together.

The wedding was a smash, from the ceremony that Kathie's minister brother, David, performed, to vocals by her sister, Michie, to the great party and the wonderful toasts for our good health and fortune. As for the honeymoon, it hardly fit its description in the book version of *Barbarians.* That had my pal Ross Johnson, then CEO of RJR Nabisco, sending us off to San Francisco on a Nabisco jet. In reality, we drove about forty miles to Gurney's Inn in Montauk—our car pursued by squads of camera-wielding paparazzi. I hadn't seen so many since Toots Shor took me to see "Sinat." But after we played with them for a while, ducking in and out of roadways and alleys, we pulled over to give them a curbside shot. After that they let us proceed in peace. And, I might add, in a whole lot of happiness.

Ever since *Live with Regis & Kathie Lee* became the talk of television, people constantly ask me the same question: Is the woman I'm married to anything like the woman they see on the screen? Not just anything like her, I always reply. She's *totally* like her. What you see is what she is. Watch Kathie for any length of time on her show, and you'll observe everything that I observe over the same period of time.

For openers, Kathie's intelligence is off the charts. I mean, nobody I know is smarter or quicker. She also doesn't hide anything: Everything that emanates from her mouth is totally honest. That's why she's so good at what she does. There's no guile there; there's no deceit to her. When she and Regis talk about some tragedy, she's genuinely sad about it, genuinely moved by it.

It's no secret that Kathie's honesty gets her into trouble at times. The title of her book is perfect: *I Can't Believe I Said That.* It could have also been *I Can't Believe I Did That* or *I Can't Believe I Thought That.* But while Kathie sometimes gets hammered right and left, she herself wouldn't hurt a soul. She wouldn't hurt an enemy if she had one. She lives her life by the Golden Rule: Do unto others as you would have them do unto you. And when they do unto her badly, when some sleazeball betrays her trust, she's stunned. She's been stunned by a lot of people, by some of the best. But she also rebounds better than anyone I know. I suspect that's because there's virtually no one she doesn't really care about. She just loves people, believes in people, wants to help people. Hell, if I weren't around, Kathie would probably give away everything we have.

Another question people ask me is, what makes Kathie so incredibly ambitious? Believe me, it's not ego. She's just an extremely talented person who, I think, feels that God intended her to maximize those talents. I find it strange when someone calls Kathie overly ambitious. How can you be overly ambitious? The people I've always liked to spend time with have invariably been ambitious, people who are curious about everything and want to be the best they can be. That's Kathie.

And once she gets involved with a project, it's always 190 percent. Sometimes she gets so caught up in it, so enthusiastic, that I
can just see her little motor overheating. So I'll put my arm around
her and turn off my imaginary switch on her shoulder—sort of like
shutting down a windup doll. "Don't you do that to me," she'll say.
Sometimes it slows things down, sometimes it doesn't, but at least
she knows what I'm thinking.

We also quite often cross swords about all her extracurricular
activities. I'm very outspoken about my feeling that she should put
on the brakes, and she generally agrees. Every moment she's involved in something away from Cody, I know she feels guilty. And
those times when she wants to help Cody do something or fix
something, and he looks at her, glares, and says, "No, Mommy,
Christine [our nanny] will do it," or "No, Mommy, Ted or Frances
[our dear housekeepers] will do it"—those times just kill her. The
main problem is, she can't say no. She never wants to let anyone
down. If she agrees to make x number of appearances for her clothing line, and there are three thousand women at the department
store to see her, and the guy who runs the clothing line says, "Please,
we got a request from so-and-so, couldn't you make just one more
appearance?"—well, off goes Kathie. The way she sees it, anything
less and she wouldn't be giving it her all.

One also has to understand that Kathie's success was hardly
handed to her. She worked her butt off. She went on all the calls,
absorbed all the rejections, underwent all the sexual harassments
that any good-looking woman who doesn't have any professional
stature is going to undergo. She's endured an awful lot of crap. Now,
all of a sudden, most anything she wants to do she can do. So having
come up that way, she has a terribly hard time not to take it all. As
much as I'd like her around more, I understand that—and I'm damn
proud of her.

People also ask me what I think of Kathie's "other" husband. You
know, the guy with the big mouth. In my opinion, Regis Philbin's
one big failing is that he graduated from Notre Dame—and won't let
America forget it. He actually suffers from the delusion that Notre
Dame is the greatest name in football. I don't think this condition is
necessarily terminal, provided Regis receives intensive treatment

from a good psychotherapist. And like most everything else, USC produced the best of those, too.

Seriously, Reege and I have a great relationship. Yet as much as Kathie and I like him and his lovely wife, Joy, we're all kind of careful not to see too much of each other. We do that for the same reason Regis and Kathie never see each other before each morning's show. It's what makes their opening "host chat" so spontaneous and funny. If we all started hanging out together, they seem to think, that spontaneity could dissolve. What's more, they have teenagers away at school, and we have little ones at home. Consequently, we have decidedly different social lives. You might say that the Giffords and the Philbins are like distant, yet very fond, relatives.

Besides, my best friend is the person I'm married to. In fact, Kathie and I spend most of each day trying to figure out how we can stay in touch, if not be together. We'll start with an early-morning discussion over coffee (and I mean early, like sixish before she goes off to work). "Where are you going to be at ten? Oh, there? Well, call me first." Sometimes she'll call me from the car on her way to the show. Or I'll call her when I leave for lunch.

Right now it's early in the morning, I've got an interesting day coming up, yet all I'm thinking about is our dinner. Kathie loves steak, so maybe I'll barbecue one. She also loves mushrooms and fried onions with her steak. That's not a big deal for me to make. And Cody, Cody's mad for "mashers" (mashed potatoes), so I'll pick up some of those, too. Now I'm starting to laugh at myself. I've been doing this stuff my entire life, yet for some reason it's all new again.

And, of course, it's more than laughs. We have some unbelievably romantic times. Recently, we went out to the Hamptons to attend a big party; all the Beautiful People were coming. But first we stopped off at Kathie's house, the one we worked so hard to fix up and couldn't bear to sell. I built a fire, and we looked out at all the trees I'd planted. They were about thirty feet tall: Everything seemed so cozy and secluded. "Look," I said. "Do you really want to go to that party?" Kathie just shook her head. So we went out and walked down our little country road, reminiscing about that Fourth of July weekend when I met her family. Then we drove over to a lovely little Southampton restaurant for dinner, came back, and sat by the fire again. We talked for hours about all the fun we'd had out there, all the warm, wonderful memories of our falling in love. Kathie had tears in her eyes, and so did I. Who would want to share that with a bunch of Beautiful People?

When Kathie and I do go to parties, we really watch out for each other. Especially when someone starts flirting with one of us. It always upsets me—in fact, it really ticks me off—when some bubbling, half-assed, macho yo-yo tries to come on to Kathie. I hate it when these bozos take her arm and try to steer her off. I've got really strong hands, so I'll just reach out, wrap my fingers around the arm or the wrist doing the steering, and just squeeze. I'll have a big, friendly smile on my face, and the guy will be smiling back—only for some reason his face is turning white. Of course, Kathie always scolds me for that. But what the hell.

By the same token, Kathie's antennae to women coming on to me may be the most acute on the planet. The thing is, I don't notice that kind of thing because I'm not interested in it—maybe for the first time in my life. I get along great with women, but there's no sexual undercurrent anymore. It's not there because I just don't want it to be there. I care about only one person in that room, and she's the one with me.

And heaven help any woman who doesn't recognize I'm Kathie's guy. Take the time we attended Kathie's first Kentucky Derby with our friends Cloyce and Ashley Box. The night before the race, we went to a huge cocktail party in an old Louisville hotel. Later, leaving the party on our way to dinner, I headed to the men's room and Kathie to the ladies' room. As I faced the urinal, unzipped, and started doing my business, I heard a female voice ask the attendant outside, "Was that Frank Gifford who just went into the men's room?" Seconds later, there she was—not terribly unattractive but not attractive, either. She plopped down on the washbasin next to the urinal and breathlessly said (with a breath minty from juleps), "I've always wanted to meet you, Frank."

As bizarre as it was, I certainly wasn't going to let her chase me out of the men's room. So I kept on peeing, and she kept on babbling. Our departure from the men's room coincided with Kathie's return from the ladies' room. One look at the fire in Kathie's eyes and I knew my newfound friend was in deep trouble. *"What the hell are you doing with my husband?"* Kathie screamed. It was one of the greatest disappearing acts I'd ever seen. The woman just vanished. I mean, she moved faster than Secretariat. Now Kathie was glaring at me, as if somehow *I* caused it all. Thank God no one else was around. Imagine what the *National Enquirer* would have made of *that*.

I'm occasionally asked if I mind some of the intimate revelations that Kathie makes on her show, particularly the ones about me. Hey, how could any guy mind being called a "human love machine" before 10 million people? Actually, though, Kathie once did go a bit too far. Our bedroom, Cody's bedroom, and the bedroom of his nanny—Christine Gardner—all adjoin. Christine came to us just before Cody was born. She's bright, fun, and attractive, and has become like family to us. But several years ago, shortly after Cody arrived, I awoke in the middle of the night and, naked and still half asleep, went in to check on him. He was fine, so I went to the bathroom down the hall and, on the way back, noticed a door open. I peeked in, and there was our dog, Chablis, curled up at the foot of a bed. Since Chabby usually slept with us, I groggily went into the room, perched on the side of the bed, and started petting her. Suddenly, I realized Chabby and I had company.

"*Frank?*" said a very concerned Christine.

I couldn't believe it. I jumped up, raced back to our room, and leaped into bed. Then I woke up Kathie and blurted out the whole embarrassing story.

Big mistake. The next morning the viewers of *Live with Regis & Kathie Lee* learned from Mrs. Frank Gifford that Mr. Frank Gifford had sleepwalked naked into the nanny's bedroom. The next thing I knew, the supermarket tabloids leaped on the story—only now it's "Kathie Lee's Hubby in Bed with Nanny!" Needless to say, that story's haunted me ever since. It's gotten into the media's computers, so every time some reporter punches in my name, the damn thing jumps out—just waiting to be embellished all over again. Everyone ribs me about it. Shortly after that headline ran, I attended an awards dinner along with Dan Burke, the chief executive officer of Capital Cities/ABC and therefore my chief, too. At the reception prior to dinner, Dan came over to me with a big grin. "Caught in bed with your nanny, huh?" he said. "And claimed you were sleepwalking? Boy, that would never sell at *my* house!"

The ironic part is, I actually do have a sleepwalking problem, something I discovered a few years ago. I'd been assigned by *Wide World of Sports* to cover the Tour de France in Paris. The day before I flew over there, I flew to California for an ABC affiliates meeting and caught the red-eye back to New York the next morning. That night I was on a flight to Paris. So by the time I checked into the Hotel George V and arrived in my room, I felt like a walking zombie. Which, it turned out, is exactly what I became.

Around four in the morning, I woke up with a very strange sensation. I sensed that I was in the Westchester County home of bandleader Peter Duchin. What made that strange was that, while Peter was a friend of mine, I'd never stayed in his home. What's even weirder, I somehow remember every detail of everything that happened next.

Following band music only I could hear, I got up, walked out the door, and began strolling the halls. Yes, I was naked this time, too. Then I took the elevator all the way down to the kitchen. There I encountered a short, swarthy guy peeling potatoes. Still thinking I was in Peter Duchin's house, I said to him, "I need to find my room." The poor guy took one look and grabbed a tablecloth, which he carefully wrapped around my waist. Then he guided me back to the elevator and pushed the button for the lobby. When the doors opened again, I walked past two cleaning women mopping the floor. They looked at me as though this happened every night. Who knows, maybe it did. By now I was standing in front of the concièrge. "I need to find my room," I repeated, still holding tight to the tablecloth.

Man, that concièrge had to be the world's coolest. "Name, *monsieur*?" he politely inquired. "Gifford," I replied. He nodded and handed me an extra key. I found my way back to my room, but just before nodding off, I wrote a note to myself and placed it by the phone. "I can't believe what happened," it said. "I walked naked in my sleep." When I awoke the next morning, I was certain the whole thing had been a very bad dream. Then I saw the tablecloth. Then the extra key. And then the note. I grabbed for the phone and called Kathie.

She caught the next plane to Paris—carrying my best pair of pajamas.

Naturally, Kathie also told that story on her show. But this time something good came out of it. A doctor called her to explain: "Your husband suffers from transglobal amnesia. He really isn't sleepwalking. He's just reacting to crossing too many time zones in too short a period." Though that still sounds crazy to me, whenever I check into a hotel these days, I always hang my bathrobe in a special spot. Over the doorknob.

One summer morning a few years after Kathie and I were married, an odd thing happened to me on the street. As I strolled along East Fifty-seventh near Park Avenue, I was accosted by an elderly Italian woman. "Whassamatta wich you?" she shouted, shaking her finger at me. *"Why don't you give your wife a* bambino?"

Huh?

That evening I mentioned the encounter to Kathie. Which is how I learned that she'd taken her campaign to have a baby to the airwaves, joking about my reluctance to become a father again during her host chat with Regis. (Ah, the never-ending surprises that come with marriage to a talk-show hostess!) In my opinion, at least, that reluctance didn't seem unreasonable for a man my age. After all, I had three children and five grandchildren at the time, so I figured I'd already done my bit to propagate the species. And I knew from experience that the enormous pleasures of rearing children come with doses of heartache and pain (hell, I had teenagers during the *sixties*). Yet, as I had told Kathie, I also believed that it's every woman's right to make the baby decision herself.

Cody Newton Gifford came into the world on March 22, 1990— and my world suddenly filled with a whole lot of joy. He was conceived on the most romantic vacation of my life, a five-day cruise along the Italian Riviera aboard one of Carnival's four-masted sailing ships. But while Kathie and I agree on the setting for Cody's conception, we disagree about the precise place. She says off Portofino. I say off Portovenere. Actually, it could have been anywhere, because in our little part of that boat there was a whole lot of rockin' goin' on.

Fittingly, we got our baby's name from a football telecast. On the previous Thanksgiving, I was sitting in my in-laws' home in Bowie, Maryland, watching the Cleveland Browns play the Detroit Lions. Kathie and I, having known for months that our baby would be a boy, were still debating what to name him. Suddenly, an offensive tackle for the Browns, an All-Pro named Cody Risien, made a big play.

"Hey, what about Cody?" I called out to Kathie, who was in the kitchen.

"Cody?" she said. "I think I love it. I *do* love it. *That's it!*" No one ever accused Kathie of lacking enthusiasm. Within seconds she had added "Newton" to Cody and was dancing around the room chanting, "Cody Newton Gifford . . . Cody Newton Gifford . . ."

Newton, of course, is my middle name, and I've hated it for a lifetime. I tried to explain my feelings to Kathie, warning her how often some bright little yo-yo at school would harass our Cody with "Ya, ya, ya . . . you're a Fig Newton . . . you're a Fig Newton." In any event, as far as Kathie was concerned, it was already etched in stone.

Now flash ahead to March 22. A few hours after Cody entered the world, a public-relations woman for Kathie's show called the Browns' front office to get the proper spelling of Cody Risien's last name. "Oh, by the way," said the person on the other end of the line, "Cody is retiring from football today to become a lay minister. And guess what? It's also his birthday." Ever since, I can't count the number of people who have told Kathie and me, "We now have a Cody, too." As far as I know, however, only two Codys have the same birthday—mine and a great offensive-tackle-turned-lay-minister who inspired his name.

I sometimes kid Kathie about my having a son so late in life. "One day," I warn her, "he's going to demand the car, and I'll have forgotten where I parked it." Yet while Cody makes me uncomfortably aware of the limited time I have left, that's made me even more appreciative of my time with him. I can't overstate the happiness he's given me. When Cody was about a year old, we established a wonderful early-morning ritual. About the time the sun rose, and after Kathie left for the studio, I'd fix him his favorite breakfast. (In fact, I still do, and we've got the kitchen stains to prove it.) Then I'd get him into his traveling clothes, pop him into the stroller, and wheel him across the street to our "secret garden." That's our name for a heavily wooded area behind three huge mansions, which were built during the eighties but never sold. I'd take Cody's hand and lead him through the "garden," pausing to observe chipmunks and deer and maybe even a circling hawk. As Cody sucked on his pacifier, I talked to him about all kinds of things. You know, *guy* things. I guess you could say we were bonding, something I never had the time—or, more accurately, never took the time—to do with my other children.

I'll never forget Cody's first Halloween night out. I dressed up as a cowboy and Kathie as something she called "Little Bo Creep." Cody put on his favorite ensemble: tiny football shoes with fake cleats, miniature shoulder pads, and a Giants jersey with the number 11, Phil Simms's number. Then, along with Christine (costumed as a Fig Newton) and her sister's two kids (Robbie, dressed as a pumpkin, and Cailin, a ballerina), we jumped in our Jeep and set off trick-or-treating.

Man, what a fiasco! Kathie would knock on a door, and we'd all stand there with big, expectant grins. And all we'd hear was, *woof, woof, woof!* There wasn't one two-legged creature home in a single house we hit. As we drove and drove, the look on Cody's face sent me an unmistakable message: C'mon, Dad, what *is* this trick-or-treat stuff? So on the next Halloween, we called all of our neighborhood friends and made sure at least a few would be home. This time Cody made a killing, and all of a sudden Halloween was right up there with Christmas.

Actually, Cody loves to wear costumes at any time of year. He went through one period permanently dressed as a fireman: You couldn't get the raincoat, boots, and fire chief's hat off him. I started taking him over to the local firehouse, where the guys would slide down poles for him, put him in the truck, all kinds of things. He just loved them, and they him. Around the third time we were there, the bell actually rang, and all hell broke loose. I pulled Cody out of the way as the firemen grabbed their boots and their hats and jumped on the truck. Damned if they didn't turn on the siren just before roaring off. Cody's eyes bulged as big as Frisbees. For the next few months, that's all he wanted to talk about. "Codes," I'd say. "What happened at the firehouse?" He'd do ten minutes of stand-up.

Though Cody and I occasionally watch football on TV together, I don't sense he has any great interest in playing it. That's just fine with me. Sure, the pro game wasn't exactly a Maypole dance in my Giants days, but the guys who play it now are so much bigger and stronger that they're far more capable of causing permanent injury. If Cody *wants* to play football, that's his choice. But I'm sure not about to stick a helmet on his head and throw him out "there." I like his profile exactly the way it is.

Besides, Cody is already showing signs of inheriting Kathie's show-biz gene. This kid's a natural performer. In fact, he actually upstaged a president of the United States. When Cody was about two, President Bush invited Kathie and me, along with some other former athletes and performers, down to Washington to help him launch a national physical-fitness program. He gave a long speech about it, which CNN carried live. I'd brought Cody along and was holding him in my arms as I stood alongside the other athletes—all of us directly behind the president. As President Bush started talking, Cody suddenly spied Millie, the First Dog, who was lolling offstage. Cody had been great until then. But all of a sudden he began furiously twisting and turning. Rather than have him start squawking, too, I gently lowered him to the floor.

Well, Cody chased after that poor dog like the Energizer bunny. Back and forth he toddled, with every eye on him instead of on the man behind the mike—who remained oblivious to the whole thing. Of course, CNN's cameras were right on top of it. When Kathie and I watched it later on tape, we totally freaked.

Now that Kathie had been proved so right about having Cody, she decided it would be just as right to give Cody a sibling. We discussed it all at home, and once again she talked about it on the air—with virtually identical results. Though the elderly woman who accosted me this time wasn't Italian, the place was again East Fifty-seventh near Park. "I know you," she shouted, jumping up and down like Doc Sweeny. "You're Mister Kathie Lee. *Why don't you give that woman another baby?*"

Actually, I needed no convincing. I wanted Cody to know what it's like to have a little sister or brother, to experience the kind of loving intimacy that Kathie has with her own sister and brother. Kathie discovered she was pregnant in July of 1992. Several weeks later, we flew to Vail, Colorado, for a much-needed vacation. Kathie was totally exhausted and fighting a heavy cold without any help from medications, which, of course, are a no-no for a pregnant woman. On a gloomy, rainy Friday, she began spotting. Late Saturday afternoon she lunged for the bathroom, from where I heard a loud moan. As she started to sob, I rushed in. She obviously had miscarried and was totally inconsolable. I took her in my arms, held her tighter than I've ever held her, and gently kissed her head. I told her, as best I could, that all was okay, this was God's will, and we'd be fine.

I knew that Saturday afternoon is one of the worst times to find a doctor, especially during off-season in a ski resort. But not only did I turn one up, he turned out to be a real-life Marcus Welby. His name is Ed Cohen, and he returned my phone message within minutes. After soothingly consoling Kathie, he told us the location of the hospital and was waiting in the parking lot when we drove up through the pouring rain. I'd put the fetal tissue in a cup, wrapped a napkin around it, and brought it along. When I gave it to Dr. Cohen, he just nodded, then turned his attention to Kathie.

"Are you the one who works with Regis?" he asked.

"Actually," I said, "he's the one who works with *her.*"

Our laughter put everyone at ease. After examining Kathie and performing a sonogram, Dr. Cohen talked to us for nearly an hour. He confirmed that we'd lost the baby, suggested some reasons for it that were beyond Kathie's control, pointed out the astonishingly high rate of miscarriages, and explained that Kathie could still give birth to a perfectly healthy child. He just made her feel better about everything, or at least took away some of the pain.

As we rose to leave, I awkwardly asked Dr. Cohen how we should pay for his services. "Let me tell you a little story," he replied, leaning forward and gazing softly at Kathie. "I lost my mother a month ago, and she was your biggest fan. You can't imagine the pleasure you gave her in the last days of her life. So I would like to do this for her. And if somewhere down the line you get a chance to do something nice for someone, do it in her memory—and tell them to pass it on." Now it was my turn to have tears in my eyes.

As fate would have it, Vail was where Kathie and I conceived again, this time during a Thanksgiving vacation in 1992. We also settled on the name of Cassidy, a name we not only both liked but one that would fit either a boy or a girl. Now for a second twist of fate. About a month later, I opened a Christmas card from Cody Risien and his family, with whom we'd started corresponding. "Oh, my God," I thought. "Cody Risien and his wife have a daughter named Cassidy! He's going to think something's *really* weird."

Later, we learned from the amniocentesis that our Cassidy will also be a girl. I can see her now: She's wearing one of those little Laura Ashley dresses with a great big bow in her blond hair, and she's adorable. Sometimes I feel as if I'm standing outside of my life looking in, watching everything unfold like a beautiful play. Now it's time for Laura Ashley to come onstage. As for Cody, he can't wait to play the role of big brother. Recently, while spending a weekend on Long Island, we called Cody to tell him we'd be home in a few hours. "You bringing Cassidy, too?" he asked.

One day, I suspect, I'll tell Cassidy about Cody's circumcision, because if there's a single story that illustrates what life with Kathie is like, that's it. As with most new mothers, Kathie couldn't bear the idea of her baby going under the knife. So on the morning of his circumcision, she wrote a little poem to the obstetrician, our friend Dr. Michael Langan, and tucked it into Cody's diaper.

> *Dear Dr. Langan:*
> *Just take a tad*
> *Please leave me most of what I already had*
> *Life is too short, so don't make ME that way!*
> *Now please hold steady and have a nice day.*
> *Love,*
> *Cody*

Dr. Langan tells me he's still laughing. Me, too. As a matter of fact, now that I think about it, my life really isn't a beautiful play. I'm actually living inside a beautiful sitcom—and there's only one name for it. *I Love Kathie.*

CHAPTER 13

TIME-OUT

*I*t was the slowest train I'd ever ridden. Then again, I'd never ridden a funeral train before, let alone one carrying a friend who was an assassinated presidential candidate.

As the train made its mournful journey from New York to Washington on that June day in 1968, I found myself sitting in a car with several of Bobby Kennedy's children. Being too young to fully comprehend their father's murder, several of them were understandably antsy. And being Kennedys, they wanted to compete at something. So I showed them one of my favorite games, a test of hand reflexes in which one person (me) drops a dollar bill between another person's thumb and index finger. The idea is to try to catch it before it hits the floor. Though the game looks easy, it's guaranteed to drive the would-be catcher crazy with frustration. And none of the kids became more frustrated that day than Michael Kennedy, Bobby's eleven-year-old son. Losing that game to me over and over just drove Michael bonkers. Maybe I should have let him win a few—because eleven years later Michael married my daughter Vicki.

Yup, I'm a member of the world's largest extended family. I'm a Kennedy in-law.

Ironically, it all began on a plane. In the spring of 1961, as I was flying home from Chicago, the first-class stewardess stopped by with a message: "Attorney General Kennedy would like to come up and join you." I said sure, absolutely, by all means.

We sat together the rest of the way to New York, mostly talking football. One subject that didn't come up was politics. I suspect Bobby knew I'd campaigned for Richard Nixon against his brother the year before. If so, he was polite enough not to mention it. In any event, we got along so well that, once the plane landed, he and I and his assistant—a federal marshal—ended up having beer and cheeseburgers at P. J. Clarke's. I drove my car from the airport, and Bobby's car followed me into the city, where we both parked outside P.J.'s on East Fifty-fifth Street. At one point in our meal, Bobby looked up and asked, "Who's in our car?"

"Nobody," said Bill Barry, his assistant and a longtime family friend.

"Well then, who's guarding the secrets?"

They stared at each other for a moment, then burst out laughing. Apparently, Bobby's car was loaded with important files on a hush-hush case he was developing. This being New York, that car could have been stolen just as quickly as the pope's limousine. As I recall, we all laughed a lot that night.

In the following months, invitations to all kinds of Kennedy events started showing up. Once, along with Ethel and Maxine, we went to one of Manhattan's swankiest French restaurants. There was quite a group of us, but the maître d' zeroed in on Bobby and did his phoniest number. I mean, he bowed so low you'd think he was greeting some king. I didn't realize how much Bobby hated that kind of pretentiousness until the maître d' started reeling off the house specials in French. Bobby never looked up from his menu. He just said, very softly, "Don't you speak English?" He wasn't being mean, really, yet there was quiet steel in his voice. Just like that—right in the middle of his spiel—the guy switched to English delivered with a distinct Bronx accent: "We also got calf brains, we also got some nice filet of sole. . . ." It broke everyone up, and we had a great night.

Over the next few years, I talked with Bobby several times and watched him in action even more. One thing continually struck me: his sincere caring for other people. He related to strangers like no one I'd ever witnessed. He'd walk into a crowd and start talking to a guy, and that guy instantly knew that he really cared. Once I told him all about my trip to Vietnam, especially about those Vietcong whose pigmentation had changed from spending years in caves and how I'd become convinced we could never beat people like that. He seemed as impressed as I was.

Unlike a lot of politicians I've met, Bobby didn't look over your head when you talked to him. He truly listened to people. By the same token, I saw Bobby totally chill out those he thought were bullshitting him—kind of the way he did that maître d'. That's probably where he got his reputation for heartlessness. Hell, he was anything but heartless. He just couldn't tolerate bullshit.

It was Ethel who brought my daughter, Vicki, into the Kennedys' orbit. When Vicki was sixteen, Ethel arranged for her to work as a summer intern in Ted Kennedy's office in Washington. Vicki, who has a super mind, wrote a paper on the inequity of women's education that Ted proudly quoted in a speech before the House of Representatives. That put her name in the *Congressional Record* (and you better believe her old man was proud of her, too). During that summer, Vicki lived with Ethel at Hickory Hill, and there she met Michael. Which helps explain why she subsequently decided to go to Boston College. Though I didn't know it at the time, Michael was attending nearby Harvard. All I know is that one fine morning I gave my only daughter away to a Kennedy—me, the guy who'd organized Athletes for Nixon!

As it turned out, Vicki made a brilliant choice. Besides bearing a spooky resemblance to his father, Michael has inherited Bobby's intelligence and charm and concern for others. Having watched him grow up, I'm especially proud of what he's accomplished. He took over his older brother's company when Joe II was elected to the House and really made it go. It's called Citizens' Energy Corporation. Basically, they buy oil on the world market and sell it at cost to poor people in housing projects in a growing number of communities across the nation.

Michael is also one of the best-known Americans in Africa. He's always over there, conferring with Africa's leaders about their horrendous problems. (That surname of his still provides a wide entree.) Then he comes back here and meets with congressional and business people to help get those problems solved. He's enormously successful at it. And like Bobby, Michael's a good daddy. He works equally hard to get home and be with his kids. I suspect one day he'll run for office, and while that obviously gives me mixed emotions, I think he has the potential to be everything his father and uncle would have been. Michael is very special among a lot of special children.

I've been around the Kennedys long enough to observe firsthand the unbelievable abuse they are confronted with by today's tabloid "journalism," both print and electronic. The lies and distortions come at them on an almost daily basis. The older members of the family have grown up dealing with this in an amazingly graceful way. But it's palpably unfair to the littlest Kennedys to encounter this garbage on the playground, on the school bus, on the beach, and, most damagingly, on their TV sets in the early evening. I know that the Kennedys, one and all, would virtually give up their lives for the First Amendment. But as far as I'm concerned, when little guys such as Vicki and Michael's three children are constantly bombarded by a heartless, sensationalizing media hiding behind the mask of journalism, I'd like to take the First Amendment and shove it you-know-where.

If there's one myth about the Kennedys that ain't no myth, it's their incredible athletic competitiveness. Playing touch football with them at Hickory Hill or Hyannis Port was insanity. Even for a guy who played twelve years with the Giants, it was dangerous. You had to stay constantly alert, because they hurled their bodies around like kamikazes. Even the littlest Kennedys would come up from behind and whack you in the back. Plus every one of them wanted to be the quarterback. They're all born leaders, I guess. Get them in a huddle, and all you heard was, "Let me throw it. No, let me throw it. No, let me . . ."

It was the same when we went sailing. The stories about Ethel and sailing are legendary. She named her boat *Resolute,* which was, I quickly discovered, an understatement. One summer afternoon, when about ten of us were on the *Resolute* off Hyannis Port (there were a couple of dogs aboard, too), Ethel's sister-in-law Eunice breezed by with a boatload of kids. We all waved, there was a lot of yelling back and forth—and then, of course, they proceeded to race.

Now both are good sailors, yet somehow, while Eunice was tacking and Ethel was going downwind, they found themselves racing toward a head-on collision. I took one look at the set of Ethel's jaw and thought, Oh, my God, she's not going to back off! The two boats drew closer and closer. I know nothing about sailing, but something told me no rule of the sea would come into play here.

At the last second, Eunice swerved. Ethel did not even blink. Had both of them been alone on those boats, I suspect that would have been the end of the boats.

A few hours later, we gathered in Ethel's living room for some pre-dinner cocktails. All of a sudden, the French doors flew open, and in strode Eunice with a garden hose. Grinning from ear to ear, she proceeded to spray Ethel and all those around her. "There!" she exclaimed, turned around, and left. Believe it or not, everyone laughed uproariously—and no one harder than a thoroughly drenched Ethel. That, you see, is another thing about the Kennedys: For all their mutual competitiveness, they're bound by an amazing amount of love and loyalty. I mean, their lives are predicated on that. And lest anyone misunderstand Eunice Kennedy Shriver, here's a story that says everything about her.

In 1968 Eunice called me with a request. She'd been running some summer day camps for children with mental retardation, boosting their self-esteem by teaching them sports. Now she was organizing an international competition to showcase those kids' surprising athletic skills. She was calling it the Special Olympics. Could I get some famous athletes to attend?

My unspoken reaction was, no way is this going to work. People don't want to know about retarded children, much less watch them compete. But I agreed to make some calls and eventually rounded up Paul Hornung, Bart Starr, Oscar Robertson, Bobby Hull, and several other great names. That first Special Olympics was held at Chicago's Soldier Field. There were a few hundred kids on the field and virtually no one in the stands.

Today there are Special Olympics programs in ninety-six countries. More than 3 million children have participated in the Games, which reach tens of millions more through television coverage. And that all happened because of the enormous drive and determination of Eunice. She has the same qualities Vince Lombardi had. She's incredibly focused, relentlessly persuasive, and doesn't want to hear anything peripheral—like why something won't work. Somehow she can get people to kill themselves to make it work. I call her my "benevolent dictator" because you simply can't turn her down. More than any other single person, Eunice has changed the world's perception of the mentally retarded, and in that respect she's changed the world. She's brought these people into the mainstream. In my view, there should be a Nobel Prize for that—and hopefully there will be.

As a member of the Special Olympics board, I've been privileged to occupy a ringside seat, and it's been an enormously emotional experience. Seeing those kids compete has moved me countless times. Never so deeply, though, as at the Games of 1972. Roone Arledge had agreed to cover them on *Wide World of Sports,* and I was the announcer.

When the gun went off for the hundred-yard dash, one boy broke way ahead of the pack. There was no question he'd win: The competition wasn't as equal as it should have been and is now. Leading by about ten yards, the young boy suddenly stumbled, staggered, and sprawled onto the track. My heart froze. The one thing you hope won't happen is for a kid like that to get hurt, not physically so much as emotionally.

But as the boy in second place caught up with him and started to run by him, he stopped. He glanced ahead at the finish line and back at the rest of the field. Then he leaned over and picked the fallen boy up as the others raced by. They came across the finish line with their arms around each other, one last, the other next-to-last. God, that touched me. Not only did it say what the Special Olympics is all about, but it showed me what those kids can teach the rest of us. That wasn't about winning. It was about simple human caring. As a matter of fact, that's what the Kennedys I've known are all about, too.

TWO FOR THE SHOW

While I'm most closely identified with *Monday Night Football,* I've had the chance to do all manner of nonfootball telecasts. Among them were four Winter Olympics, three Summer Olympics, and several hundred installments of *Wide World of Sports.* All of that landed me in many memorable places to work with a lot of terrific people, especially Jim McKay, who has been so good at what he does for so long that he inhabits a league of his own. Still, it's the athletes who haunt the mind. The thrill of victory, the agony of defeat—clichés, perhaps, yet they've left behind a kaleidoscope of indelible images.

For completely different reasons, two moments will always stand out. One was the most dramatic athletic performance I've ever witnessed. The other starred the most outrageous performer I've ever encountered.

Innsbruck, 1976: As a widely traveled skier, I've long known that Alpine skiing is to Austrians what pro football is to Americans. I also know that they regard an Olympic men's downhill as the World Series, Super Bowl, and heavyweight championship fight all rolled into one spectacular event. Nothing, however, prepared me for the scene on Innsbruck's Mount Patscherkofel on that partly sunny day in 1976. From its very top to its very bottom, the course was lined with cheering, waving, singing fans, mostly Austrians. The whole mountain seemed alive. Someone estimated the crowd at 75,000, but I'd bet at least 150,000 were there, along with almost as many bottles of schnapps.

The man virtually everyone was cheering for was Franz Klammer, a twenty-one-year-old Austrian skier whose recent streak of victories had made him a national hero. Klammer didn't ski with anything approaching classic style. He just skied to win, and he took enormous physical risks to do it. Add to that charm, intelligence, and an irresistible smile, and you can see why the Austrians were engaged in a love affair with Franz. Very few, though, considered him mature enough to grab the gold at Innsbruck. On top of that, he'd drawn the fifteenth position, which meant fourteen other racers would chew up the course before he hit it.

My announcing partner for the race was Bob Beattie, a dear friend, fellow traveler, and former coach of the U.S. ski team. To feed the pictures in the typical European style, Austrian television had cameras at the top and bottom of the course. ABC's cameras covered the middle section, but since Bob and I could see only the Austrian feed in our broadcast booth, we could not call the race as it unwound. Later in the day, when we had tape coverage spliced from every part of the course, we would add our voice-over commentary to it and prepare the whole package for broadcast.

The heavy favorite and defending Olympics champ, Bernhard Russi of Switzerland, came down first. He skied so flawlessly that, by the time Klammer stepped into the start house, Russi held a six-tenths-of-a-second lead. That doesn't sound like much, but when you're reaching speeds of 80 mph or more, it's virtually insurmountable.

By now the course was torn up and laced with shadows. Bob and I felt kind of bad, because this was going to be a tremendous disappointment for the hometown folks, and we'd been having a hell of a time with them. As we watched on our monitors, Klammer crouched in the start house, his face like a rock. You could almost feel the electricity surging from him. Then he came flying out of there, virtually in free-fall. He hit the first little knoll so fast that he literally dove off it, nearly hitting the hay bales they'd stacked alongside it to keep skiers from going into the trees. I mean, he was flying. He almost lost it a couple of more times before disappearing from the view of the Austrian cameras at the top of the course.

Of course, we could still see Klammer's running clock on the electronic timer. We checked his time at the two intermediate checkpoints: still behind Russi's, but not by all that much. Klammer had a chance. Suddenly, we saw him again on the Austrian feed at the bottom third of the course. As he soared into view, everything seemed to be flailing, his arms, his poles, even his skis. Now he was at a spot with a grim mystique. It was called the "Dead Soldier," because they'd found one frozen there many years after World War I. It's basically a narrow, roadlike traverse leading to a steep left turn and into the final schuss. The racers could not afford to hit that last turn too fast, or they might find themselves in the trees. Consequently, almost all of them had taken the top side of the traverse's slope so they could hit the turn in control—sort of like cornering a race car by easing high and wide.

Not Klammer. He went diving into that traverse on the bottom side, which was the fastest side because it was icy and hadn't been chewed up. He came into the final turn carrying every bit of his speed.

"My God!" I couldn't help yelling to Bob. "He's going to blow it out."

He damn near did. Yet miraculously enough, he got through it. He had one ski up in the air—which just about nicked a hay bale—before throwing himself into the tuck and crossing the finish line. Up flashed his time: Klammer had edged Russi by exactly $33/100$ of a second.

Needless to say, the mountain erupted. The Austrians poured onto the course and carried their hero off on their shoulders. Somehow Bob and I ended up among them. It was unreal. Cowbells were clanging and an oompah band was oompahing as everyone headed to the nearby little village of Igles to celebrate. Bob and I, always eager to promote goodwill between nations, joined them at the local pub for some schnapps. Well, make that a lot of schnapps. Pretty soon we were all parading around this little plaza, shouting "Yay, Franz!" as the Austrians waved their flags and blew on their horns and got totally shitfaced.

Suddenly, I remembered something. "Uh-oh," I said to Bob. "We still have to do the commentary." We jumped in our car and somehow made it back down the mountain to the broadcast center. Some twenty cups of coffee later, our guys had meshed the Austrian tape of the race's beginning and end with the ABC tape of its middle for a complete picture of Klammer's incredible run. Once Bob and I looked at that, it was easy re-creating our amazement for our commentary.

Several years ago, when *TV Guide* chose the most exciting live sports moments over the past twenty-five years of television, Franz Klammer's 1976 gold-medal run was a runaway winner. *TV Guide* pointed out that this was what sports television was all about—being there live and in color at just the right moment. Of course, it wasn't live at all: Writers and commentators just kept writing and saying that it was. In any case, it's taken on a life of its own. Every time there's a Winter Olympics, they trot out that tape as an Olympics classic. And every time I see it, I get chills.

London, 1975: Evel Knievel was very good to *Wide World of Sports.* Of the ten highest-rated shows in the history of the series, no fewer than three starred the man who billed himself as "a professional life-risker." Even Evel's failures fueled his legend. His unsuccessful attempt to clear the Snake River Canyon in a rocket (his parachute started opening almost before he left the launch pad) drew such enormous coverage that Evel decided to make an international tour. First stop: London, where he announced he would jump over thirteen double-decker buses at Wembley Stadium.

To Evel's astonishment, London greeted the news with near-total apathy. Just a few days before the jump, the stadium had sold only a couple of hundred cheap seats. Clearly, the British didn't have a clue to who Evel Knievel was and didn't care to find out. So the master of hype started drumming up some ink, as only he could. First he raced his motorcycle down the wrong side of a London street. When the police pulled him over, Evel complained, "You people over here drive funny."

That got him arrested, which got him in the papers, which got him a live interview on the BBC. He even brought along his favorite cane. When he unscrewed the top, it dispensed shots of Wild Turkey, Evel's drink of the moment. But it was Evel's words that stirred things up that night.

"Why on earth, may I ask, would anyone want to ride a motorcycle over a row of buses?" said his oh-so-proper female interviewer.

"Ma'am," replied Evel, "I can tell just from looking at you that you wouldn't understand."

"Oh, you Americans," she sniffed. "You're all so brash."

"Let me tell you something, lady," Evel shot back. "If it hadn't been for us Americans, I'd be jumping for the Germans."

That did it. Suddenly, London became very much aware of this crazy cowboy with the big, boozy cane and the even bigger mouth. Wembley sold out.

The night before the jump, Evel called my hotel room. "Frank, whatcha doin'? Let's have some dinner and check out some lights."

It turned out to be a very long night. By now England regarded

Evel as the most famous American since Eisenhower, and crowds attended his every move. There must have been two dozen people at our dinner table. Every now and then, between bites, Evel would unscrew his cane, pour himself a blast of Wild Turkey, and give me a wink. Meanwhile, he was telling unbelievable lies to these poor people. He even claimed he'd actually cleared the Snake River Canyon, but the wind had shifted and blown his parachute all the way back. Everyone solemnly nodded.

Later, we hopped in his rented Rolls-Royce and began touring the pubs. "Come on, Evel," I finally said, "you've got to get back to your hotel and get a little rest. It's going to be a tough day tomorrow."

Evel threw his arm around me. "Just one more stop, old pal. There's something I always wanted to try."

Five minutes later, we're parked on a kind of lookout over the Thames River. From somewhere Evel produced a five-iron and a caddie sack full of golf balls. "I've wanted to do this ever since I heard about this river," he mumbled. Then he lurched over to a narrow railing, climbed on top of it, and began whacking balls into the darkness. He was trying to hit one across the Thames.

"That's it," I said. "I'm out of here." And off I went to look for a cab.

Miraculously, Evel didn't fall into the Thames. But his eyes looked like crimson spotlights when I next saw him a few hours before his big jump. He'd driven to Wembley in his huge van, which he parked in one of the stadium's tunnels. I accompanied him through the tunnel for his first look at the dimensions of his challenge. They'd built a towering ramp going to the very top corner of the stadium, the bottom of which turned upward to launch Evel over the thirteen double-decker buses. At the far end of the line of buses stood another ramp that was optimistically intended for his landing.

Evel calmly took it all in, thought for a moment, and then just as calmly said, "I can't make that."

I felt myself turning pale. *Wide World* had really been promoting this show, which was being beamed back to the United States. "Look," I said to Evel. "Just tell them to pull one or two of the buses out. Nobody's going to question you for not killing yourself."

"I can't do that, either," muttered Evel. Then he turned around and headed back to his van.

I frantically sought out Doug Wilson, our producer. "Doug," I informed him, "we've got a major problem. Evel says he can't make it, and I don't think we should be a part of what's going to happen."

Now it was Doug's turn to blanch. "What, what, what?" he sputtered. "How do you know that?"

"Because he flat-ass said he can't make it. And he's too proud to pull out even one of those buses."

"Let's go talk to him."

By now the stadium was filling up, and the acts preceding the main event—daredevil acts, of course—were on the field. We knocked on the door of Evel's van. No answer. We knocked again. Still no answer. So we opened the door, and there, sprawled on a cot in blissful sleep, was our star. I gently shook him awake.

"What are we going to do about the jump, Evel?" I pleaded. "What are we going to do about the telecast?"

"Aw, don't worry, old pal," he said with a groggy grin. "I'm changing the bike's gear ratio to get more speed."

If that was good enough for Evel, it was fine with Doug and me. Two hours later, I'm standing with a microphone before one hundred thousand people at the entrance to the up ramp. Doug gives me a "Five-four-three-two-one . . . go!" And as the camera light goes red, I say something like, "We're live at London's Wembley Stadium, where Evel Knievel will be jumping thirteen double-deck buses. In all honesty, I've spoken to Evel, and he's not sure this jump will be successful."

As we cut to a commercial, Evel comes roaring up behind me and slams on his brakes, raising so much dust I start coughing. Even so, I can see his eyes through his helmet's visor. They're still bloodshot.

"Great crowd, huh?" he says.

"You honestly think you can do this?"

"I don't know," he replies. "But I'm really going to jack 'em up. I'll make two fake passes and go on the third one. I'll flip you my thumb when I'm ready to take off."

So he roars around a bit, does a couple of wheelies, and then zooms to the crest of the up ramp. The entire crowd inhales. Evel stops right at the very top of the stadium and sits there, revving his engine. The crowd is on its feet, and the people can't believe what they're about to see. All of a sudden, here he comes . . . but no, he backs off right at the edge of the descent. He repeats the teasing process again as the crowd turns near-hysterical. On the third approach, just as he promised, he flips me his thumb and down the ramp he zooms.

Well, Evel was right. He cleared twelve-and-a-half buses, but the rest of the thirteenth knocked him ass-over-teakettle. The most bizarre part was that, as he rolled over and over down the exit ramp, the bike seemed to chase after him—finally landing atop his crumpled body in a cloud of dust and dirt. Horrified, I ran over and helped his mechanic pull the bike off. The first thing I noticed was a bone sticking out of his hand. The second was the blood pouring from his mouth. My God, I thought, he's got to be dying.

Then Evel's eyes opened, and his lips started to move. I bent my ear to his mouth, figuring he was about to make a last request.

"Frank," he whispered.

"Yeah, yeah, I'm here, Evel. What is it?"

"Get that broad out of my room!"

Needless to say, I was dumbstruck. Finally, I said, "Evel, don't move, just stay there. They've got a stretcher coming. They've got medics coming."

"Get away from me!" he yelled. "I walked in here, and, goddammit, I'm walking out!" Covered with blood, mud, and oil, Evel staggered to his feet, put one arm around my shoulders and the other around his mechanic's. Then he dragged himself into the tunnel and passed out.

I caught up with him in an intensive-care unit later that night. He had an arm and a leg elevated and was swathed in bandages. The first thing he said to me was, "I was only kidding when I told you to get that broad out of my room. My wife's on her way over."

Then Evel gave me a big wink.

A QUESTION OF FOCUS

Perhaps because some viewers think I've been around since the first test pattern, I'm often asked about the state of television sports. One thing I'm certain of is that I came along at the right moment. When I broke into TV, the average set offered about seven channels. That was a wonderful time to be in television, because you were forced to learn the business from the ground up. I edited my own film (later videotape), wrote my own copy, produced my own segments, and got a hands-on feel for what made it all work. In contrast, many of today's announcers have no idea what goes on down in the "basement." To them the technology is just something that functions. They would have difficulty even imagining that at one time everyone did a lot of everything: We were real people rather than voices in a headset, people who shared wonderful moments together as well as discovered how this great TV machine works.

These days, mainly because of the complex technology, some of my colleagues look to their producers for every conceivable kind of direction. And that can be a major problem, because that constant voice in their ears often wields too much power. If you think there are big egos in front of the cameras, you should meet some of the guys behind it. They're absolutely dying to put their stamp on the broadcast, to read their names in the local TV critic's column the next day.

I have a great observation post on some of this because I hear and see a lot of regional telecasts. Whenever I look at tapes of the teams that will meet on next week's Monday-night matchup, the feeds of regionally telecast games, I frequently hear what goes on in the booths during commercials, the off-air feed. I often overhear the play-by-play and color guys conversing with their producer. Many times they'll be discussing what their focus will be when they come out of a commercial. And too often, that focus will be purposely negative. A running back's great move will be characterized on the upcoming replay as a terrible tackle. A superb block becomes a poor defensive effort. A quarterback sack, bad protection—when in fact someone made an outstanding defensive move. And on and on.

I can only assume that this slant on a game is done in the name of journalism. But, I suspect, it's really done for the shock value and the attention it might garner. What bothers me most is that there is little or no consideration for the individuals involved. A casual, sarcastic (not to mention inaccurate) critique of a player offered to tens of millions of viewers may make for laughs in the truck or back at the home office in New York, but it can have a devastating impact on its target.

Try coming home—as I did on too many occasions—to find a young son who's been harassed by his schoolmates asking why you blew the game. Yeah, maybe there'd been a fumble or a dropped pass. But what was left out of the TV commentary was that the fumble was caused by a brutal yet great hit, and the pass I dropped was so poorly thrown I shouldn't have been anywhere near the ball.

Too many producers also want to turn the game into a sociological tract. I look at sports as entertainment first and the cutting edge of change second. A very distant second. Sure, there are times when you must deal with the racism in sports, the greed in sports, the drugs, and all its other ills. But somewhere along the line, a few of my more ego-driven colleagues have gotten fun and games confused with their personal mission to right the wrongs of the world—once again, I suspect, only for the attention it will command.

To me, the typical football viewer is a guy who's had his ass chewed at the office, who's figuring out how to afford another baby, whose wife just presented him with three overdue bills, and whose teenager busted up the car and then sulked all week. Now he wants to forget all that. He wants to sit back and enjoy the sheer beauty of a perfectly delivered pass or watch a linebacker stomping someone the way he'd like to stomp his boss. Yet a lot of TV people want to pump that poor guy with more problems. Maybe that's how they get their identity. While I'm convinced that something like the Howard & Don show would never work on television today, perhaps we should all lighten up a bit and enjoy the sport as much as our viewers are trying to. Hey, the game of football is not war, recession, catastrophe, or the changing of the guard at Buckingham Palace. It's only a game played by grown-up boys. Let's not make it any more than it is.

I'm not entirely alone on this score. When Bill Walsh decided to leave NBC to return to college coaching at Stanford, he spoke very candidly about why. He explained that he couldn't wait to escape the negative drift of network sportscasting. He got sick of people who didn't know what they were talking about telling him to "shoot from the hip," and to aim those shots at the guys on the field. He couldn't stand all the politicizing and all the manipulating. Bill's real problem, I suspect, was that he had the clout of a rookie punter.

Believe me, no producer's going to tell John Madden what to say. From what I hear, Madden would squish him and toss him out. But a guy coming into this game nowadays can't be that way. Bill Parcells wasn't that way, and neither was Bill Walsh. John Madden just happened to break in during a different period, and he now reigns on one of those rare, untouchable thrones.

There's one more thing that bugs me about my business these days, and that's information overload. It's all over our computer-driven society—all those charts and graphs laying out all that statistical minutiae—and now it's swept across the TV screen. We've gone totally stat-happy. We're like little kids obsessed with a new toy, and the toy, of course, is the computer.

At the risk of sounding self-serving, I think we handle this access to excess better on *Monday Night Football* than any other telecast. Steve Hirdt, the executive vice president of the Elias Sports Bureau, the official statisticians for the NFL, the NBA, and major-league baseball, has done some brilliant work on *MNF* week in and week out. His information (in concert with our producer, Ken Wolfe) is put together in a very judicious way, designed to complement a given game—not *become* the game. However, on a recent *MNF* broadcast, even we got into some complex numerical comparison of Troy Aikman's career and Terry Bradshaw's career. When the graphic came up, I couldn't help myself. I said to Al, "I hope you can explain all that, because there's sure a lot of lines up there." I was also thinking of the guy at home who's sipping his beer and scratching his head. We now have the capability to absolutely numb that guy's mind with statistical overkill. We should be very careful how we deal with it.

Of course, the biggest problem with the marriage of television and sports is money. Soaring players' salaries and rights fees, shrinking ad sales and market share—they're all putting tremendous pressure on the bottom line, not to mention the relationship. I'm sure that Dan Burke, the chief executive officer of ABC, spoke for his counterparts at NBC, CBS, and the other TV entities when he told the press, "The burden of saying 'no' begins with us. If this means no Olympics [on TV], we accept the consequences of no Olympics. If it's no World Series, it's no World Series, even if it means getting pushed around for a week or two in the household ratings. But we've decided that's better for everyone's future than huge losses."

While network football isn't in as dire shape as network baseball, football has its own big financial problems. CBS's estimated loss on the last baseball contract of more than half a billion dollars has been widely bandied about. But losses on the NFL's TV contract have been very quietly reaching some scary numbers of their own. For the 1993 season, the fourth and final year of the contract, the three networks and the cable operators—ESPN and Turner—will lose a combined estimate of $250 million on pro football.

The best guess is that baseball and football will face some major revenue reductions from television, even with baseball's dramatic new partnership deal with NBC and ABC. All this is happening at a time when players' salaries have gone bonkers in both sports. Multimillion-dollar, multiyear deals have become so commonplace that NFL players the casual fan never even heard of, along with journeymen baseball players, are making more than their game's superstars of just a couple of years ago.

In my view, the answer to this changing economic world is rather obvious: pay-per-view (PPV). Of the two sports, pro football seems more likely than baseball, with its plummeting ratings, to be in the best position to take advantage of PPV.

ABC Sports has provided a guideline for the NFL with its PPV package of college football. On any given Saturday, games with top viewer appeal are televised by ABC's affiliates to regional areas, while other games are made available in that same area over cable to people with special interests. For instance, a New York viewer like myself might receive Ohio State vs. Michigan free over WABC-TV. I might prefer, however, to see USC vs. Washington—a game being telecast "free" on the West Coast. So that game would be carried on cable in my area, and I could dial it up on PPV. The NFL could do something very similar. In the New York area, an avid Chicago Bears fan might be able to see his Bears play Detroit over cable, rather than watch the networks' free matchups slated for the New York region on that game day.

The problems, of course, are multitudinous, beginning with the network sponsors who might complain about their audience deterioration because of all the additional viewing opportunities. Then there's always the specter of a congressional crackdown on both television *and* sports. Politicians love to tell their constituents about how they're saving them from the greedy clutches of those who would take away their "free sports." Baseball, of course, has operated under an antitrust exemption for decades, based on a seventy-year-old Supreme Court decision declaring that the sport is not a business. (Today CBS could testify that baseball is indeed a business, not to mention a damned expensive one.)

However it plays out, pay-per-view will not go away—and, in effect, that's what "free" TV is all about anyway. When a sponsor pays $850,000 for a thirty-second spot on the Super Bowl show, it doesn't require an MBA to figure out that the sponsor's product is going to cost the viewer a whole lot more in the marketplace.

Nor is it just economics that will dictate the use of PPV: The technology is ready, and expanding at an incredible rate. Everywhere one looks, plans are being laid for a much more diverse video menu for the public. It's both exciting and scary to contemplate the five hundred channels that will probably be operational by the mid-nineties. And then there's the Direct Broadcast Satellite system (DBS), which will also be part of the big video picture, along with those ugly yet relentlessly proliferating backyard satellite dishes.

All this new technology will impact on sports—most likely, to its benefit. Perhaps a bigger concern, however, is how these changes will affect our society. As a recent father and a grandfather five times over, this worries me even more. There was a time when mass network television could bring us all together, whether it be in horror or delight. Now, because this country is so incredibly diverse, we need that electronic bond as never before. Someone recently told me that in New York City alone there are over thirty different languages spoken daily. But while mass communications has historically been the fuel that has fired this American melting pot, we confront a future in which hundreds of specialized video options may tempt us to slip back into our safe, all-too-cozy ethnic cocoons.

Can our changing society cohere into a caring, understanding one? Or will the lack of a mass media as we have known it contribute to an increased fragmentation? Only the Codys of the world will know the answer to that.

HERE'S TO GOOD FRIENDS

Toots Shor had a favorite line about friends. "I don't want any more of them," he'd say, "because I don't have time for the ones I've got now."

What he meant is that real friendship requires loads of TLC, and you can give that only to a few. There's a lot of truth to that. Show me somebody who's a "close friend" of everybody, who's on every scene and at every party, and I'll show you a very unhappy man or woman. Because these people don't have the time, or they're not making the time, to share intimate things with others, which forges the bond of true friendship.

Although I'm not a person who makes friends easily, the ones I have are very close. A few, in fact, are as much family to me as my real family. They're the people I'm in constant touch with. If more than a week goes by and I haven't talked to them, I sense something missing from my life. I treasure them.

For some odd reason, my friends tend to come in pairs. Take Bob Karpe and Les Richter, those two All-Americans I palled around with in high school and college. A few years after I joined the Giants, the three of us sat down together, had a few beers, and talked about how we were going to preserve our friendship despite living on different coasts. Bob was very involved in southern California real estate, so he suggested that we form a real estate investment partnership. That way we'd always have a reason to stay in touch. Each of us put up what he could afford at the time. Then we needed a name for it. Since both of them were University of California grads, they proposed calling it CAL. I said, "Hell, no! I'm an equal partner here and I went to USC." So we ended up calling our partnership CALSC, and it's been highly successful. As has our friendship—except when Cal plays USC.

Then there are Marty Davis and Herb Siegel. Marty is the chairman of the Paramount Communications conglomerate, which owns everything from Paramount Pictures to Madison Square Garden. When I met him more than twenty years ago, he was trying to do something for the Multiple Sclerosis Society. He wanted to set up an annual Dinner of Champions to drum up money for MS research, and he enlisted my help in organizing it. These New York dinners have raised more than $25 million. Over the years, Marty and his wife, Louella, and Kathie and I have shared some great times. Although he's been described as "one of the toughest bosses in America," the Marty Davis I know is a self-effacing, extremely funny man who picks his friends as carefully as he protects his stockholders.

Herb Siegel is the head of Chris-Craft, another big conglomerate. Back in the mid fifties, when our paths first crossed, Herb was a successful young talent agent, and I liked him and his wife, Ann, right off. Like Marty, Herb is a brilliant businessman. But somewhere along the line, the two of them crossed swords, and their wounds didn't heal for many years. When I invited them to our parties, dinners, and other affairs, they hardly spoke to each other. I never noticed any of this, so I just kept inviting them. Gradually, they became good friends. Believe it or not, Herb is just as shy and funny as Marty—at least out of the boardroom. Whenever the Davises, Siegels, and Giffords get together, it sounds like a sitcom laugh track.

In sad contrast, I've also watched two of my most cherished friends engage in a long and bitter family feud. When Jack Mara, Wellington's brother, died in 1965, his will left his 50 percent share of the New York Giants to his wife, daughter, and son—my dear friend Tim. In effect that made Tim, who represented the combined interests of his side of the family, and his uncle Well, who held the other 50 percent, co-owners of the team—a match definitely not made in heaven. Talk about total opposites.

Well Mara lives the perfect spiritual life. For all the years I've known him, and they number more than forty, I've never heard him utter a swear word. He goes to mass almost every day and has put all eleven of his children through Catholic colleges. Well pours the same devotion into the Giants, showing up at virtually every practice, attending to the tiniest detail of the team's operation. That's Well's life: his family, his church, and his Giants.

Tim Mara is more like his father: charming, extroverted, and fun-loving. He was that way from the moment I met him, that sixteen-year-old kid I played Ping-Pong with at my first training camp, the kid who befriended me when I most needed a friend. Later, Tim became the quintessential man-about-town, squiring the prettiest women to the best restaurants and always leaving laughter in his wake. Everyone who knows him, and he knows everyone, likes him enormously. In fact, both of his ex-wives are two of his best friends. Now *that's* a likable man.

As for my own relationship with the two Maras, a couple of incidents say it all. When I traveled to Canton, Ohio, in 1977 to be inducted into the Pro Football Hall of Fame, everyone warned me that the induction ceremony would leave me in tears. No way, I told them.

Then Well Mara walked up to the microphone to formally present me. "For twenty-five years," he told the crowd, "Frank Gifford has personified the son all of us dream of." Sure enough, I felt a tear rolling down my cheek. For me, it was the most moving moment of a very moving day.

Two years later, my younger son, Kyle, was seriously injured, and two of his friends instantly killed, when their car crashed into a tree on a New Jersey highway. The news reached me just as I stepped out of a private plane in Lake Placid, New York, where I had gone to broadcast a pre-Olympics ski race. The pilot offered to fly me to New Jersey, which left me just enough time to make one phone call. I called Tim Mara. After I explained what had happened, he said he'd meet me at the hospital. By the time I got there about an hour later, Tim had consulted with Kyle's doctors, talked to the police, arranged for Kyle to be taken to a better-equipped hospital for a brain scan, and contacted one of New York's top medical experts on serious head injuries, who quickly took over the case. Though Kyle was unconscious for about three weeks, he eventually recovered almost completely. Needless to say, I picked the right person to call.

Imagine, then, how I felt to discover that some well-meaning words of mine helped set off the much-publicized "War of the Maras." It happened during an evening with Tim in the late seventies, a time when the Giants had hit the depths of their futility and their followers the absolute apex of their wrath. It was like the early fifties again, except now the New York fans, ever alert for new ways to make a statement, had reached to the skies. They'd hired a private plane to fly over a Giants home game. Behind it trailed a long streamer with scarlet lettering: 15 YEARS OF LOUSY FOOTBALL. WE'VE HAD ENOUGH.

All of this obviously consumed Tim's mind when we met for dinner, because he did something highly uncharacteristic. He became so upset about the Giants' plight that he began disparaging his uncle's management of the team. That prompted me to do something equally uncharacteristic. I flashed at Tim.

"Let me tell you something," I said. "You're bad-mouthing a guy who's been doing all the work and taking all the heat. You represent fifty percent of this ball club, but you basically don't do anything. So you have no right to criticize your uncle unless you get involved with the team and find out what's going on."

Man, I touched off a rocket. Tim, I later learned, not only started making waves, he began kicking ass. He demanded that Well give him a 50 percent say in major decisions affecting the team. Not surprisingly, that struck Well as an affront, particularly coming from someone with such a totally different lifestyle. What had been a politely standoffish relationship quickly deteriorated into a down-and-mean feud.

Although Pete Rozelle arranged for a compromise by bringing in George Young to run the football operation as general manager, there was no such truce off the field. Both sides became permanently alienated, right down to the wives and children and grandchildren. There were no more family get-togethers at Thanksgiving and Christmas. Well and Tim would pass each other in the office hallway without speaking. In the owner's box at Giants Stadium, a partition was erected to shield their seats from each other's eyes. It just broke my heart. Finally, Tim got tired of it all, sold his half share in the team, and settled in Florida.

What makes their estrangement even more tragic is that both men are so much alike in the ways that truly matter. Tim is the most caring person I know other than Well, and Well is the most caring person I know other than Tim. They're both unbelievably generous and very quiet about their generosity. I can't count the number of former Giants players for whom either Well or Tim has gotten jobs or paid the rent or sent their kids through college. As Well likes to put it, and he's really putting it for Tim, too: "Once a Giant, always a Giant."

Perhaps that's why I still hold out hope for a reconciliation. In the back of my mind, I see these two people whom I love so much sitting down and saying, "Look, we both profited from what our fathers did. Our fathers put their hearts and souls and guts into keeping this franchise alive. Maybe we owe them something, maybe we owe our grandchildren something. Maybe we should apply that motto of ours to ourselves: 'Once a Mara, always a Mara.'"

FOURTH QUARTER

Recently, Kathie gave me a pillow embroidered with the words OLD AGE DOESN'T MATTER UNLESS YOU'RE A WINE. It's a clever line, but I'd bet my bifocals that whoever thought it up never fathered a son at fifty-nine. These days old age matters a *lot* to me.

When Cody was born, I confronted my mortality for the first time. All it took was some simple addition. When he's finishing college, I told Kathie, I'll be eighty-two, and I'll probably be gumming everything to death and hobbling to the drugstore. The good news is that having Cody has done wonders for my workout ethic. I lift weights virtually every day, and while I'm not obsessed with it, I feel almost as healthy as in my days as a Giant. I also finally had surgery on my back, which was injured during my football career and got so bad I couldn't even pick up my new baby. So when people tell me, "Cody will keep you young," they're right for the wrong reason. He's keeping me in shape so I'll still be around when *he's* no longer young.

Not that things don't get a trifle bizarre. A few years ago, I had a reunion dinner with some old Giants teammates. All they wanted to talk about was their knee implants, and all I wanted to talk about was "binkies." Then there are my five grandchildren. Imagine how they feel when they have to call a three-year-old "Uncle Cody"!

If my biggest concern is not being around for Cody, my biggest regret in life is not being at home more for my other kids. My daughter, Vicki, and I have had some heavy discussions about that. One night it just burst out of her: "Why weren't you around more when I was young?" That hurt, not only because it was true but because there wasn't much I could have done to change it.

I can imagine what it was like for Vicki as a little kid. All the other dads on the block went to the office every morning and came home every evening. Her daddy went out the door, the door hit him in the ass, and the next time she saw him, he was running around on television. Vaguely, in the back of her mind, she probably remembers that Dad had to be in Cleveland for a football game, do his radio show, make a speech, go to Hawaii for a commercial, or some damn thing. But she really had no idea what I was doing or why I was doing it. To her, I was just never at home.

Of course, from my point of view, remembering the way I grew up, I felt I *had* to do all that. I got into a game and turned it into a profession and then into a livelihood and finally into something out of the American Dream. The demands of doing and achieving and becoming just took over. Yet in all honesty, I should have been perceptive enough to realize whom that was going to hurt. I should have known it was going to hurt Vicki and Vicki's mother and Vicki's brothers. Maybe that's why Vicki became such a terrific mother herself. She learned from her own mom how to do things when Dad wasn't around much. I look at my daughter as the very best in the very best profession there is. She's the greatest mother I've ever known.

As for my two sons by Maxine, both turned out better than I had any right to expect. Jeff is a successful builder of houses and condos in Las Vegas and a wonderful family man. While Kyle still has some residual impairment from that horrible auto accident, he lives on his own very happily, commuting to his job in New York and spending a lot of time with both his real mother and his stepmother. Although I can never rectify what I did wrong as a father, it's a great feeling to get another chance with another child. You might say that Cody is the beneficiary of everything I didn't give Vicki, Jeff, and Kyle.

As for myself, I've been lucky enough to see an awful lot of life. I can't think of anyone I wanted to know whom I didn't end up knowing. For all that, my greatest thrill, and I've had more than my share, was being inducted into the Hall of Fame. This probably sounds somewhat trite, but the enormity of it still hasn't fully registered.

When you start playing a sport, you never imagine winding up in a Hall of Fame. Then you get a break here, you get a break there, and one day you're staring at a bronze bust of yourself above a list of your achievements. To say that's forever is nonsense, because nothing is forever. But it certainly will outlast a lot of other things, like some huge estate some eighties zillionaire acquired before his debts caught up with his greed. One day my grandchildren may come to see me in that Hall. And maybe their grandchildren. And maybe even their grandchildren's grandchildren. Damn, that gives me goose bumps.

As for my biggest satisfaction in life, and this may sound equally trite, nothing brings me a greater reward than helping someone else. I can't describe the kick I get out of doing something for somebody. It sure beats the hell out of buying yet another creature comfort when you're already as comfortable as anyone deserves. And thankfully, I'm now in a position to help big time. People call almost every day: Someone they know has MS, and whom can they turn to? Or they need a guy to emcee a fund-raiser or visit a hospital or work on a telethon. The fascinating part is that Kathie's the same way. She's almost fanatical about trying to help others.

Kathie and I are also very spiritual. I'm not one to go around preaching to people, but I guess all that haphazard religious training I encountered while growing up left its mark—as did Kathie's on her. We pray together at least once a day. We'll be at the dinner table and Kathie will reach out her hand and I'll take Cody's hand and we'll pray. Kathie is as impulsive about that as she is about most everything else. One day, while I was driving us home on a Connecticut highway, a voice on the radio reported that Howard Cosell had cancer. Kathie asked me to pull over onto the shoulder of the road. Then she clasped my hand, and we said a prayer for Howard. We're still praying.

Actually, Kathie and I have different philosophies about prayer. She believes in a highly personal God who cares about each of us. She feels it's okay to ask Him for things. I, on the other hand, believe that God's got a much bigger job on His hands than worrying about me. I feel we should confine our prayers to just thanking Him for our blessings. When we discussed all this, Kathie came up with a classic Kathie solution. "You do the thanking," she said, "and I'll do the asking."

While Kathie is as much a minister of her faith as she is an entertainer (and she's great at both), I'm less outgoing about my own spirituality. I'm convinced, however, that if the entire world—whether they believe in Jesus Christ or not—lived by His teachings, it would be a far better world.

Other than being with my family, some of my favorite moments come aboard airplanes. Or to be more specific, aboard the pre-sunrise "red-eye" flying home from a Monday-night game on the West Coast. I always arrange for a window seat. It's usually brilliantly clear at that time of year, and as you sweep across America, you can see forever. You can see all those cities with all those tiny lights glowing inside all those homes. Then I always think the same thought. Just a few hours ago, something like one in every five of those homes—tens of millions of people—were listening to the roughneck's kid from Bakersfield.

Suddenly, I become that kid again. It's a Friday night in autumn, and I'm standing behind a fence that looks so high gazing at a football field that seems so far away. Everything rushes back, the smell of the grass and the brightness of the lights, and, above all, the intensity of my longing. At those moments, my heart fills with emotion—and the emotion I feel is a mixture of awe and gratitude.

Come to think of it, that's exactly the way I feel when I look back on my life.

ABOUT THE CO-AUTHOR

HARRY WATERS is an award-winning senior writer at *News-week*, where he currently serves as the television critic. His work has appeared in *The New York Times Magazine*, *New York* magazine, *GQ*, *Penthouse*, *Reader's Digest*, and other publications. He lives in Manhattan with his wife, Ruth.